Body Counts

Body Counts

THE VIETNAM WAR AND MILITARIZED
REFUGE(ES)

Yến Lê Espiritu

UNIVERSITY OF CALIFORNIA PRESS

University of California Press, one of the most distinguished university presses in the United States, enriches lives around the world by advancing scholarship in the humanities, social sciences, and natural sciences. Its activities are supported by the UC Press Foundation and by philanthropic contributions from individuals and institutions. For more information, visit www.ucpress.edu.

University of California Press
Oakland, California

Library of Congress Cataloging-in-Publication Data

Espiritu, Yen Le, 1963– author.
    Body counts : the Vietnam War and militarized refuge(es) / Yến Lê Espiritu.
        pages   cm.
    Includes bibliographical references and index.
    ISBN 978-0-520-27770-0 (cloth : alk. paper)
    ISBN 978-0-520-27771-7 (pbk. : alk. paper)
    ISBN 978-0-520-95900-2 (ebook)
    1. Vietnam War, 1961–1975—Refugees.   2. Refugees—Vietnam.
3. Refugees—United States.   4. Vietnamese Americans.   5. Collective
memory—United States.   6. Militarism—United States.   I. Title.
    DS559.63.E87   2014
    959.704'31—dc23   2014003088

Manufactured in the United States of America

23   22   21   20   19   18   17   16   15   14
10   9   8   7   6   5   4   3   2   1

In keeping with a commitment to support environmentally responsible and sustainable printing practices, UC Press has printed this book on Natures Natural, a fiber that contains 30% post-consumer waste and meets the minimum requirements of ANSI/NISO Z39.48–1992 (R 1997) (*Permanence of Paper*).

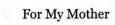

For My Mother

Contents

Illustrations

Acknowledgments

Perched atop a military vehicle, the boisterous American soldiers tossed handfuls of candy to a group of Vietnamese schoolchildren who went scrambling to pick them up from the littered ground. This was a familiar scene on the busy streets of Saigon during the Vietnam War. As a child, I instinctively recoiled at the sight of the smug soldiers doling out their sugary gifts, disturbed that the uniformed and gunned men were literally looking down on the scurrying children. In return, I glared angrily at the soldiers—and always pointedly refused the candy. I draw attention to this scene—what I came to see as the covering up of U.S. military violence via candy—because it captures the intent of this book: to expose the hidden and disguised violence behind the humanitarian term "refuge," what I term *militarized* refuge.

My journey, from being an object of rescue to becoming a critic of the rescue fantasy, has not been simple. To be a Vietnamese refugee in the United States is to be subjected to prying questions about "the war," denigrated as an unwanted burden on state resources, and featured as evidence of U.S. benevolence. But I have come to see that refugee life also constitutes a site of social critique that disrupts the U.S. "rescue and liberation" myth—a major argument of this book. Some key influences on my journey from there to here: the underfunded junior high and high schools that I attended in Perris, California, which taught me about racial and class inequality; Rubén Rumbaut's course on refugees that I took as an undergraduate student way back when, which introduced me to the field of refugee studies; and the Asian American Studies Center at UCLA, which opened up for me the world of critical scholarship and pedagogy.

Since 1990, I have been a faculty member in the Ethnic Studies Department at the University of California, San Diego. I have done all my *real* learning here, alongside brilliant colleagues and students. The inspired work of our junior faculty, such as the award-winning *Aloha America* by recently tenured Adria Imada, bodes well for the future of ethnic studies. Special thanks to Fatima El-Tayeb, Dayo Gore, Curtis Marez, and Shelley Streeby for joining the department when we most needed them; to Ross Frank for being the most generous person I know; and to Ana Celia Zentella for her infectious and indefatigable fighting spirit. Although they have since left UCSD, Lisa Sun-Hee Park and Denise Ferreira da Silva, scholars extraordinaire, helped me connect immigration and refugee studies to war and violence studies. I am also grateful to Yolanda Escamilla, Samira Khazai, and Mary Polytaridis for being so good at their jobs, so committed to the Ethnic Studies Department, and so supportive of me. I wish to acknowledge the insightful comments on earlier drafts of this book from Jody Blanco, Tak Fujitani, Sara Johnson, Curtis Marez, Nayan Shah, Shelley Streeby, Kalindi Vora, and Danny Widener. I am forever indebted to Lisa Lowe and Lisa Yoneyama for their life-giving friendship and intellectual companionship. I mourn their departure from UCSD, and feel their absence every day, in every way. And all my love to my dear friend, Rosemary George, who left us all too soon.

Teaching ethnic studies at UCSD has been most rewarding. This book has benefited from discussions with the students in my graduate seminars on History and Memory; War, Race, and Violence; and Critical Immigration and Refugee Studies. I have also learned much about racial violence, refugeehood and U.S. imperialism from the work of and conversations with Mohamed Abumaye, Long Bui, Lisa Cacho, Ofelia Cuevas, Kyung-Hee Ha, Lisa Ho, Cathi Kozen, John Marquez, Jennifer Mogannam, Kit Myers, Linh Nguyễn, Ayako Sahara, Lila Sharif, Davorn Sisavath, Jennifer Kim-Anh Tran, Tomoko Tsuchiya, Ma Vang, and Thúy Võ Đặng. I thank Sally Le for being the best research assistant ever.

Since I began this book in 2005, the field of Southeast Asian American Studies has flourished, thanks to the labor and pioneering scholarship of an inspired and inspiring group of scholars: Lan Duong, Mariam Lam, Fiona Ngô, Cathy Schlund-Vials, Nguyễn-võ Thu-hương, Mimi Nguyen, Viet Thanh Nguyen, Isabelle Thuy Pelaud, Linda Trinh Vo, and Khatharya Um. Meeting and working with Nguyễn-võ Thu-hương on the special *Amerasia Journal* issue, *30 Years AfterWARd: Vietnamese Americans and U.S. Empire* (2005), was a formative experience. I have continued to cherish our friendship and collaborations. I am also grateful to chị Kim-Loan Hill and chị Lan Phó for sharing their wisdom of experience with me. Special thanks to Thúy Võ Đặng for co-hosting the annual *Tết-together* at my house to celebrate the Vietnamese New Year, complete with *lô-tô* and *bầu cua cá cọp*. We have been at this for over a decade now—our way of building community for Vietnamese American scholars and allies in Southern California.

Pierrette Hondagneu-Sotelo, my writing partner in the last stage of my writing, deserves special acknowledgment for keeping me to a chapter-a-month schedule, for giving me timely and helpful feedback, and for insisting that I pay as much attention to immigrant lives as to immigration theories. She is the main reason that I was able to complete the book during my sabbatical year. I also thank Diane Wolf for our collaborations over the years, especially our most recently published piece on the public commemorations of the Vietnam War and the Holocaust in the United States. At the University of California Press, I thank Naomi Schneider for believing in the project, Julia Zafferano for her meticulous copyediting, and Chris Lura and Jessica Moll for bringing the book through production.

The research for this book has been supported by a number of funding institutions: the American Sociological Association—Fund for the Advancement of the Discipline (FAD), the U.C. Institute of Global Conflict and Cooperation, the U.C. Pacific Rim Research Program, the UCSD Center for the Humanities, the UCSD Academic Senate, and the UCSD Institute for International, Comparative, and Area Studies. Parts of chapter 2 were previously published as "Militarized Refuge: A Transpacific Perspective on Vietnamese Refuge Flight to the United States," in *Pacific and American Studies* 12 (2012): 20–32, and an earlier version of chapter 2 will be published as "Militarized Refuge: A Critical Rereading of

Vietnamese Flight to the United States," in *Transpacific Studies: Framing an Emerging Field*, edited by Janet Hoskins and Viet Thanh Nguyen (Honolulu: University of Hawaii Press, 2014). An earlier version of chapter 4 was published as "The 'We-Win-Even-When-We-Lose' Syndrome: U.S. Press Coverage of the Twenty-Fifth Anniversary of the 'Fall of Saigon'" in *American Quarterly* 58, no. 2 (2006): 329–52. Thanks to the publishers for permission to reprint.

Outside of academia, I thank Delia Goodwin and Leticia Schrupp for their steadfast friendships; Antoinette Charfauros-McDaniel and Leigh Ann Farmer for our shared daughters; Sonja de Lugo for our many long conversations over the years; and Michael de Lugo for his big heart. And special thanks to Tyler Davenport, wise beyond his years, for showing me that we do not have to be related by blood to be family. He has my deepest affection—always.

Finally, my family—my reason for everything. I thank my husband, Abe, for the gift of our children. People often ask how I balance it all. My answer: it has never been a balancing act. The children have always been my priorities; nothing else comes close. I admire Evyn for her keen intellect, deep understanding of social inequalities, and genuine commitment to social justice; Maya for her quick wit, artistic talents, and love of family; and Gabriel for his agile mind, quiet strength, and cautious nature. A special shout-out to Maya for creating the striking book cover, which beautifully captures the mixture of violence and joy of refugee life: in this case, a refugee camp that is surrounded by barbed wires and exploding bombs, but also adorned by flowers and brightly clothed children. I am confident she will realize her dream of becoming a children's book illustrator. I also want to acknowledge my extended family in Việt Nam for their abiding love—no matter the elapsing time and distance. And lastly, this book is dedicated to my mother, Hồ Ngọc Hoa, for all that she has endured as a refugee in the United States but also for all that she has managed to build for her daughter—and her beloved grandchildren—in this very space of militarized *refuge*.

1 Critical Refuge(e) Studies

> There were things about us Mel never knew or remem-
> bered. He didn't remember that we hadn't come running
> through the door he opened but, rather, had walked, keep-
> ing close together and moving very slowly, as people often
> do when they have no idea what they're walking towards or
> what they're walking from.
>
> lê thi diem thúy, *The Gangster We Are All Looking For*

At this moment of reinvigorated U.S. imperialism and globalized militarization, it is important to interrogate anew public recollections of the
U.S. war in Vietnam—"the war with the difficult memory."[1] As a "controversial, morally questionable and unsuccessful"[2] war, the Vietnam War
has the potential to unsettle the master narratives of World War II—in
which the United States rescued desperate people from tyrannical governments and reformed them "into free and advanced citizens of the
postwar democratic world."[3] It is this "good war" master narrative of
World War II, in which the United States is depicted as triumphant *and*
moral, that legitimizes and valorizes U.S. militaristic intervention
around the world then and now. This book thus asks: how has the United
States dealt with the "difficult memory" of the Vietnam War—a war that
left it as neither victor nor liberator? Having lost the Vietnam War, the
United States had no "liberated" country or people to showcase, and, as
such, the Vietnam War appears to offer an antidote to the "rescue and
liberation" myths and memories. Yet, in the absence of a liberated
Vietnam and people, the U.S. government, academy, and mainstream
media have produced a substitute: the freed and reformed Vietnamese
refugees.

1

Calling attention to the link between the trope of the "good refugee" and the myth of "the nation of refuge," this book argues that the figure of the Vietnamese refugee, the purported grateful beneficiary of the U.S. "gift of freedom,"[4] has been key to the (re)cuperation of American identities and the shoring up of U.S. militarism in the post–Vietnam War era. As I will show, Vietnamese refugees, whose war sufferings remain unmentionable and unmourned in most U.S. public discussions of Vietnam,[5] have ironically become the featured evidence of the appropriateness of U.S. actions in Vietnam: that the war, no matter the cost, was ultimately necessary, just, and successful. Having been deployed to "rescue" the Vietnam War for Americans, Vietnamese refugees thus constitute a *solution*, rather than a *problem*, for the United States, as often argued. The conjoined term *"refuge(es)"* is meant to encapsulate this symbiotic relationship: that *refuge* and *refugees* are co-constitutive, and that both are the (by)product of U.S. militarism—what I term "militarized refuge(es)."

On the surface, the image of thousands of Vietnamese risking death in order to escape "communism" and resettle in the United States appears to affirm U.S. uncontested status as a nation of refuge. Yet, as Vietnamese American writer lê thi diem thúy reminds us in the epigraph, not all Vietnamese came running through the door that the United States allegedly opened. Rather, many moved very slowly, with much confusion, ambivalence, and even misgivings, uncertain about what they were walking toward or what they were walking from. And a few, in fact, travelled in the opposite direction, away from the United States.[6] In other words, the refugee flight-to-resettlement process was full of detours and snags, characterized "by chaos at the end of the war, confusion, and the stark absence of choice for many of those who had 'evacuated.'"[7] The messiness, contingency, and precarious nature of refugee life means that refugees, like all people, are beset by contradiction: neither damaged victims nor model minorities, they—their stories, actions, and inactions—simultaneously trouble *and* affirm regimes of power.

During the Vietnam War, the U.S. Army employed "body counts"—the number of confirmed Vietnamese kills—to chart U.S. progress in the war.[8] Accordingly, I use this very term, *body counts,* as the book's title in order to expose the war's costs borne by the Vietnamese and to insist that bodies—Vietnamese bodies—should *count.* Focusing on the politics of war memory and commemoration, *Body Counts* examines the connections between

history, memory, and power, and it refashions the fields of American studies, Asian American studies, and refugee studies not around the narratives
of American exceptionalism, and immigration, and transnationalism but
around the crucial issues of war, race, and violence—and of the history and
memories that are forged from the thereafter. Explicitly interdisciplinary,
Body Counts moves between various disciplines in the humanities and
social sciences, drawing on historical, ethnographic, cultural, and virtual
evidence in order to trace not only what has disappeared but also what has
remained—to look for the places where Vietnamese refugees have managed to conjure up social, public, and collective remembering.

Although this book recounts the wounds of social life caused by the
violence both before and after the Vietnam War, its primary objective is to
reveal the social practices that have emerged to attend to these wounds.[9]
Body Counts thus moves decisively away from the "damage-centered"
approach so prevalent in the field of refugee studies and focuses instead
on how first- and second-generation Vietnamese have created alternative
memories and epistemologies that unsettle but at times also confirm the
established public narratives of the Vietnam War and Vietnamese people.
Emphasizing the range of Vietnamese perspectives both before and after
the war, it critically examines the relationship between history and memory, not as facts but as narratives. Like other communities in exile,
Vietnamese in the United States feel keenly the urgency to forge unified
histories, identities, and memories. Against such moral weight of "the
community," *Body Counts* asks what happens to events that cannot be narrated. What lies just underneath the surface? Which memories are erased,
forgotten, or postponed and archived for future release? Where and how
then do these "nonevents" fit into the narration of history?[10] In sum, how
would refugees, not as an object of investigation but as a site of social critique, "articulate the incomprehensible or heretofore unspeakable"?[11]

SOCIAL SCIENCES: PRODUCTION OF THE "REFUGEE PROBLEM"

In the devastating aftermath of Hurricane Katrina in 2005, reporters,
politicians, and media commentators used the term "refugee" to describe

the tens of thousands of storm victims, many of them poor African Americans, who were uprooted from their homes along the Gulf coast and forced to flee in search of refuge. Almost immediately, prominent African American leaders, including Jesse Jackson and Al Sharpton, charged that the use of *refugee* to refer to Katrina survivors was "racially biased," contending that the term implies second-class citizens—or even non-Americans.[12] For these critics, "refugeeness" connotes "otherness," summoning the image of "people in a Third World country" who "carried the scraps of their lives in plastic trash bags," wore "donated clothes," and slept "on the floor of overpopulated shelters."[13] In this context, calling U.S.-born African Americans *refugees* was tantamount to stripping them of their citizenship—"their right to be part of the national order of things."[14]

As the Katrina controversy reveals, and as the following review makes clear, the term "refugee" triggers associations with highly charged images of Third World poverty, foreignness, and statelessness. These associations reflect the transnationally circulated representations of refugees as incapacitated objects of rescue, fleeing impoverished, war-torn, or corrupt states—an unwanted problem for asylum and resettlement countries. As "refugeeism" has become a prominent feature of our times, Trinh T. Minh-ha urges us to "empty it, get rid of it, or else let it drift"—to prevent the word "refugee" from "being reduced to yet another harmless catchword."[15] Trinh tells us that words have always been effective weapons to assert order and win political combats but that, when we scrutinize their assertions, "they reveal themselves, above all, as awkward posturing, as they often tend to blot out the very reality they purport to convey."[16] This section scrutinizes the assertions of the word "refugee," as propagated in the social sciences, especially in the discipline of sociology, in order to empty it of its power. In reviewing the literature on Vietnamese refugees, I pay close attention to its role in interpellating and producing the Vietnamese subject, in naturalizing certain understandings of their resettlement in the United States, and in reinforcing specific ideologies about the U.S. role before and after the Vietnam War. In particular, I am interested in how and why the term "refugee"—not as a legal classification but as an *idea*—continues to circumscribe American understanding of the Vietnamese, even when Vietnamese in the United States now constitute multiple migrant categories, from political exiles to immigrants to transmigrants, as well as a large number of native-born.

I initiated this book project in part because I was troubled by what Eve Tuck calls damaging and "damage-centered" social science research that reinforces and reinscribes a one-dimensional notion of racialized communities as "depleted, ruined, and hopeless."[17] Emphasizing the traumas of war, flight, and exile, social scientists have constructed Vietnamese refugees as "only lives to be saved,"[18] a people "incapacitated by grief and therefore in need of care."[19] As a people fleeing from the only war that the United States had lost, Vietnamese refugees have been subject to intense scholarly interest—an "overdocumented" yet ironically un-visible population when compared to other U.S. immigrant groups. Indeed, the 1975 cohort, as state-sponsored refugees, may be the most studied arrival cohort in U.S. immigration history.[20]

Soon after Vietnamese refugees arrived in the United States in 1975, the federal government, in collaboration with social scientists, initiated a series of needs assessment surveys to generate knowledge on what was widely touted as a "refugee resettlement crisis." Viewing the newly arrived refugees as coming from "a society so markedly different from that of America," government officials and scholars alike regarded the accumulation of data on Vietnamese economic and sociocultural adaptation essential to "protect[ing] the interests of the American public."[21] Other substantial data sets on Vietnamese refugee adaptation followed: from the Bureau of Social Science Research Survey, the Institute for Social Research Survey, the National Institute of Child Health and Human Developmen (NICHD) funded survey, and other government records, including the 1980 U.S. Census.[22] Constituting the primary data sources on Vietnamese and other Southeast Asians from the mid-1970s and throughout the 1980s, these large-scale surveys, which cumulatively portrayed the refugees as a *problem* to be solved, delimited and conceptually underpinned future scholarly studies and popular representations of these communities in the United States. This hyper-focus on the refugees' needs and achievements has located the *problem* within the bodies and minds of the refugees rather than in the global historical conditions that produce massive displacements and movements of refugees to the United States and elsewhere.

Prescribing assimilation as the solution to the "refugee problem," subsequent studies have imposed a generalized narrative of immigration on

Vietnamese refugees, thereby reducing the specificities of their flight to a conventional story of ethnic assimilation.[23] The assimilation narrative constructs Vietnamese as the "good refugee" who enthusiastically and uncritically embrace and live the "American Dream."[24] Christine Finnan's 1981 study of the occupational assimilation of Vietnamese in Santa Clara County provides a telling example. In Finnan's account, the oft-exploitative electronics industry becomes a "symbol of opportunity" in which Vietnamese technicians "are eager to work as many hours of overtime as possible."[25] Even while praising the hardworking and enterprising Vietnamese, Finnan discursively distances them from normative American workers by reporting that "occupations that may seem undesirable to *us* may be perfectly suited to [the refugees'] current needs" and that Vietnamese become technicians "because they are patient and can memorize things easily."[26] Finnan also contends that Vietnamese, even those who were the elite in Vietnam, prefer working as electronics technicians in the United States to working in Vietnam "because there is more potential for advancement here."[27] In the same way, Nathan Caplan and colleagues optimistically characterize Vietnamese economic pursuits as "conspicuously successful" even while reporting that the overwhelming majority (71 percent) held "low-level, low-paying, dead-end jobs" and that slightly more than half (55 percent) were employed in the periphery rather than in the core economic sector.[28]

By the late 1980s, scholars, along with the mass media and policy makers, had begun to depict the Vietnamese as the newest Asian American "model minority." Published in 1989, *The Boat People and Achievement in America,* which recounts the economic and educational success of the first-wave refugees who came to the United States during the 1970s, was among the first and most influential texts to document Vietnamese "success," likening it to the larger Asian American process of assimilation: "The refugees have now begun to share in the Asian American success stories we have become accustomed to find reported in the news media," and "The success of the Indochinese refugees are, in a broad framework, also part of the overall achievement of Asian Americans."[29] Subsequent publications were particularly effusive about the "legendary" academic accomplishments of Vietnamese refugees' children who "came to America as boat people . . . survived perilous escapes and lost one to three years in refugee camps."[30]

CRITICAL REFUGE(E) STUDIES

Together, these studies present the United States as self-evidently *the* land of opportunity, which then allow the authors to conclude that, even when Vietnamese are underemployed and barely eking out a living, they are still better off in the United States than if they had remained in Vietnam. Because the word "refugee" conjures up images of a desperate people fleeing a desperate country, Vietnamese workers are presumed to be naturally suited and even grateful to work in boring, repetitive, monotonous, low-paying, and insecure jobs. Such tidy conclusions dispense with questions about U.S. power structures that continue to consign a significant number of Vietnamese Americans to unstable, minimum-wage employment, welfare dependency, and participation in the informal economy years after their arrival.[31] Moreover, this ahistorical juxtaposition of opportunities in Vietnam and in the United States naturalizes the great economic disparity between the two countries, depicting the two economies as unconnected rather than mutually constituted. As I will elaborate in chapter 4, the production of the assimilated and grateful refugee—the "good refugee"—enables a potent narrative of America(ns) rescuing and caring for Vietnam's "runaways," which powerfully remakes the case for the rightness of the U.S. war in Vietnam.

REFUGEES AS A SOCIO-LEGAL OBJECT OF KNOWLEDGE

Departing from the emphasis on refugee resettlement in sociology, some scholars in the interdisplinary field of international relations have stressed the significance of the "refugee" category, especially in the twentieth century, for the practice of statecraft.[32] This scholarship thus conceptualizes the refugees not as a problem but, in a sense, as a *solution* for resettlement countries. As Nevzat Soguk muses, for all that states denounce refugee outflows as a problem, the precarious condition of "refugeeness" in fact provides "affirmative resources for statist practices," fostering a better appreciation of what it means to enjoy state protection.[33] In Susan Carruthers's words, the refugees' insecurity is "at once a rebuke and a reminder that there's 'no place like home.'"[34] As reviewed below, the more critical and interdisciplinary scholarship in the field of international relations undercuts the traditional social science conceptualization of refugees as a problem to be solved and scrutinizes instead the economic, cultural, and political foundations of the modern nation-state.

In her generative book on the cultural politics of international encounter, international affairs scholar Melani McAlister urges us to bring "the cultural analysis of empire into the heart of U.S. foreign policy studies."[35] Emphasizing the complex connections between cultural and political narratives, McAlister contends that foreign policy itself is a meaning-making activity that has helped to define the nation and its interests.[36] The more critical international relations literature on refugee policies reveals that the provision of asylum has constituted an important foreign policy tool to tout the appeal of the U.S. brand of "freedom."[37] As such, refugee policies are active producers of meaning—a site for consolidating ideas not only about the desperate refugees but also about the desirability of the place of refuge.[38]

The figure of the refugee, as a socio-legal object of knowledge, has been metaphorically central in the construction of U.S. global power. According to Randy Lippert, during the Cold War years, "*refugeeness* became a moral-political tactic," demarcating the difference between the supposed uncivilized East and the civilized West, and fostering "cohesion of the Western Alliance nations."[39] In 1951, prodded by the United States, whose paradigmatic refugee was the East European and Soviet escapee, the U.N. Convention Relating to the Status of Refugees officially defined "refugee" as a person who "is outside the country of his nationality" and who harbors a "well-founded fear of being persecuted for reasons of race, religion, nationality, membership of a particular social group or political opinion."[40] Although this definition focused on the plight of individuals rather than groups and emphasized the causes of flight, it unduly privileged victims of *political* oppression above victims of natural disaster or other types of oppression.[41]

During the Cold War, the term "refugee" became interchangeable with "defector," as the "provision of asylum became a foreign policy tool" awarded by Western countries primarily to European anticommunists who fled or refused to be repatriated to Communist countries.[42] The propaganda value of accepting refugees fleeing communism—deemed the living symbols of communism's failure—was central to U.S. foreign policy goals, providing the nation with an alleged advantage over the Soviet

Union. Historian Carl J. Bon Tempo reports that, in 1948, following the admission of more than 250,000 displaced Europeans, Congress passed the Displaced Persons Act, which provided for the admission of an additional 400,000 European refugees. Reflecting the anticommunist imperative of the time, subsequent refugee laws granted admission primarily to persons escaping from Communist governments, largely from Hungary, Poland, Yugoslavia, Korea, and China, and in the 1960s from Cuba.[43] Until the mid-1980s, more than 90 percent of the refugees admitted to the United States came mainly from countries in the Communist Eastern bloc.[44] Tempo thus concludes, "It is little wonder, then, that for much of the post–World War II era, Americans, from presidents to the public, associated refugees with anticommunism."[45]

The association of refugees with anticommunism influenced U.S. policies on refugees from Southeast Asia. Soon after the 1975 "Fall of Saigon,"[46] Congress, at the urging of President Gerald Ford, passed the Indochina Migration and Refugee Assistance Act, granting refugees from South Vietnam and Cambodia unprecedented large-scale entry to, and resettlement in, the United States. Between 1975 and the mid-1980s, some 360,000 refugees from Southeast Asia entered the United States through a series of parole authorizations by the president. In the face of continuing outflows of refugees from Southeast Asia as well as from the Soviet Union and Cuba, Congress passed the landmark Refugee Act of 1980, which adopted the 1951 United Nations' definition of "refugee" and established for the first time a uniform procedure for the admission and resettlement of refugees of "special concern" to the United States. Although the purported goal of the 1980 act was to drop any reference to communism and eliminate the previous geographic restrictions on granting of refugee status to only Europeans, the actual admissions proposals for fiscal-year 1980 continued to prioritize refugees who had "close ties to the United States," whose resettlement would further U.S. foreign policy objectives, and for whom the "United States has stood uniquely as a symbol of freedom from oppression."[47] In other words, the 1980 act remained most hospitable to refugees fleeing communism, which resonated with then-president Ronald Reagan's ardent anticommunist foreign policy.[48]

According to Ambassador Victor H. Palmieri, U.S. Coordinator for Refugee Acts, refugees from Southeast Asia were the main beneficiaries of the 1980 act. Characterizing the Southeast Asian refugee outflows as "a human tragedy of staggering dimensions," the United States proposed to admit a total of 168,000 refugees from "Indochina" in fiscal-year 1980, in comparison to the proposed 33,000 from the Soviet Union and 19,500 from Cuba.[49] Palmieri espoused that these refugee admissions constituted a "major commitment by [the U.S.] government and by the American people" to help "these persecuted and uprooted persons begin new lives in our country."[50] Senator Ted Kennedy likewise praised the legislation: "In the Refugee Act of 1980, Congress gave new statutory authority to the United States' longstanding commitment to human rights and its traditional humanitarian concern for the plight of refugees."[51] Palmieri's and Kennedy's statements encapsulate the argument of this section: that U.S. refugee policy constitutes a key site for the production of Vietnamese refugees as grief-stricken objects marked for rescue and the United States as the ideal refuge for the "persecuted and uprooted" refugees. This representation of the conjoined refuge(es) "write[s] out the specificities of forced migration and the legacy of the Vietnam War," enabling Americans to remake themselves from military aggressors into magnanimous rescuers.[52]

CRITICAL REFUGEE STUDIES

Though distinct in purpose and methodology, the scholarship on refugee resettlement and on refugee policies construct the refugees as out-of-place victims and the nation-state as the ultimate provider of human welfare. In these studies, the rooted citizen constitutes both the norm and the ideal, whereas the refugee is described as uprooted, dislocated, and displaced from the national community.[53] These studies thus treat state borders as geographical givens rather than territorial boundaries constructed by law and regulated by force. In this section, I chart an interdisciplinary field of *critical refugee study*, which conceptualizes "the refugee" not as an object of investigation but rather as a *paradigm* "whose function [is] to establish and make intelligible a wider set of problems."[54] This field begins with the premise that the refugee, who inhabits a condition of statelessness, radically calls into question the established principles of the nation-state and the idealized goal of inclusion and recognition within it. Critical refugee studies thus flip the script, positing that it is the existence of the displaced refugee, rather than the rooted citizen, that provides the clue to a new politics and model of international relations. Yet I also argue that critical refugee studies scholars need to do more than critique; we need to be attentive to refugees as "intentionalized beings"[55] who possess and enact their *own* politics as they emerge out of the ruins of war and its afermath. As T. Fujitani and colleagues argue in an influential volume on Asia-Pacific War(s), it is important "to move beyond a strictly deconstructive mode, to intervene positively in the recovery and reinterpretation of events, experiences, and sentiments that have been pushed to the margins of the past."[56] In short, critical refugee study scholarship conceptualizes the "refugee" as a critical idea but also as a social actor whose life, when traced, illuminates the interconnections of colonization, war, and global social change.

Political Philosophy Critique of the Citizen/Nation/State Hierarchy

A place to begin would be Hannah Arendt's brief but important 1943 essay, "We Refugees," in which she proposes that the condition of being a refugee, which brings into serious question the assumption of rights, constitutes the paradigm of a new historical consciousness.[57] Refugees, as those who have lost all rights, are the anomalies that expose the contradiction at the heart of the liberal democratic nation-state: the principle of national sovereignty implies the right to exclude anyone from citizenship or entry, but such exclusion from rights is at odds with the professed commitment of the liberal democratic state to universal individual rights. Extending Arendt's insight, Giorgio Agamben considers the displaced refugee to be the central figure of our political history: the "one and only figure" that exposes most deeply the "original fiction" of modern national sovereignty.[58] Indeed, the three primary solutions to the "refugee crisis"—repatriation, integration into the first-asylum countries, or resettlement in a third country—all affirm that the refugees represent an aberration of categories in the national order of things.

Arrendt's and Agamben's theoretizations of the refugee reveal the limits of the liberal effort to assimilate refugees to the nation-state and thus of the social science studies that focus on refugee resettlement reviewed above. For these political philosophers and their followers, a normative theory of global justice fails to grasp that the reform of existing institutions can only reinforce the system of nation-states that produces refugees in the first place.[59] For example, Robyn Liu warns that the desire to provide a durable solution to the "refugee problem"—"to create or restore the bond between a person as a citizen and a state as her legal protector"—ends up affirming the status of the nation-state as the ultimate protector and provider of human welfare.[60] In the same way, Soguk maintains that humanitarian interventions on behalf of refugees—represented as "citizens gone aberrant"—"enforce intergovernmental regimentation that reinscribes the statist hierarchy of citizen-nation-state."[61] As Viet Thanh Nguyen succinctly states: although immigrant studies affirm the nation-states the immigrant comes from and settles into, critical refugee studies challenge the very viability of the nation-state.[62]

In a world imagined to be composed of mutually exclusive, territorially bound spaces, refugees, lacking the qualities of the citizen, do not properly belong anywhere because they "constantly remind others of the arbitrariness and contingence of identity borders and boundaries."[63] Since refugees represent an aberration in the national order of things, nations tend to externalize refugees ideologically, constituting them as objects of state suspicion, threats to security, and a *problem* in need of therapeutic intervention—thus the overemphasis on refugee resettlement outcomes discussed above.[64] In other words, as critical refugee studies scholars point out, refugees are a "problem" not because they are pathetic victims who drain the state's resources but because they make visible "a transgression of the social contract between a state and its citizen."[65] As someone "out of place"—that is, without the protection of the state—a refugee is an anomaly whose status needs to be brought back into place by either naturalization or repatriation. When these options do not materialize, as I discuss in chapter 3, refugees are held in detention camps for an indeterminate amount of time, their liberty suspended "for no other reason than having arrived within a territory which is not their own."[66]

"Complex Personhood" and "Intentionalized Beings"

The political philosophy literature, which calls into question the fiction of modern sovereignty, provides an effective epistemological critique of the discourse on refugee resettlement by pointing out that liberal resettlement programs are a form of "geopolitical humanitarianism" that end up affirming the state-citizen hierarchy.[67]

Still, epistemological critiques, however powerful, risk rendering the refugee "only as a lack."[68] I am more persuaded by Patricia Owens's argument that political philosophy critiques of the modern nation-state can appear both "arrogant and irrelevant" to the lives of real refugees who are often seeking, above all, the right to belong to a political community.[69] I argue that an engaged critical refugee studies project needs to do more than critique; it also needs to integrate sophisticated theoretical rigor with the daily concerns of real people as they navigate their social worlds. To be clear, I am not privileging resistance or agency; I am aware of the pitfalls of analyses that romanticize and reify marginalized subjects while eliding the complexity and multiplicity of their lives. I am also cognizant of the poststructuralist insistence that social beings are always culturally and politically constructed. As Sherry Ortner ruminates on what she terms "the crisis of representation in the human sciences":

> When Edward Said says in effect that the discourse of Orientalism renders it virtually impossible to know anything real about the Orient (1979); when Gayatri Spivak tells us that the "subaltern cannot speak" (1988); when James Clifford informs us that all ethnographies are "fictions" (1986:7); and when of course in some sense all of these things are true—then the effect is a powerful inhibition on . . . seeking to understand other people in other times and places, especially those people who are not in dominant positions.[70]

Yet, as Ortner also eloquently argues, it is possible to acknowledge that subjects are constructed and that oppression is damaging, and *still* recognize the ability "of social beings to weave alternative, and sometimes brilliantly creative, forms of coherence across the damages."[71] Tuck calls this recognition "desire-based" research, which "accounts for the loss and despair, but also the hope, the visions, the wisdom of lived lives and communities."[72]

With some notable exceptions, the literature on forced displacement has ignored the refugees' rich and complicated lived worlds, the ways in which they labor to have resilient, productive, and even heroic lives in displacement.[73] I agree with Ortner that dominated subjects do more than simply oppose or react to domination, that "they have their *own* politics," which has been forged through the logic of their "own locally and historically evolved bricolage."[74] In other words, even when refugees are reduced to an "aberration of categories" or "a zone of pollution,"[75] they are, to cite Avery Gordon, never, never just that.[76] In Tuck's eloquent words: "Even when communities are broken and conquered, they are so much more than that—so much more that this incomplete story is an act of aggression."[77] What I hope to show is that Vietnamese refugees are "intentionalized beings" who enact their hopes, beliefs, and politics, even when they live militarized lives.[78] My intent is not to valorize Vietnamese refugees but to note their "complex personhood,"[79] to be attentive to how they manage their lives, and to take seriously, rather than dismissively, their differing and different subject positions and political perspectives. I also hope to show, as Trinh notes, that "the state of indeterminateness and of indefinite unsettlement" that characterizes the refugees' life in transit *persists* in resettlement, even when the "happily resettled" tout their feelings of gratitude or flaunt their material success.[80] In short, the aspiration of the book is to call attention to lives that have been ravaged by war: to mark the broken trajectories as well as the moments of action as refugees search for and insist on their right to *more*.

VIETNAMESE AMERICAN STUDIES: ABOUT MILITARIZED REFUGE(ES)

"For general western spectatorship, Vietnam does not exist outside of the war," observes Trinh.[81] Concerned that Vietnam exists only as a spectacle for the West, many Vietnamese proclaim that Vietnam is a country, not a war. Tired of being associated "only with *that* war" in which Vietnamese are represented most often as pathetic and passive victims, some Vietnamese American studies scholars have insisted that we move the field beyond the parameter of the war in order to study Vietnamese in all their complexities.[82] The past four decades have seen a proliferation of articles and books that cover Vietnamese lives from more complex and critical perspectives. Nazli Kibria's ethnographic study of Vietnamese families in Philadelphia in the early 1980s remains the richest study of the changing family dynamics within the Vietnamese American community.[83]

Following Kibria's example, subsequent studies began to conceptualize Vietnamese not as a refugee group in transit but as a new racial or ethnic group that is deliberately and gradually embedding themselves in their new communities.[84] Moving beyond demographic and needs assessment studies, an emerging generation of Vietnamese American scholars shifted the focus of study to the linguistic, cultural, and literary expressions of the Vietnamese diasporic communities.[85] As an example, a 2003 *Amerasia Journal* special issue on Vietnamese Americans emphasized the transnational dimensions of their experience, including studies on transnational cultural flows and forms of collaboration between Vietnamese American and Vietnamese music makers, transnational marriages between women in Vietnam and overseas Vietnamese men who live in Western countries, and transnational assembly work.[86]

These studies also open up the category "Vietnamese American" by addressing the gender, sexual, class, political, religious, cultural, and generational diversity of the population and by articulating the localistic, familial, national, and transnational linkages of Vietnamese lives. As a group, these works on the Vietnamese diaspora integrate isolated studies of the "Vietnamese experience" into the larger field of migration studies and enable Vietnamese studies scholars to join postmodern theorists and others in cultural studies in the larger discourse about diaspora, exile, transnationalism, ethnicity, and identity.[87] In sum, these promising developments in the field of Vietnamese studies provide us a rare glimpse into how Vietnamese have created their worlds and made meaning for themselves—and in so doing, to restore, in Amitava Kumar's words, "a certain weight of experience, a stubborn density, a *life* to what we encounter in newspaper columns as abstract, often faceless, figures without histories."[88]

Although I am certainly sympathetic with this desire to move beyond the war, I worry that such a decoupling of Vietnamese Americans from the Vietnam War risks assimilating Vietnamese into the apolitical and ahistorical category of "cultural diversity," in which Vietnamese become represented as just one more marker of cultural difference in the U.S. multicultural landscape. I am also concerned that, even some forty years after its "end," a "determined incomprehension" remains the dominant U.S. public stance on the history and legacy of the Vietnam War.[89] Despite the profusion of text and talk on the Vietnam War in Vietnam(ese) studies, I contend that the field has yet to critically engage the war as an important historical and discursive site of Vietnamese subject formation and of the shaping and articulation of U.S. nationhood. This book thus asks us to return once again to *that* war and its "refugees." Although I recognize that Vietnam is a country and not a war, and that Vietnamese lives do not begin and end with the Vietnam War, I agree with Viet Thanh Nguyen that its/our "history still demands an ongoing engagement with what that war meant, if we are not to concede its meaning to revisionist, nationalist agendas in the United States."[90] Accordingly, I suggest that, rather than doing away with the term "refugee," we imbue it with social and political critiques that call into question the relationships between war, race, and violence, then and now.

Militarized Refuge(es)

Since the 1993 publication of the landmark collection *Cultures of United States Imperialism,* in which Amy Kaplan called out the glaring conceptual and ideological "absence of empire from the study of American culture,"[91] studies of colonialism and imperialism have proliferated as American studies scholars shifted attention away from nationalist paradigms and foregrounded America's embeddedness within transnational and hemispheric cultures and histories.[92] Included in this critical scholarship is a growing body of work that examines the ways in which empire and war, especially the Cold War, have intersected in American culture.[93] Moving away from the voluminous military and diplomatic histories that focused on war's political leaders, military planners, and policymakers, these newer studies conceptualize war as a cultural phenomenon, paying particular attention to how "policy-making, intelligence-gathering, war-making, and mainstream politics might be profoundly shaped by a social and cultural world beyond the conference table or battlefield."[94] Most provocative are studies that reveal how colonial histories and cultures constitute the conditions of possibility for ongoing forms of militarization.[95]

I recognize the value of conceptualizing war as a "knowledge project or epistemology,"[96] but I also believe that we need to continue to think of war in terms of "militarized violence"—not only epistemic or symbolic violence but the actual physical violence of "guns and bombs" unleashed on "expendable nonpersons," those devoid of names and faces, family and personal histories, dreams and hopes, politics and beliefs. According to U.S. Department of Defense statistics, close to six million U.S. troops served in Southeast Asia and/or South Vietnam during the Vietnam War. The number of U.S. troops in Vietnam peaked at 543,000 in April 1969.[97] The My Lai Massacre, in which U.S. forces massacred about 400 unarmed women, children, and elderly men in the village of My Lai in South Vietnam, is widely considered "the most shocking episode of the Vietnam War."[98] U.S. military policies (e.g., search-and-destroy missions in the South, carpet-bombing raids in the North, free-fire zones, and chemical defoliation) cost Vietnam at least three million lives, the maiming of countless bodies, the poisoning of its water, land, and air, the razing of its countryside, and the devastation of most of its infrastructure. Indeed, more explosives were dropped on Vietnam, a country two-thirds the size of California, than in all of World War II. According to Heonik Kwon, the war in Vietnam was a culmination of technological advancement in the weapons of mass destruction and was a philosophical "total war." Whereas the war in North Vietnam was a "conventional war" with a clear division of labor between armed combatants and unarmed civilians, the war in the South was an unconventional one in which villagers had to fight as hard as any armed soldiers—not necessarily to win the war, but just to survive. In the southern context, war death could be the death of anyone.[99]

U.S. scholarship has largely separated war studies and refugee studies into different fields of study. This decoupling obscures the formative role that U.S. wars play in structuring the displacements, dispersions, and migrations of refugees to the United States and elsewhere. As Setsu Shigematsu and Keith Camacho contend, "U.S. war waging has become an integral, if not naturalized, part of the grammar of . . . (im)migration narratives."[100] And yet, in the U.S. academy, popular media, and published autobiographies and memoirs, Vietnamese flight to the United States is most often portrayed as a matter of desperate individuals fleeing political persecution and/or economic depression, or simply fleeing "the Communists," completely discounting the aggressive roles that the U.S. government, military, and corporations have played in generating this exodus in the first place. It is not that the history of U.S. military, economic, and political intervention in Vietnam is excluded in studies on Vietnamese Americans; rather, it is often included only as background information—

as the events that *precede* the refugee flight rather than as the actions that *produce* this very exodus, the refugee subject, and the U.S. nation-state.

Juxtaposing refugee/immigration studies and war/international studies, I contend in this book that it is the presence of the refugees—Vietnam's runaways—that enables the United States to recast its aggressive military strategy as a benevolent intervention. As Jodi Kim argues, the refugee simultaneously is a product of, a witness to, and a site of critique of the gendered and racial violence of U.S. wars.[101] I thus situate my discussion of refuge(es) within a specific frame of reference: the long, long durée of U.S. colonial expansion and war making in Asia. In chapter 2, I coin the term "*militarized* refuge(es)"—with its intended jarring juxtaposition—in order to expose the hidden violence behind the humanitarian term "refuge," thereby challenging the powerful narrative of America(ns) rescuing and caring for Vietnam's discarded that erases the role that U.S. foreign policy and war played in inducing the "refugee crisis" in the first place.

History and Memory

In the United States, public discussions of the Vietnam War often skip over the history of militarized violence inflicted on Vietnam and its people. It is not that the Vietnam War has been forgotten. Partly due to the lack of a national resolution, the Vietnam War "is the most chronicled, documented, reported, filmed, taped, and—in all likelihood—narrated war in [U.S.] history."[102] But, as Ralph Ellison reminds us, the highly visible can actually be a type of invisibility such that the profusion of text and talk on the Vietnam War actually conceals the costs borne by the Vietnamese[103]— the lifelong costs that turn the "Fall of Saigon" and the exodus from Vietnam into "the endings that are not over."[104] As scholars, public historians, and the media have repeatedly documented, Americans have been obsessed with the Vietnam War as an *American* tragedy. As a result, most American writings on the war involve the highly organized and strategic forgetting of the Vietnamese people: "They are conspicuously absent in their roles as collaborators, victims, enemies, or simply the people whose land and over whom (supposedly) this war was fought."[105] As an example, the highly controversial Vietnam Veterans Memorial, the very site where U.S. cultural memory of the Vietnam War is represented and debated, disallows any acknowledgment of the war's effects on the Vietnamese. As Nguyên-Vo Thu Huong observes, "Vietnamese Americans as refugees occupy the position of self-mourners because no one else mourns us."[106]

The nonrecognition of Vietnamese losses raises the question: what makes for a grievable life? As Judith Butler asks, how does mourning take place for those who never "were," who "fit no dominant frame for the human," and whose lives do not count as lives?[107] Butler is not simply talking about the process of dehumanization, where humans are not regarded as humans; rather, she asks us to be attentive to the "racial differential that undergirds the culturally viable notions of the human"—notionsthat open up questions at the level of ontology: "What is real? Whose lives are real? . . . What, then, is the relation between violence and those lives considered as 'unreal'?"[108] Butler argues that this failure of recognition—the insistence that there was no event, no loss—"is mandated through an identification with those who identify with the perpetrators of the violence."[109] Relatedly, in a book on the boom in testimonies, autobiographies, and memoirs emanating from Iran, Iraq, and Afghanistan, Gillian Whitlock notes that some life narratives move quickly into and within Western media, whereas others are "epistemologically disabled" and remain "trapped" within the immediate community that has suffered the pain; he argues that this disparity has everything to do with "whose lives count, and under what circumstances."[110] To have traction, Whitlock contends, the refugee narrative needs "national history on its side" and must become linked to "civic virtue and the national good."[111]

As a consequence of "the masculinist hypervisibility of American representations of the Vietnam War"[112] and the concomitant discounting of Vietnamese (especially of South Vietnamese) accounts of the war, the most that we have are fragmented "flashes" of memory, of partial and imperfect recollections. Looking for and calling attention to the lost and missing subjects of history are critical to any political project. In a different context, Toni Morrison has instructed us to be mindful that "invisible things are not necessarily not-there."[113] How do we write about absences? How do we compel others to look for the things that are seemingly not there? How do we imagine beyond the limits of what is already stated to be understandable? To engage in war and refugee studies, then, is to look for the things that are barely there and to listen to "fragmentary testimonies, to

barely distinguishable testimonies, to testimonies that never reach us"[114]—
that is, to write ghost stories.

Attentive to "the ghostly" and "the afterlives" of Vietnamese refugees,[115]
this book gathers accounts of Vietnamese exilic remembrance and represents them as events that disrupt what Khatharya Um calls "the too-
early foreclosure upon the wounds of war and dispersal."[116] Amid so much
organized forgetting, I feel keenly the need to note Vietnamese American
presence, rather than its absence, and to find different ways of knowing
and writing about history outside of the realm of state-sanctioned commemorative discourses and practices. I also pay more attention to strategic and self-imposed silence than to the power-laden process of silencing,
to the ways that subjugated histories are told "quietly" or told without
words or sometimes safeguarded for future tellings, whether or not I grasp
the reasons behind these decisions.[117] At the end of the day, I concur with
Grace Cho that "there is as much power in uncertainty as in knowing the
truth," and I am grateful for what I have been able to glimpse and learn
from these gaps and empty spaces.[118]

BOOK OVERVIEW

As a critical refugee studies project, *Body Counts* examines the ways in
which the mutually constituted processes of remembering and forgetting
work in the production of official discourses about empire, war, and violence as well as in the construction of refugee subjectivities. Throughout, I
grapple with the difficulties and risks inherent in the methods and tech-
niques of reading, writing, and sharing "ghost stories"—or "truths" that are
unspoken or unspeakable. By paying special attention to Vietnamese
American histories whose traumatic consequences are still actively evolving
in today's space and time, *Body Counts* "is looking not so much for answers
as for new *enabling questions*, questions that would open new directions for
research and new conceptual spaces for the yet unborn answers."[119]

Body Counts critically engages the social science literature on refugees
through an interdisciplinary and intersectional perspective that "deliberately unravel[s] seemingly stable distinctions among identificatory
categories and disciplinary divisions."[120] Placing various critical fields in

conversation with each other, I aim to open up new avenues for critical investigation of structures of violence, power, and identity as well as new means of seeing and charting what Neferti Tadiar terms "alternative ways of becoming human":

> The tangential, fugitive, and insurrectionary creative social capacities that, despite being continuously impeded, and made illegible by dominant ways of being human, are exercised and invented by those slipping beyond the bounds of valued humanity in their very effort of living, in their making of forms of viable life.[121]

Although not explicitly about women's lives, *Body Counts* adopts a feminist approach to the study of militarized refuge(es): it examines the intersection between private grief and public commemoration, listens for unsaid things by relying on other senses such as feelings and emotions, and looks for the hidden political forces within the site of intimate domestic and familial interaction. In all, *Body Counts* engages in what I term "critical juxtaposing": the bringing together of seemingly different and disconnected events, communities, histories, and spaces in order to illuminate what would otherwise not be visible about the contours, contents, and afterlives of war and empire. Whereas the traditional comparative approach conceptualizes the groups, events, and places to be compared as already-constituted and discrete entities, the critical juxtaposing method posits that they are fluid rather than static and need to be understood in *relation* to each other and within the context of a flexible field of political discourses. I argue that it is through the methodology of critical juxtaposing that we can best see that Vietnamese commemorative practices occur not in a vacuum but at the intersection of familial, local, national, international, and transnational dynamics.

Focusing on refugee camps in Southeast Asia, the very site of the construction of Vietnamese as "passive, immobilized and pathetic,"[122] chapter 2 views the refugee flight—from Vietnam to the Philippines to Guam and then to California, all of which routed the refugees through U.S. military bases—as a critical lens through which to map, both discursively and materially, the legacy of U.S. military expansion into the Asia Pacific region and the military's heavy hand in the purportedly benevolent resettlement process. I make two related arguments: the first about military colonialism, which contends that it was (neo)colonial dependence on the United States that turned the Philippines and Guam into the receiving centers of the U.S. rescuing project; the second about militarized refuge, which emphasizes the mutually constitutive nature of the concepts "refugees" and "refuge" and shows how both emerge out of and in turn bolster U.S. militarism. Following chapter 2's investigation of the militarized nature of refugee camps, chapter 3 focuses on the social life that refugees forged and nurtured in the camps. The first part of the chapter shows how Vietnamese lives were subsumed into the biopolitical and necropolitical logics of organized camp life, and the second half details how Vietnamese refugees created new lifeworlds within the camp, not only to survive but to claim a life within it.

Chapters 4 and 5, as tandem chapters, examine the narrative of the "good refugee"—the successful, assimilated, and anticommunist newcomers. Chapter 4 argues that it is the narrative of the "good refugee," deployed by refugee studies scholars, mainstream U.S. media, and Vietnamese Americans themselves, that has been key in enabling the United States to turn the Vietnam War into a "good war." Chapter 5 tells the Vietnamese refugee version of this story, explaining how and why South Vietnam's war dead and anticommunism had become so central to the refugees' retellings of their war losses in the United States. Moving beyond the exclusionary commemorative sites, it focuses on two quotidian memory places—Internet memorials and commemorative street names—that Vietnamese Americans have improvised in order to remember their dead.

Chapter 6 focuses on the postwar generation, detailing how their experiences are mediated by their own "postmemory" of the Vietnam War, by their parents' direct experiences with the war, and by the politics of war commemoration practiced by both Vietnam and the United States. In chapter 7, the book's conclusion, I emphasize the war's irreconcilability and ongoingness, insisting that we pay attention to the living effects of what seems to be over and done with.

.   .   .   .   .

Given that the American public continues to perceive Vietnamese in the United States principally as war *refugees,* many Vietnamese Americans understandably bristle at the pigeonholing of their community as perpetual foreigner. While I agree that it is politically important to insist that Vietnamese have always been inside of and played absolutely crucial roles in the building and sustaining of the U.S. nation-state, I also believe that it is equally important to claim the critical space outside of the nation—to inhabit that space between countries from which we can articulate the tensions, irresolutions, and contradictions of the promise of citizenship and belongingness for those on the social margins. This "space between" also enables us to interrupt existing notions of "rescue and liberation" as it calls attention to the discarded who emerge from the brutal dislocations produced by war, colonization, and globalization as well as by the persistence of racialized discourses and practices in the United States.[123] Yet this critical stance of refusing incorporation is not necessarily the same as denying the need for refuge. Following Trinh, *Body Counts* thus asks: what is involved in maintaining this balance between "refuse and refuge"?[124]

lê thi diem thúy writes that Vietnamese refugees are a "people larger than their life situation."[125] To take seriously Vietnamese evolving perspectives of the war is to remember Vietnam as a historical site, Vietnamese people as genuine subjects, and the Vietnam War as having its own integrity that is internal to the history and politics of Vietnam. In all, *Body Counts* interrupts and disrupts the mutually constituted notions of "rescue and liberation" and the "good refugee" by calling attention to the lives that could or would have been, as well as the lives that did emerge from and out of the ruins of war, and "peace"—all the while insisting that we become tellers of *ghost stories*, that we pay attention to what modern history has rendered ghostly, and to write into being the seething presence of the things that appear to be not there.[126]

Amid the organized forgetting of the Vietnam War and its people, this book is an act of remembering—and remembrance.

2 Militarized Refuge(es)

> As battles become bases, so bases become battles; the bases
> in East Asia acquired in the Spanish American War and in
> World War II, such as Guam, Okinawa and the Philippines,
> became the primary sites from which the United States
> waged war on Vietnam. Without them, the costs and logis-
> tical obstacles for the U.S. would have been immense.
>
> Catherine Lutz, *Bases of Empire*

Just days before the Fall of Saigon,[1] my mother and I were among the thousands of people who were waiting anxiously at Tân Sơn Nhất International
Airport to board overloaded U.S. military cargo carriers that were evacuating
American personnel and their South Vietnamese allies. Since cargo carriers
are not designed for passengers, we crouched uncomfortably on the aircraft
floor, packed tightly against other exhausted bodies, as the carrier hurriedly
exited the city, heading toward the Pacific. Approximately three hours later,
the aircraft landed in the Philippines, where a group of Catholic nuns greeted
us with refreshments and prayers; after refueling and a brief rest, the carrier
flew us to a hastily assembled refugee center on the U.S. territory of Guam.
The next evening, in our makeshift "tent city" on Guam, we heard on the
radio that the Communist North Vietnamese and Viet Cong troops had captured Saigon, forcing the South Vietnamese government to surrender. To
this day, I remember the stillness of a stunned people, suddenly without their
quê hương (homeland). After a short stay on Guam, where we spent our days
waiting in long lines for just about everything, we boarded a commercial
aircraft and flew about 6,000 miles to our final destination: California.

In all, U.S. military aircraft carriers airlifted approximately 130,000
Vietnamese citizens out of the city in the final days before the Fall of

Saigon. It was only in conducting research for this chapter that I discovered that the route my mother and I took was the one most frequently used for airlifted refugees: from Vietnam to Clark Air Force Base in the Philippines to Andersen Air Force Base on Guam to Marine Corps Base Camp Pendleton in California; over 41 percent traveled it.[2] An additional 19 percent went from Vietnam to Guam and then on to Camp Pendleton; another 32 percent traveled to Camp Pendleton, making stops in the Philippines, Guam, or Wake Island. My research also revealed the oft-hidden *colonial* and *militarized* nature of these evacuations. With the Defense Department coordinating transportation and the Joint Chiefs of Staff–Pacific Command in charge of the military moves necessary for the evacuation, Vietnamese were airlifted from Saigon on U.S. military aircrafts, transferred to U.S. military bases in the Philippines, Guam, Thailand, Wake Island, and Hawaii, and delivered to yet another set of military bases throughout the United States: Camp Pendleton in California, Fort Chaffee in Arkansas, Eglin Air Force Base in Florida, or Fort Indiantown Gap in Pennsylvania. Moving from one U.S. military base to another, Vietnamese refugees in effect witnessed firsthand the reach of the U.S. empire in the Asia-Pacific region. That few scholars, including myself, have questioned these military connections speaks to the power of the myth of U.S. "rescue and liberation" to make un-visible the militarized nature of the evacuations.

In chapter 4, I will argue that the narrative of the "good refugee" has been key in enabling the United States to turn the Vietnam War improbably into a "good war"—an ultimately necessary and moral war. Here, I show that the good-war narrative requires the production not only of the good refugee but also of the good *refuge*. The making of the "good refuge" was launched in April 1975 as U.S. media and officials extolled and sensationalized the last-ditch efforts to evacuate and encamp the shell-shocked refugees at military bases throughout the Pacific archipelago. Ayako Sahara has argued that the end of the Vietnam War and its aftermath were the moments that the Ford and Carter administrations represented Southeast Asian refugees as the white man's burden, and the United States as the magnanimous rescuers, in order to facilitate national rehabilitation for the loss of the Vietnam War.[3] U.S. efforts to reposition itself as the savior of Vietnam's "runaways" suggest that humanitarian interventions are not merely about resolving a problem; they are also practices that "work principally to recuperate state sovereignty in the face of specific historical challenges."[4]

To upend U.S. self-presentation as the good refuge, this chapter exposes the militarized nature of what has been dubbed "the largest humanitarian airlift in history."[5] Methodologically, I trace the most-traveled refugee route via military aircraft as a critical lens through which to map, both discursively and materially, the transpacific *displacement* brought about by the legacy of U.S. colonial and military expansion into the Asia Pacific region. I make two related arguments: the first about military colonialism, which contends that it was the region's (neo)colonial dependence on the United States that turned the Philippines and Guam—U.S. former and current colonial territories, respectively—into the "ideal" receiving centers of the U.S. rescuing project; the second about militarized refuge(es), which shows that *refugees* and *refuge* are mutually constituted and that both emerge out of and in turn bolster U.S. militarism. American studies scholars have written extensively on the epistemic and symbolic violence of war making, but this chapter examines war in terms of "militarized violence": the raw, brutal, and destructive forces that Western imperial powers unleash on the lands and bodies of racialized peoples across time and space.

MILITARY COLONIALISM: ABOUT ISLANDS

As indicated above, about 92 percent of the first-wave Vietnamese refugees who fled to the United States in 1975 trekked through the Philippines, Guam, or Wake Island—all islands, all with prominent U.S. military bases.[6] Not mere happenstance, these stopovers followed the dictates of a "militarized organizing logic"[7] that reflected—and revealed—the layering of past colonial and ongoing militarization practices on these islands. Since the Spanish-American War in 1898, the United States had colonized islands—Cuba and Puerto Rico in the Caribbean, and Guam, Eastern Samoa, Wake Island, Hawaii, and the Philippines in the Pacific—and transformed them into strategic sites for advancing American economic and military interests. In all these islands, the United States established coal stations, communication lines, and naval harbors, wreaking havoc on the local population, economy, and ecology in the process.[8] Calling attention to the connections between colonialism and militarization, Robert Harkavy reports that, from the nineteenth century until and beyond World War II, most overseas bases throughout the world were "automatically provided by colonial control and were an important aspect and purpose of imperial domination."[9]

The Philippines: America's "First Vietnam"

In 1898, in the aftermath of the Spanish-American War, the United States brutally took possession of the Philippines over native opposition and uprising, thereby extending its "Manifest Destiny" to Pacific Asia. Linking U.S. war in the Philippines to that in Vietnam, Luzviminda Francisco dubs U.S. imperial aggression in the Philippines the "first Vietnam" in order to dispute the contention that the violent U.S. war in Vietnam was an "aberration" of American foreign policy.[10] It was during the Philippine-American War (1899–1902)—which resulted in the death of about a million Filipinos, the destruction of the nationalist forces, and the U.S. territorial annexation of the Philippines—that the United States established its first military bases there. For the next century, the Philippines hosted, often unwillingly, some of the United States' largest overseas air force and naval bases. As a consequence, the Philippines was key to U.S. power projection capabilities in the Pacific Basin, serving as its prime military outpost and stepping stone to China and the Asian mainland.[11]

Established as a direct consequence of the U.S. colonial occupation of the Philippines, Clark Air Force Base (AFB) was initially a U.S. Army Calvary post, Fort Stotsenburg, until the creation of the Air Force in 1947. From 1903 to 1979, Clark provided a vital "umbrella of security and surveillance to the Pacific region."[12] Even after the Philippines' formal independence in 1946, the Military Bases Agreement, signed one year later, formalized the establishment of twenty-three air and naval bases in strategic parts of the Philippines, the most important of which were Clark AFB and the Subic Naval Base.[13] Although the agreement was signed in 1947, its preliminary terms had been arranged before World War II, in effect making it an agreement between the United States and its colony, not between two sovereign states. In comparing this Military Bases Agreement with similar postwar military arrangements between the United States and other countries, Voltaire Garcia II concluded that "the Philippine treaty is the most onerous" and that its provisions "made the bases virtual territories of the United States."[14] In 1951, the United States and the Philippines signed the Mutual Defense Treaty, which obligated both countries to provide joint defense against any external military attack in the Pacific on either country, further entrenching U.S. military control over the Philippines.[15] Although the treaty was purportedly about military cooperation for the good of both nations, it was in effect a colonial project, with the American military machine allegedly "protecting a feminized, brown Pacific."[16]

During the Cold War, Clark grew into a major American air base. At its peak, it had a permanent population of 15,000, making it the largest American base overseas.[17] In 1979, pressed by Filipino intellectuals and nationalists who objected to the pervasive U.S. military presence, the Philippines and the United States signed a new agreement that established Philippine sovereignty over the bases but still guaranteed the United States "unhampered" military use of them. It was not until a 1991 vote for national sovereignty by the Philippine Senate that the U.S. Air Force transferred Clark back to the Philippine government, some ninety years after the first U.S. troops landed in the Philippines.[18]

Guam: "Where America's Day Begins"

After World War II, colonialism and militarism converged in the Pacific. Willfully aborting the decolonization movement in Micronesia, American military leaders turned the region's islands into a Pacific "base network" that would support U.S. military deployment in allied Asian nations as part of the containment of communism.[19] Once they had secured American hegemony in the Pacific, military leaders proceeded to build permanent facilities on key islands in Micronesia, primarily Guam and Kwajalein Atoll. As the largest of more than 2,000 islands scattered between Hawaii and the Philippines, Guam's role in the geopolitics of the Pacific was transformed from the prewar situation, "in which Guam was a lonely American outpost surrounded by hostile Japanese islands, to one in which Guam was the center of an American-dominated lake that encompassed the entire western Pacific Ocean," second in importance only to Hawaii. By 1956, Andersen AFB, a 20,000-acre site located on the northern end of the island of Guam, had become Strategic Air Command's chief base in the Pacific, one of thirty-eight overseas bases that encircled the Sino-Soviet Bloc.

The militarization of Guam was swift and expansive. On August 11, 1945, Admiral Chester Nimitz informed the U.S. chief of naval operations that to convert Guam into a "Gibraltar of the Pacific" would require 75,000 acres, or 55 percent of the island. About a year later, the Land Acquisition Act was passed, authorizing the Navy Department to acquire private land needed for permanent military installations on Guam.[20] By the beginning of 1950, the U.S. federal government controlled close to 60 percent of the island. Today, the U.S. military maintains jurisdiction over approximately 39,000 acres, or one-third of Guam's total land area;[21] given Guam's location relative to the International Date Line, it seems fitting that the island's motto is "Where America's Day Begins." According to anthropologist Catherine Lutz, "Guam, objectively, has the highest ratio of U.S. military spending and military hardware and land takings from indigenous U.S. populations of any place on earth."[22]

MILITARIZED *REFUGE*: RESOLVING THE REFUGEE CRISIS

The Philippines and Guam—Pacific Stopovers

Grafting the colonial histories of the Philippines and Guam onto the history of the Vietnam War, this section illuminates how residual and ongoing effects of colonial subordination "constitute the conditions of possibility for ongoing forms of militarization."[23] Therein lies the crux of what I term militarized *refuge*: it was the enormity of the military buildup in the Pacific that uniquely equipped U.S. bases there to handle the large-scale refugee rescue operation. Felix Moos and C. S. Morrison describe the U.S. decision to use the military infrastructure in the Pacific for the rescue operation as "inevitable": "An operation of this magnitude, and one requiring immediate execution, eliminated any alternative."[24] In short, U.S. evacuation efforts were not a slapdash response to an emergency situation that arose in Vietnam in 1975 but rather part and parcel of the long-standing militarized histories and circuits that connected Vietnam, the Philippines, and Guam, dating back to 1898.

A seemingly humanitarian gesture, the U.S. designation of Clark AFB as a refugee staging point was intimately linked to, and a direct outcome of, U.S. colonial subordination and militarization of the Philippines. Because of that base's prominence and proximity to Saigon, U.S. officials promptly designated it the first refugee "staging area": a temporary housing site for Vietnamese en route to the continental United States to complete the necessary screening and paperwork.[25] Flown there by military aircraft C-141s and C-130s, more than 30,000 refugees, including over 1,500 orphans, transited through Clark AFB in the spring of 1975.[26] At its peak, in April and May, as many as 2,000 refugees at a time were housed in a tent city adjacent to the base's Bamboo Bowl sports stadium.[27] However, as the flow of refugees surged, Philippine president Ferdinand Marcos informed the U.S. ambassador on April 23 that the country would accept no more Vietnamese refugees, thus foreclosing the most promising staging area in the Asia-Pacific region.[28] In response, that very same day, U.S. officials moved the premier refugee staging area from the Philippines to Guam, and they ordered the local Pacific Command representative on Guam and the Commander Naval Air Forces Marianas to prepare to accept, shelter, and process the refugees as they were being evacuated from South Vietnam.[29]

The swift U.S. decision to designate Clark AFB as a refugee staging area, and the Philippines' equally quick refusal to accept any more refugees, reflected the ambiguous nature of the 1947 Military Bases Agreement: though the United States had control of the bases, the Philippines had sovereignty over them. In the case of Guam, there was no such ambiguity. Since Congress had passed the Organic Act in 1950, which decreed Guam an unincorporated organized territory of the United States under the jurisdiction of the Department of the Interior, the federal government had held plenary powers—that is, full authority—over the island.[30] On an island where the U.S. military controlled one-third of its territory, Guam—more specifically, its air and naval bases—became the "logical" transit camps for the processing of evacuees.

With total land area of about 200 square miles and meager local resources, Guam was hardly an ideal location for the large-scale refugee operation. That it became *the* major refugee staging point in the Pacific had more to do with the U.S. militarization of Guam than with U.S. humanitarianism. Directed by the Joint Chiefs of Staff–Pacific Command's local area commander, Operation New Life was a massive undertaking, requiring the resources and manpower of all military branches on Guam as well as those of neighboring Pacific and mainland bases.[31] In all, nearly 20,000 military personnel, including the crews from visiting ships and aircrafts, were directly involved in the Guam refugee operation. Military bases, as the largest and most resourced institutions on Guam, doubled as refugee shelters. Refugees were initially housed in temporary barracks on Anderson AFB, on the Navy field at Agana, and at the U.S. Marine Corps Camp at Asan Point, and subsequently in the hastily constructed but massive tent city on Orote Point within the U.S. Naval Station, which provided tent space for about 50,000 people, including my mother and me.[32]

At the onset of the refugee influx, the Pacific Command representatives on Guam estimated that, even with the use of all military structures and all available civilian rentals, Guam could shelter a *maximum* of 13,000 people for a *short* period of time.[33] However, in all, more than 115,000 evacuees passed through Guam, a number that exceeded Guam's civilian population at that time by at least 25,000.[34] At its peak, as many as 3,700 evacuees were processed through and airlifted out of Andersen on any given day.[35] The sheer volume of refugees overwhelmed Guam's limited resources. Locals found their access to lagoons and beaches reduced, their water supply rationed, and their travel restricted as military vehicles jammed busy roads. Children had no transportation to school because all of the 181 school buses were being used to transfer refugees from the various air and ship terminals to the temporary military housing and campsites. Overall health conditions also deteriorated, as mosquito and sewage-borne diseases proliferated.[36] Not only did more refugees come than expected, but they also stayed longer than anticipated, thereby pushing the actual refugee population on Guam beyond an acceptable limit. Begun on April 23, 1975, Operation New Life was not officially closed until October 16 that year, and it was not until January 15, 1976, that the last evacuee left Guam. According to a local newspaper, however, even as of April 1976 Washington had yet to reimburse Guam for refugee-related costs that totaled nearly $1 million.[37]

The Vietnamese refugees were not supposed to linger on Guam; they were to be processed almost immediately and then sent on to the continental United States. However, some U.S. states initially refused to accept the refugees or postponed the arrival date, in part because of a lack of planning and proper facilities but also because of adverse reactions by the public and strong opposition by state officials to the influx of refugees. As an "unincorporated territory of the United States" with second-class citizenship status, Guam had little choice but to continue housing the refugees until U.S. states decided to receive them.[38] Thus, the U.S. decision to designate Guam the primary staging ground for refugees, even when the island's resources were severely stretched and its inhabitants adversely affected, repeats the long-standing belief that indigenous land is essentially "empty land"—that is, land empty of its indigenous population. During the late 1940s and early 1950s, faced with strong public opposition to the influx of Russian and East European refugees, U.S. Cold War strategists likewise attempted to resettle the refugees on what they considered to be empty—or, more accurately, emptied—land on the Virgin Islands, or on "some other insular possession."[39] Commenting on U.S. intentions to reconstitute these "empty lands" as new homelands for refugees, Susan Carruthers opines: "Shut out by the 'paper wall' that immigration restrictionism erected around the United States, [Eastern Bloc] escapees were imagined reenacting the founding drama of a territory similarly conceived by its first colonists as 'unused' land."[40] In some ways, the U.S. carpet bombing of Vietnam was also symptomatic of an empty-land mentality—a flagrant dismissiveness of the country "as a worthless piece of land."[41]

In short, the refugee situation on Guam bespoke the intertwined histories of U.S. military colonialism on Guam and its war in Vietnam: it was the militarization of the colonized island and its indigenous inhabitants that turned Guam into an "ideal" dumping ground for the unwanted Vietnamese refugees, the discards of U.S. war in Vietnam. Moreover, the refugee presence bore witness not only to the tenacity but also to the limits of U.S. empire, critically juxtaposing "the United States' nineteenth-century imperial project with its *failed* Cold War objectives in Southeast Asia."[42]

California's Camp Pendleton—Refugees' First U.S. Home

From Guam, many Vietnamese refugees journeyed to the other side of the Pacific—to Marine Corps Base Camp Pendleton, a 125,000-acre amphibious training base on the Southern California coast, in San Diego County. There, at a U.S. military base, the largest Vietnamese population outside of Vietnam got its start in America. Like Clark and Andersen AFBs, Camp Pendleton emerged out of a history of conquest: it is located in the traditional territory of the Juaneno, Luiseno, and Kumeyaay tribes, which had been "discovered" by Spanish padres and voyagers who traveled to Southern California in the late eighteenth century, "owned" by unscrupulous Anglo-American settlers for about a century as the California state legislature repeatedly blocked federal ratification of treaties with native communities, and ultimately "acquired" by the U.S. Marine Corps in 1942 in order to establish a West Coast base for combat training.[43] Camp Pendleton's prized land—its varied topography, which combines a breathtakingly beautiful seventeen-mile shoreline and "extensive, diverse inland ranges and maneuver areas," makes it ideal for combat training[44]—is thus "stolen land," an occupied territory like Guam.[45] This fact remains unacknowledged, replaced with the myth of empty land. According to the official website of the Marine Corps Base Camp Pendleton, "Spanish explorers, colorful politicians, herds of thundering cattle, skillful vaqueros and tough Marines have all contributed to the history of this land."[46] Conspicuously absent in this official origin story is an account of the stolen land and of the San Diego native communities that have been made landless and destitute as a result. Nonetheless, this buried past has continued to surface—sometimes literally. As of 2001, there had been seventeen inadvertent discoveries of Native American remains and objects involving three major military projects on Camp Pendleton, including "complete burials, human bone fragments, and funerary objects."[47]

The first military installation on the U.S. mainland to provide accommodations for Vietnamese evacuees, Camp Pendleton temporarily housed over 50,000 refugees between April and August 1975. Like other refugee centers in the Pacific, setting up the tent city to house the refugees was a massive undertaking: nearly 900 Marines and civilians worked for six days to erect the 958 tents and 140 Quonset huts.[48] Heavily covered by national and international media, Camp Pendleton's participation in the U.S. military's 1975 relocation effort, dubbed Operation New Arrivals, was key to U.S. efforts to recuperate after the defeat in Vietnam; its importance to the nation was underscored by First Lady Betty Ford's May 21 visit to the camp to greet newly arrived Vietnamese children.[49] For a nation still reeling from the shock of defeat and the agony of a deeply divisive war, watching images of U.S. Marines—the central players in that very war—working "around the clock to build eight tent cities and to provide water, food, clothing, medicine, electricity, power, and security for the first 18,000 refugees"[50] must have been cathartic, a step toward reclaiming faith in America's goodness and moving beyond the extremely unpopular war. For American soldiers like Lewis Beatty, a Camp Pendleton Marine with two tours in Vietnam who "helped put up tents, built latrines, [and] hauled clothes and diapers," assisting the refugees provided a sense of redemption. Looking back on his war experiences in Vietnam thirty-five years later, Beatty confided that "we saw things that no person should ever see." Yet the arrival of the Vietnamese and their touted assimilation into the United States turned his sorrow into joy, enabling him to put the war behind him and to revel in their (presumed) shared experience of parenthood: "Here it was joy. In their kids, I could see my kids. . . . The hard times those people had to go through to assimilate into our society."[51]

These warm images, replayed on every anniversary of the Fall of Saigon—of soldiers caring for Vietnamese evacuees, of Vietnamese spouting gratitude for American generosity—tell only half-truths. They conveniently erase the fact that the majority of Americans did not welcome the refugees' arrival. A Gallup poll taken in May 1975 indicated that 54 percent of the respondents opposed the settlement of Vietnamese in the United States. In numerous letters and phone calls to public officials, many Americans urged that little or no government assistance be allocated to the refugees.[52] This opposition was racially charged. In California, then-governor Jerry Brown actively opposed Vietnamese settlement, even attempting to prevent planes carrying refugees from landing at Travis Air Force Base near Sacramento, claiming that the Vietnamese would add to the state's already-large minority population.[53] California's Republican representative to Congress, Burt Talcott, exclaimed to his constituents, "Damn it, we have too many Orientals."[54] In the communities near Camp

[handwritten note in margin: so Vietnam are complex and not US??]

Pendleton (and the three other refugee receiving centers), which were bat-
tling high unemployment rates, residents loudly opposed the settlement
of refugees in their neighborhoods, spurring the State Department to dis-
perse the refugees as widely as possible throughout the country in order to
minimize the financial burden on any single locality.[55]

The warm images also made un-visible the connection between the
refugee recovery mission and the military violence that preceded it—the
fact that both were executed by the same military outfit: Camp Pendleton's
1st Marines. Indeed, the same individual, General Paul Graham, directed
both combat and rescue efforts, further blurring one into the other. In
1967, Graham served as assistant chief of staff of the 1st Marine Division
in South Vietnam and, later, as commanding officer of the 5th Marine
Regiment. In April 1975, now advanced to the rank of brigadier general,
Graham, as the West Coast Marine Corps coordinator, processed over
50,000 Vietnamese and Thai refugees from Southeast Asia at Camp
Pendleton. While serving in this capacity, Graham was awarded a Gold
Star. Upon his retirement, he was presented with a personal Certificate of
Appreciation from President Gerald Ford for "meritorious service in the
resettlement of Indo Chinese refugees in the United States, as well as the
Distinguished Service Medal."[56] Graham's "meritorious service" in the
resettlement of the refugees included setting up a tight security system in
the tent city, making sure that "there were MPs [military police] everywhere," and "quell[ing] all the conflicts immediately. He was keeping it in
total control."[57] Graham's illustrious career, his promotions and recogni-
tions, was thus built in part on the role that he played in executing both
the violence against and the recovery of Vietnamese bodies.

MILITARIZED REFUGE: PRODUCING THE REFUGEE CRISIS

The material and ideological conversion of U.S. military bases into places
of *refuge*—places that were meant to *resolve* the refugee crisis, promising
peace and protection—discursively transformed the United States from
violent aggressor in Vietnam to benevolent rescuer of its people. In this
section, I challenge the logic of this "makeover" by detailing the violent

roles that these military bases—these purported places of refuge—played in the Vietnam War, in order to hold them accountable for the war-induced displacement of the Vietnamese people. The term *militarized refuge*—its intended jarring juxtaposition and accent on "militarized"—exposes the hidden violence behind the humanitarian term "refuge," thereby challenging the powerful narrative of America(ns) rescuing and caring for Vietnam's "runaways" that erases the role that U.S. foreign policy and war played in spurring the refugee exodus. These militarized refugee camps had precedents, most notably in the hundreds of work and concentration camps in Germany that were converted into "Assembly Centres" for refugees—the very victims of these camps—in postwar Europe.[58]

In the Philippines, Clark AFB was the backbone of logistical support for U.S. involvement in Southeast Asia. Soon after the United States proclaimed its campaign to contain communism in the late 1940s, Clark became the headquarters of the 13th Air Force and played a key logistical role in support of the U.S. forces in the Korean War (1950–53). From 1965 to 1975, as the largest overseas U.S. military base in the world, Clark became the major staging base for U.S. involvement in Southeast Asia, providing crucial logistical support for the Vietnam War. Air traffic at Clark reached as high as 40 transports per day, all bound for Vietnam. At the same time, in an exercise of its fledgling sovereignty, the Philippines refused to permit the United States to mount B-52 bombing runs from Clark: the aircraft had to fly from Guam but were refueled from Clark. U.S. troops at Clark also provided vital support to the war because they spent a significant portion of their alleged "temporary duty" in Vietnam. The large number of temporary-duty troops who were sent to Vietnam from Clark, as well as from other U.S. bases in the Pacific, was part of the Pentagon's illicit design to mislead Congress about the number of troops that were officially assigned to Vietnam's combat zone.[59]

The United States could not impose its military will on the Philippines, a sovereign nation, but it could and did on Guam, its unincorporated territory. When the United States was not permitted to mount B-52 bombing runs from Clark, it turned to Anderson AFB, which came to play a "legendary" role in the Vietnam War, launching devastating bombing missions over North and South Vietnam for close to a decade.[60] In this way, Guam's fate was linked to that of the Philippines as U.S. military decisions often triangulated these two vital nodes in the Pacific base network. The two air force bases also joined efforts in providing crucial medical support for U.S. troops during the Vietnam War. Beginning in November 1965, four times a week, C-141 aircraft would fly from Clark into Da Nang to load casualties, return for a two-hour stop at Clark, and then fly on to Guam. The close proximity of these three sites—Vietnam, the Philippines, and Guam, linked via U.S. militarism in the Pacific—meant that injured soldiers were transferred to Guam within two or three days of injury, as flight times between Da Nang and Clark was about two and a half hours and between Clark and Guam was about four hours.[61]

After it became operational as North Field in 1945, Andersen AFB played vital roles in U.S. wars in the Pacific, launching daily bombing missions over Japan during World War II, serving as a focal point for aircraft and material flying west during the Korean War, and supporting rotational bomber deployments from stateside bases after that war—first with B-29s, and eventually hosting B-36, B-47, B-50, B-52, KC-97, and KC-135 units. From 1945 to 1951, Strategic Air Command used Andersen to train and practice its wartime skills, which would be deployed time and again in Southeast Asia.[62]

Guam's involvement in the Vietnam War began in 1962, when it first served as a support base for the American advisers that President John F. Kennedy dispatched to South Vietnam. In mid-1965, after the United States deployed ground combat units in South Vietnam, Guam's role in the war was greatly expanded: "The number of bombing runs over North and South Vietnam required tons of bombs to be unloaded, for example, at the Naval Station in Guam, stored at the Naval Magazine in the southern area of the island, and then shipped to be loaded onto B-52s at Andersen Air Force Base every day during years of the war."[63] A hornet's nest of intense activity, Andersen rapidly became the largest U.S. base for B-52 bombers—"the eight-engine behemoths that attempted to bomb the Vietnamese communists into submission."[64] Given Guam's proximity to Vietnam, a B-52, which carries 108 500-pound bombs, could fly from Guam to Vietnam and back without refueling.[65] On June 18, 1965, Andersen launched twenty-seven B-52s against suspected Viet Cong base operations and supply lines, the first of thousands of conventional "iron bomb" strikes—dubbed Operation Arc Light—over North and South Vietnam as well as Cambodia and Laos. The Nixon Doctrine, announced on Guam on July 25, 1969, initiated the withdrawal of U.S. ground troops from Vietnam but also immediately escalated the U.S. air war, with B-52 bombing missions from Guam increasing in tempo and ferocity.[66] In 1972, Andersen was the site of the most massive buildup of airpower in history, with more than 15,000 crews and over 150 B-52s lining all available flight line space—about five miles long. At its peak, Andersen housed about 165 B-52s.[67] During Operation Linebacker II (named after Nixon's favorite sport), the round-the-clock "Christmas bombing" against the cities of Hanoi and Haiphong in December 1972, bombers stationed at Andersen flew 729 sorties in eleven days. On December 18, 87 B-52s were launched from Andersen in less than two hours. Dubbed the "11-day war," Operation Linebacker II is credited for forcing the North Vietnamese to return to the stalled Paris peace talks and to sign a cease-fire agreement in January 1973.[68] The Nixon Doctrine was thus a racial project: by withdrawing American troops but intensifying the air raid, the United States prioritized American lives over Vietnamese lives, preserving the former while obliterating the latter, racialized to be dispensable, via carpet bombing.

The U.S. air war, launched from Guam, decisively disrupted life on the island, underscoring once again the total disregard for the island's inhabitants. Richard Mackie, a Public Health Service officer, describes the thundering impact of the air war on everyday life:

> There was no announcement. There was no warning. It just started happening. Every hour, day and night, every house . . . would almost shake off its foundation as the deafening roar of three B-52s and a refueling plane would pass a few hundred feet over our heads. . . . Life became tedious, sleep was almost impossible. Conversations were continually interrupted. We found ourselves constantly gritting our teeth and staring angrily at the ceiling as each 'sortie' passed overhead. Guam's main highway was jammed day and night with trucks hauling bombs from the port to the airbase.[69]

Finally, the Department of Defense's busiest training installation, California's Camp Pendleton, trained more than 40,000 active-duty and 26,000 reserve military personnel each year for combat.[70] During the Vietnam War, Marines arriving at the Camp were given fifteen intensive training days, complete with a fabricated Vietnamese jungle village with deadly booby traps, and then sent to Vietnam. Camp Pendleton also was (and is still today) the home base of the illustrious 1st Marine Regiment, whose battalions began arriving in Vietnam in August 1965. The regiment's battalions participated in some of the most ferocious battles of the war, including Harvest Moon in December 1965, the Utah, Iowa, Cheyenne I and II, and Double Eagle battles in the succeeding months, and Operation Hastings in July 1966. Between January and March 1968, the 1st Marines, along with other U.S. Marine and South Vietnamese units, fought to regain control of Hue, the old imperial capital, engaging in street fighting and hand-to-hand combat, killing nearly 1,900 "enemies" in the process. The regiment continued heavy fighting through the rest of the year, culminating in Operation Meade River, which killed nearly 850 Vietnamese. In 1971, the regiment was ordered back to Camp Pendleton—the last Marine infantry unit to depart Vietnam.[71] In all, during the course of the Vietnam War, via its satellite military bases, the United States dropped more explosives on Vietnam—a million tons on North Vietnam, and four million tons on South Vietnam—than in all of World War II.[72] Four times as many bombs were dropped on South Vietnam as on North Vietnam because the U.S. goal was to decimate the Viet Cong in the South in order to preserve South Vietnam as a non-Communist, pro-American country.[73]

As such, the Pacific military bases, Clark and Andersen AFBs, and California's Marine Corps Base Camp Pendleton, credited and valorized for resettling Vietnamese refugees in 1975, were the very ones responsible for inducing the refugee displacement. The massive tonnage of bombs, along with the ground fighting provided by Marine units like Camp Pendleton's 1st Marines, displaced some twelve million people in South Vietnam—almost half the country's total population at the time—from their homes. Although there are no statistics on how many North Vietnamese were forced to flee their homes, it is likely that the percentage of the displaced there must have been even higher, because North Vietnam coped with the relentless American air war by evacuating major population centers to the countryside.[74] Yet the literature on Vietnamese refugees seldom mentions the internally displaced. By recognizing only the refugees fleeing Vietnam after 1975, U.S. officials and scholars have engaged in the "organized forgetting" of the millions of long-term refugees who stayed in Vietnam, whose dislocation was the direct consequence of

[handwritten margin note: logistically, who else to use? Those were pacific bases]

U.S. military's "high-technology brutality."[75] Together, the hyper-visibility of the post-1975 refugees who left Vietnam and the un-visibility of the internal refugees who had been displaced throughout the war enabled the United States to represent itself as a refuge-providing rather than a refugee-producing nation.

"OPERATION BABYLIFT": VIOLENCE AND RECOVERY WITHOUT A PAUSE

In April 2010, marking the thirty-fifth anniversary of the Fall of Saigon, the Camp Pendleton Historical Society unveiled the exhibit "Images at War's End," which features a series of black and white photographs and paintings by Colonel Charles Waterhouse, depicting life at the "Tent City" refugee camp in 1975. One photograph particularly stands out: dated May 5, 1975, it depicts two Vietnamese children walking barefoot around the camp, their bodies engulfed in extra-long military jackets (figure 1). Undoubtedly, the gesture was meant to be kind; the jackets were intended to warm their little bodies against the morning cold. Yet the picture encapsulates so vividly the concept of *militarized refuge(es)*, with young Vietnamese bodies literally wrapped in U.S. protective military gear as they wandered the grounds of their new home in America—a military base that housed the same 1st Marines who had waged ferocious battles in Vietnam, leaving high numbers of combat deaths in their wake.

The military jackets photo symbolizes the unsettling entanglement between military acts of violence and recovery, with recovery overlaying and at times disappearing (the memory of) violence. As discussed above, Clark AFB, Andersen AFB, and Marine Corps Base Camp Pendleton were all integral to the U.S. war in Vietnam, and all doubled as refugee camps. The photo also brings to mind Operation Babylift, the controversial U.S. emergency initiative that airlifted over 2,500 Vietnamese infants and children out of war-torn Vietnam in April 1975.[76] Coined by some as "one of the most humanitarian efforts in history," Operation Babylift was hastily arranged and executed. On April 3, 1975, in an effort to reposition the United States as a do-gooder in Vietnam, President Ford pledged $2 million to airlift the children from orphanages to new homes in the United

Figure 1. Young Vietnamese refugee children, wearing "extra-long" field jackets, walk through one of the refugee camps aboard Camp Pendleton, California. Photo taken on May 5, 1975, by Major G. L. Gill. (Photo courtesy of Camp Pendleton Archives.)

States and granted all parolee status. The majority of the flights were military cargo planes, ill equipped to carry passengers, especially infants and young children. On some flights, the babies were placed in temporary cribs, empty crates or cardboard boxes, lined up corner to corner inside the cargo bays of Air Force planes.[77]

In the Babylift mission, the changeover from acts of violence to recovery occurred *without even a pause.* On April 4, 1975, initiating Operation Babylift, a U.S. Air Force aircraft C-5, "which was returning to the Philippines after *delivering war material,*" immediately flew to Saigon to airlift Vietnamese orphans to Clark AFB.[78] In other words, the C-5 was performing two seemingly opposing missions—warring and rescuing—back to back, and yet seemingly without contradictions. In the chaotic days of the rescue mission and even long after, no one noted the irony, or what should be the incongruity, of transporting Vietnamese displaced children in the very aircraft that delivered the war material that triggered

how else to accomplish logistically??

war is just violence. only after the bloodshed has stopped do we get to symbolize ? romanticize their displacement in the first place. Unfortunately, the initial Babylift mission proved to be a disaster, because the C-5 aircraft crashed minutes after takeoff, killing 138 people, most of whom were Vietnamese children. Despite the tragic accident, however, the appropriateness of the recovery mission was so self-evident that Operation Babylift resumed almost immediately.

Without a pause—that was how Operation Babylift was executed. A congressional investigation of the operation concluded that there was "a total lack of planning by federal and private agencies."[79] The emergency nature of the evacuation, stemming from the perceived urgency to get the children out of Vietnam at all costs, rushed not only the transport of the young evacuees but also the safety checks to ensure that they were bona fide orphans. When available, the children's birth records were stowed with them for the flight. But for many children swept up in the hasty evacuation from Vietnam, documentation of their family status was sketchy or incomplete at best. Bobby Nofflet, a worker with the U.S. Agency for International Development in Saigon, detailed the tumultuous days of Babylift: "There were large sheaves of papers and batches of babies. Who knew which belonged to which?"[80] It appears that, on nearly every level, "from the original decisions about which children would be airlifted to the protocols for finalizing adoptions, Operation Babylift suffered from acute disorder and a nearly complete lack of oversight."[81] The hasty and slipshod evacuation, even of children with uncertain family status, reflects the racialized belief that the United States is self-evidently a safer and better home than Vietnam for the children—a belief fortified by years of war and war propaganda waged in the region. As Vietnamese American journalist Tran Tuong Nhu, one of a small number of Vietnamese living in San Francisco at the time who assisted with Babylift arrivals, wondered, "What is this terror Americans feel that my people will devour children?"[82]

On April 29, 1975, at the urging of Tran Tuong Nhu and on behalf of three Babylift siblings, a group of California attorneys filed a class-action lawsuit in the Federal District Court in San Francisco seeking to halt the Babylift adoptions, asserting that many of the children did not appear to be orphans but had been taken from South Vietnam against their parents' wills, and that the U.S. government was obligated to return them to their families.[83] Because so much documentation was missing or fraudulent,

how many Falsified docs out of
hope For a better life in USA?

MILITARIZED REFUGE(ES)   43

the plaintiffs' attorneys claimed that, out of the 2,242 children who had arrived in the United States, 1,511 were ineligible for adoption. The Immigration and Naturalization Service disputed this claim, but its own investigation found that over 10 percent of the evacuees—263 children— were ineligible for adoption.[84] After ten months of wrangling, as the law-suit was becoming unwieldy and no documentation was forthcoming, Judge Spencer Williams threw out the case and sealed the records.[85] Eventually, after many years and lengthy lawsuits, only twelve children were reunited with their Vietnamese parents.[86]

As the Babylift children arrived in the United States, with their Vietnamese names imprinted on a bracelet around one wrist and the name and address of their adopted American parents on the other, the violence that brought about their orphanhood—and even their birth, since many were fathered and abandoned by American military personnel— was all but forgotten. Instead, they were celebrated as the lucky ones, bound toward a new life in America.[87] As a testament to the ideological importance of Operation Babylift for the war-weary nation, President Ford appeared on the tarmac at San Francisco airport and, standing before a horde of television cameras, welcomed to the United States the plane full of Vietnamese infants and children (figure 2).

A picture of Ford cradling a Vietnamese infant on board an Air Force bus shortly after carrying her off the plane in his arms—the white father protecting his brown baby—circulated widely and eventually became immortalized in a painting now housed in the President Gerald R. Ford Museum in Grand Rapids, Michigan.[88] With the arrival of the Babylift children, America became the white loving parents welcoming the arrival of their brown charges; the transition from warring to humanitarian nation thus completed—all without a pause.

OPERATION FREQUENT WIND: ABOUT GRATITUDE
AND AMBIVALENCE

On April 30, 2010, the U.S.S. Midway Museum in San Diego held a spe-cial ceremony on its flight deck to commemorate the thirty-fifth anniver-sary of Operation Frequent Wind—a widely publicized mission when

Figure 2. President Gerald R. Ford welcoming Vietnamese infants and children to the United States at the San Francisco airport, April 5, 1975. (Photo courtesy of the Gerald R. Ford Presidential Library.)

U.S.S. Midway sailors reportedly rescued more than 3,000 Vietnamese refugees fleeing the Fall of Saigon. Billed as a "remarkable rescue mission" where "untold lives were saved,"[89] the commemoration was a salute to militarized refuge, celebrated on the very ship that had launched tens of thousands of combat missions—that had struck military and logistics installations in North and South Vietnam, downed a number of MiGs, and laid minefields in ports deemed of significance to the North Vietnamese.[90] Indeed, Admiral Larry Chambers, who was captain of the ship on that fateful day, choked up when he recounted the heroic deeds of his crew, causing a newspaper reporter covering the commemoration to begin her article with the following: "The U.S.S. Midway may be made of iron and steel, but deep down it was 'all heart.'"[91]

Named "Honoring Freedom in America," the event drew not only the "young brave men of U.S.S. Midway"[92] but also thousands of Vietnamese Americans, hundreds of whom credited their escape from Vietnam directly to Operation Frequent Wind.[93] American valor and Vietnamese gratitude were the day's central themes: the daring American soldiers "who made it all possible,"[94] and the indebted Vietnamese refugees "who were plucked to safety."[95] Indeed, many Vietnamese—at the Midway event and elsewhere—have ardently expressed gratitude to their American rescuers, heaping praise on the very militarized refuge that I critique here. For instance, when a public radio talk show host asked Dzung Le, whose family landed on the Midway in 1975, to recount "what it was like to travel on this U.S. military helicopter and land on this flight deck," Le responded by thanking the soldiers of the Midway aircraft carrier for their gentleness and tenderness:

> I remember, it was chaotic but, strangely enough, it's also a feeling of comfort, of safety, because I knew that at the time, as we land, we are saved. . . . One of my sister[s] was quite ill at the time from dehydration, I guess, so the soldier helped carry her down there. They are very tender. And to us, we pretty much weighed about 100 pounds at the time for all of us, and these are 200 pound soldiers. They are like a gentle giant at the time, very tender. Very tender.[96]

The refugees' performances of gratitude risk recasting the history of military-induced refugee flight into a benign story of voluntary migration. They enable historians like Abe Shragge, when asked to comment on the proper tone for the Midway commemoration, to link the 1975 Operation Frequent Wind to the 1886 unveiling of the Statue of Liberty:

> I think somberness, seriousness, some joy as well that we can remember back to 1886 when we opened the Statue of Liberty to the public, that this is a nation that was created by immigrants. It was a nation that was supposed to support and nurture and welcome immigrants. And to have relived that in 1975 in this particular way under these circumstances, I think, is a very fitting tribute to a long historical process and a long heritage and tradition.[97]

Shragge's comment encapsulates the myth of immigrant America, a narrative of voluntary immigration that ignores the role that U.S. world power has played in inducing global migration.

Given the military backgrounds of many of the 1975 Vietnamese refugees and the long-term presence of U.S. military personnel in Vietnam, this instilled appreciation for the American military machine and personnel—for militarized refuge—is unsurprising. In her generative work on the figure of the grateful refugee, Mimi Nguyen has shown how Vietnamese refugees were subject to the gift of freedom twice over: first as an object of intervention in the Cold War, and second as an object of rescue in the aftermath of military defeat. According to Nguyen, to receive the U.S. gift of freedom was to be indebted to the U.S. empire.[98] However, these performances of gratitude are rooted not only in U.S. rhetoric of liberalism and freedom but also in the harsh material reality of Vietnamese refugee life. In light of the staggering losses that Vietnamese had to endure, their grateful words constitute genuine expressions of thanksgiving for having managed to get here, to *this* life, when so many others perished. Between these repetitions of thanksgiving, however, other narratives lie in wait, postponed and archived—and sometimes released.[99] For instance, on the thirty-fifth anniversary of Operation Frequent Wind, refugees interspersed their praise for the rescue mission with laments about being uninformed regarding American evacuation plans, torn from loved ones, and, in some cases, left behind by American rescuers—all of which constitute critiques, however muted, of the American rescue efforts.[100] It is important to note that most refugees, even as they express gratitude for their lives in America, mourn the tattered conditions of their beloved Vietnam and the fact that, thirty-five years later, "millions of millions of our people [in Vietnam] are still suffering."[101] Although this sentiment foremost indicts communism in Vietnam and validates life in America, it nevertheless reminds the public that the Vietnam War is *not* over, as Americans have repeatedly claimed, but that it has continued to exact an untold toll on Vietnamese in Vietnam and in the diaspora.

At the very least, these public sentiments underscore the ambivalence that many Vietnamese harbor about the role of the American military in Vietnam. A 1.5 generation Vietnamese American described this ambivalence: on the one hand, he regarded Americans in Vietnam "as crucial allies who sometimes made mistakes as they helped South Vietnam"; on the other, he "became disillusioned" with American actions:

> They talked of freedom; [but] they bombed "the hell" out of many villages
> as they attempted to destroy their enemy. They often did not respond to calls

from South Vietnamese soldiers for air support, which resulted in the loss of many lives among those they called "allies." That hypocrisy reflected the American disrespect for Vietnamese lives.[102]

Some Vietnamese have acted on these ambivalent feelings. For instance, during their stay on Guam, some refugees opted to bypass the United States and applied for asylum in France, Canada, England, or Australia because "they asked themselves why they should go to America if the Americans were directly or indirectly the cause of their downfall."[103] In a more openly defiant act, in September 1975, more than 1,500 men and women in a refugee camp on Guam staged a highly choreographed demonstration, demanding that they be repatriated to Vietnam—an "unsettling counternarrative" to the pervasive story of Vietnamese gratitude for U.S. benevolence.[104] These forms of critical remembering, however irresolute and mixed with the politics of gratitude, are key to the potential formation of counternarratives on the Vietnam War and "to the imagination and rearticulation of new forms of [Vietnamese] political subjectivity, collectivity, and practice."[105]

.   .   .   .   .

This chapter has covered seemingly unrelated topics: U.S. colonialism in the Philippines, U.S. militarism in Guam, settler colonialism in California, and the Vietnam War. However, in tracing the most-traveled refugee route via military aircraft, I have knitted these different events together into a layered story of militarized refuge(es)—one that connects U.S. colonialism, military expansion, and transpacific displacement. This is not a traditional comparative approach that treats these events as discrete, equivalent, and already-constituted phenomena. Rather, I have adopted a *relational comparative* approach, which posits that historical memories are fluid rather than static; they need to be understood in relation to each other and within the context of a flexible field of political discourse. My methodology thus revolves around the concept of *critical juxtaposing*:the deliberate bringing together of seemingly different historical events in an effort to reveal what would otherwise remain invisible—in this case, the contours, contents, and limits of U.S. imperialism, wars, and genocide in the Asia-Pacific region and on the U.S. mainland.[106] In connecting Vietnamese displacement to that of Filipinos, Chamorros, and Native Americans, and making intelligible the military colonialisms that engulf these spaces, this chapter has attempted to expose the hidden violence behind the humanitarian term *refuge*, thus undercutting the rescue-and-liberation narrative that erases the U.S. role in inducing the refugee crisis in the first place.

3 Refugee Camps and the Politics of Living

> The place of foreclosed humanity is also the place of improvised, experimental social making and organization, . . . the place of different human becoming, which threatens the order of a proper (and propertied) humanity.
>
> Neferti Tadiar, "Lifetimes in Becoming Human"

The artist team Lin + Lam reports that, whenever a Vietnamese internee was discharged from a refugee camp in Hong Kong or Malaysia, the beloved Vietnamese song "Biển Nhớ" ("The Sea Remembers"),[1] with its familiar refrain "Tomorrow, You Leave," would be played over the intercom to broadcast the pending departure.[2] Even though resettlement was a coveted opportunity for refugees, many of whom had languished for years in refugee camps, "Biển Nhớ" is not a celebratory song. Sung from the perspective of the one who stays behind, this melancholic song mourns the abrupt leave-taking and the interrupted relationships, as departing refugees often had just forty-eight hours to get ready for their trip.[3] Given such little time, this tender song took the place of extended goodbyes—a rueful reminder that refugees in transit had little control over their intimate affairs.

I open this chapter with the farewell song "Biển Nhớ" in order to pay homage to the social life that Vietnamese refugees managed to forge and nurture during their prolonged stay in refugee camps in Southeast Asia. Here and elsewhere in this book, I am deeply interested in how Vietnamese refugees, as devalued people, scripted new life histories— and indeed new lives—on the margins of sovereign space. Whereas chapter 2 focused on the military-bases-turned-refugee-camps that provisionally housed some 140,000 Vietnamese who left in April 1975 as part of the U.S.-organized evacuation,[4] this chapter examines the makeshift camps in Southeast Asia that mostly sheltered the "boat people" who fled Vietnam in the late 1970s and 1980s on crowded and leaky fishing vessels. From the mid-1970s to the mid-1990s, the United Nations High Commissioner for Refugees (UNHCR) registered a total of 839,228 refugees from Vietnam in numerous refugee camps throughout East and Southeast Asia.[5] For a large number of these second-wave refugee migrants, their stay in Asia was *not* temporary; they had remained stranded in asylum centers or, in rare cases, settled in these first-asylum countries. And yet, most accounts on Vietnamese refugees have continued to privilege settlement in the West. For the first-wave refugees, their camp stay was brief; all were processed and resettled in the United States or other Western countries in a matter of months. In contrast, the vast majority of the second-wave escapees languished in overcrowded camps, waiting uncertainly, sometimes indefinitely, to be reviewed and then resettled or repatriated. This chapter pays particular attention to the creative capacity of these second-wave refugees to make social and political lives in a context that was not supportive of, and often actively hostile to, their intimate lives.

Studies of refugee camps constitute the bulk of early scholarship on Vietnamese refugees. Researchers have repeatedly portrayed refugees as passive objects of sympathy that suffered not only the trauma of forced departure but also the boredom, uncertainty, despair, and helplessness induced by camp life.[6] However well intentioned, this crisis model, which fixates on the refugees' purported fragile psychosocial and emotional state, discursively constructs Vietnamese as "passive, immobilized and pathetic."[7] Catch phrases used to characterize the refugees' journey—such as "no-man's land," "midway-to-nowhere," "transition to nowhere," "the limbo state," and "half way to nowhere"—underscore the refugees' perceived learned helplessness and demoralized mental state.[8] Tellingly, studies of refugee camps often pair the construct of Vietnamese refugees as passive objects of sympathy with a plea for the West to "assume an *active* role in caring, counseling, or intervening."[9] Here is an example of one such call to action:

The immediate moral responsibility of the Western World to relieve the increasing intensity of the sufferings of thousands of Indochinese refugees in transit camps in Hong Kong as well as those in the other major countries of first asylum in South East Asia, cannot be over-exaggerated. Any further delay on the part of the western countries . . . will certainly allow an experience in transit to degenerate into one of "no exit."[10]

Such calls to action treat the Vietnamese as only passive recipients of Western benevolence and generosity. Focusing on U.S. refugee policies, this chapter shows that U.S. resettlement was not the benevolent, generous system touted by mainstream media and authorities but rather a stringent process that prolonged the refugees' stay in first-asylum countries. I then detail Vietnamese efforts to create new lifeworlds within the camp, not only to survive but to claim a family, a community, a life within it. In short, this chapter is an effort to understand not only the bio- and necropolitics within the camp but also the "politics of living"[11]—the practices of generating forms of viable life, or what Neferti Tadiar calls "remaindered life"—in this designed-to-be barren space.[12]

RESETTLEMENT POLICIES, "SURROGATE REFUGE," AND "PROTRACTED REFUGEES"

Testifying before a U.S. Senate subcommittee on Immigration, Refugees, and International Law in July 1979, Secretary of State Cyrus Vance evoked the mantra "We are a nation of refugees" to make his case for admitting more Southeast Asian refugees into the United States: "Most of us can trace our presence here to the turmoil or oppression of another time and another place. Our nation has been immeasurably enriched by this continuing process."[13] Vance's statement is disingenuous because it collapses the specificities of the war-induced Vietnamese flight into the general myth of "immigrant America" and promotes refugee resettlement as an example of the U.S. tradition of goodwill toward the downtrodden. It is also disingenuous because it implies that the granting of refugee status was automatic to persons fleeing "the turmoil or oppression of another time and another place," when in reality it was a highly contested and protracted process, with first-asylum countries—designated a

Table 1   Arrivals of Vietnamese Boat People by Country or Territory of First Asylum, 1975–1995

Country/Territory of First Asylum	1975–79	1980–84	1985–89	1990–95	Cumulative 1975–95
Malaysia	124,103	76,205	52,860	1,327	254,495
Hong Kong	79,906	28,975	59,518	27,434	195,833
Indonesia	51,156	36,208	19,070	15,274	121,708
Thailand	25,723	52,468	29,850	9,280	117,321
Philippines	12,299	20,201	17,829	1,393	51,722
Singapore	7,858	19,868	4,578	153	32,457

SOURCE: United Nations High Commissioner for Refugees 2000, fig. 4.3.

"dumping ground" for unwanted refugees—bearing the brunt of the work (see table 1).

In 1977, some 15,000 Vietnamese left Vietnam by boat and sought asylum in neighboring countries. By the end of 1978, nearly 62,000 boat people had taken refuge throughout Southeast Asia, overcrowding already packed refugee camps.[14] As an example, by June 1979, Pulau Bidong refugee camp in Malaysia was said to be "the most heavily populated place on earth with about 40,000 refugees crowded into a flat area hardly larger than a football field."[15] The massive outflow of refugees crystallized what had already become a problem: resettlement opportunities in Western countries had not kept pace with the refugee tide. By mid-1979, of the more than 550,000 refugees who had arrived in Southeast Asia since 1975, only 200,000 (or 36 percent) had been resettled. Over the previous six months, for every refugee who moved on to resettlement, three more had arrived in the camps.[16] As the number of arrivals grew and resettlement offers slowed, local hostility escalated. When more than 54,000 arrived in June 1979 alone, boat "pushbacks" became routine.[17] At the end of 1979, there was a backlog in the refugee camps of over 360,000 people. The five member states of the Association of Southeast Asian Nations (ASEAN)—Indonesia, Malaysia, the Philippines, Singapore, and Thailand—announced that they would not accept any more new arrivals.[18] With little control over Western governments' resettlement decisions, these countries, as the largest recipients of refugees in the region, feared that in the end they would be saddled with responsibility over these unwanted refugees in overcrowded camps. Whereas Western countries, especially the United States, had ideological reason to regard the boat people as *refugees* fleeing communism, the ASEAN countries considered them primarily as "illegal immigrants/displaced persons."[19]

With the principle of asylum under direct threat, in July 1979 the U.N.secretary general invited sixty-five governments to attend a two-day international conference in Geneva on "refugees and displaced persons in Southeast Asia." The 1979 international agreement formalized a *quid pro quo:* the ASEAN countries pledged to provide temporary asylum to Southeast Asian refugees, and the Western countries agreed to accelerate the rate of resettlement. As worldwide resettlement pledges increased from 125,000 to 260,000, first-asylum countries halted the pushbacks of Vietnamese boats.[20] However, by locating refugee sorting and processing centers *only* in Southeast Asia, this international arrangement granted resettlement countries, but not first-asylum nations, the right to manage the admission of refugees—that is, the right to control their borders from afar by denying admission of the unwanted.[21] In so doing, the international communities accorded more respect to Western resettlement countries' sovereignty rights than to those of ASEAN first-asylum countries. Irked by this asymmetry, the ASEAN countries ramped up pressure on Western countries, especially the United States, to resettle *all* the refugees, not just the most desirable ones. As an example, the deputy prime minister of Malaysia—the country that received the largest number of Vietnamese refugees from 1975 to 1979—excoriated the United States for expecting ASEAN countries to accept *all* refugees arriving on their shores but allowing itself "the luxury of spending several months asking the refugees if they have tuberculosis, if they speak English, and so on, before it decides whether to accept them or not."[22] The international division of the task of refugee resettlement thus replicated the power hierarchy between the "Third" and "First" worlds, as the poorer Southeast Asian countries assumed the role of a "surrogate refuge"—performing the civilizing work of "sanitizing" the cultures, languages, and bodies of the Vietnamese objects of rescue—for the sole benefit of Western resettlement countries.[23]

As a result of the 1979 Geneva conference agreement, between 1970 and 1988 more than a million refugees were given temporary asylum in Southeast Asia and then resettled in over twenty countries. The United States accepted the largest share of refugees (56 percent), followed by Australia, Canada, and France.[24] However, by the end of 1988, the number of fleeing Vietnamese had surged again, prompting seventy-four countries to convene the 1989 International Conference on Indo-Chinese Refugees in Geneva, where they adopted the Comprehensive Plan of Action. Previously, the international community had in effect agreed to recognize all Vietnamese arrivals to first-asylum countries as *prima facie* refugees, guaranteeing them *eventual* resettlement to third countries.[25] The CPA ended this presumptive refugee status and required that all Vietnamese arriving after March 14, 1989 (June 1988 in Hong Kong), be screened in order to determine whether, as individuals, they had a "well-founded fear of persecution." Those who could establish past persecution were entitled to resettlement in third countries; those who could not were deemed "economic migrants" and repatriated to Vietnam.[26] For the most part, the refugees regarded the screening interview as a mystery: they debated at great length over what to say and how to behave, offering and soliciting advice from each other on the "magic words" that would gain them a resettlement offer.[27] Given the seemingly arbitrary nature of screening decisions and the high rejection rate, human rights organizations and refugee advocacy groups, particularly those composed of overseas Vietnamese, widely condemned the CPA screening procedures, characterizing them as "long, arduous, and often punishing" and "arbitrary, restrictive, and often corrupt."[28] By the time the CPA formally ended in 1996, of the 120,000 Vietnamese who had been screened, about 33,200—only 27 percent— were granted refugee status and resettled in third countries; in contrast, about 75,000—63 percent—were screened out and eventually repatriated to Vietnam.[29]

However, gaining refugee status in and of itself did not guarantee resettlement; refugees also had to be individually screened and accepted by resettlement countries before they could leave the camps. By the mid-1980s, faced with a rising tide of refugees, Western countries began to reduce resettlement numbers by introducing more selective admission criteria. Refugee resettlement became a highly contested and often arbitrary process of dividing displaced persons into those worthy and unworthy of resettlement. During the Cold War, admission to the United States was determined almost exclusively on the refugees' ability to produce a documented history of fear of and flight from *communist* repression or persecution. From 1965 to 1980, and even after the passage of the more expansive Refugee Act of 1980, 95 percent or more of those awarded asylum in the United States came from communist countries.[30] By May 1982, the United States had stopped admitting all refugees fleeing Vietnam and begun to implement more restrictive resettlement policies, establishing these priorities: "former South Vietnamese government officials and members of the military; persons formerly closely affiliated with the U.S. or Western institutions; those sent to re-education camps, or to New Economic Zones because they were considered politically or socially undesirable; members of certain ethnic or religious groups; and family members of the above."[31] These criteria were not neutral; they tended to favor men (e.g., former members of the military) over women, South Vietnamese over North Vietnamese applicants, and nuclear over nonnormative families.[32] According to the Immigration and Naturalization Service's 1983 refugee processing guidelines, the burden of proof of refugee status rests with the applicants. The priority and the unequivocal value assigned to the noncommunist identity effectively required all applicants to prove to the skeptical examiners that they were fleeing communism, thereby reducing the multifaceted histories of the Vietnam War and their flight into a single story about communist persecution. Thus, at the very inception of their incorporation into the U.S. nation, Vietnamese refugees were interpellated foremost as anticommunist subjects.

According to U.S. refugee laws, family members of qualified refugees or of persons already in the United States were also eligible for resettlement. But the broader array of what constituted "family" in Vietnamese refugee life—common law relationships, in-camp marriages, and separated family members—bumped up against the narrower concept of a nuclear family specified in U.S. laws.[33] Most contentious was the issue of common-law relationships developed in camp. The United States often refused to recognize refugee status on the basis of family unity for these in-camp families, requiring the applicants to provide "serious" proof of cohabitation, children, or pregnancy.[34] Family members of Amerasians, whom the U.S.

government began accepting for immigration in 1982, also had difficulty passing the emigration screening. Although U.S. refugee laws allowed mothers to emigrate with their Amerasian children, the practical problem was that of proof. Since many of these births were the product of "illicit" affairs and thus not registered, no birth certificates existed to confirm their biological ties. In the end, without documentation, some of these birth mothers, and/or grandparents and half-siblings, were refused resettlement to the United States.[35] In delineating who was—and was not—worthy and deserving of resettlement, U.S. family unity resettlement policy actively framed and reinforced ideas of (im)proper family, kinship, and sexuality.

Media and human rights organizations widely publicized and even sensationalized the plight of repatriated Vietnamese refugees, but they largely ignored the hardship of *protracted refugees* who were warehoused for years and even decades in refugee camps, their prospects for resettlement in limbo. Refugee advocates have traditionally promoted three solutions to refuge outflows worldwide: repatriation, resettlement, and permanent integration in first-asylum countries. However, refugee warehousing— "the practice of keeping refugees in protracted situations of restricted mobility, enforced idleness, and dependency"[36]—has become a de facto and undiscussed *fourth* solution to dispose of refugees. In the Vietnamese case, the long-stayers were typically those who had gained refugee status but could not leave the camps because they had been rejected, sometimes more than once, for resettlement.[37] In 1984, about 600 Vietnamese remained in a refugee camp in Phanat Nikhom, Thailand, without any resettlement offers. More than half had been there for over two years, and some for up to five.[38] Similarly, in 1986, 71 percent of the residents at Palawan refugee camp in the Philippines had been declined admission at least once, and 30 percent of the camp population had been living there for more than two years.[39] When photographer Brian Doan visited the Palawan camp in 2004 to document the flight of the last remaining refugees, he reported that some refugees had spent more than a generation in the camp in "suspended existence" as they awaited resettlement.[40] According to a 1988 report, the majority of refugees in both the open and the closed camps in Hong Kong had been denied permanent admission multiple times. Over a thousand children had spent their entire lives in

(handwritten margin note: isn't this proof we've been making shit decisions)

these closed camps.[41] During the 1980s, Thailand also established detention camps to house long-stayers, and it even stopped processing resettlement claims for new arrivals until the Vietnamese already in Thailand had
been resettled.[42] This prolonged internment of Vietnamese refugees
explodes the myth of the United States as a nation that welcomes *all* refugees. Discriminating resettlement decisions also recall earlier U.S. detention policies, such as the confinement of Native Americans in reservations,
the internment of Japanese Americans during World War II, and the
detainment of Chinese immigrants on Angel Island between 1910 and
1940.

BIOPOLITICS AND NECROPOLITICS: REFUGEE PROCESSING CENTERS AND CLOSED CAMPS/DETENTION CENTERS

Toward the end of World War II, the refugee camp, with its spatial concentration and ordering of camp inhabitants, first became a standardized
technology of power for the management of displacement, simultaneously
caring for and dominating displaced subjects via medical/hygienic programs and quarantining; perpetual accumulation of documentation on
camp inhabitants; law enforcement and public discipline; and schooling
and rehabilitation. According to Liisa Malkki, through these processes
"the modern, postwar refugee emerged as a knowable, nameable figure
and as an object of social-scientific knowledge."[43] In this section, I show
how the living conditions of the refugee camps in Southeast Asia varied
considerably. According to oral accounts told by former Vietnamese refugees, refugee camps were most habitable in Singapore and least livable in
Hong Kong. This difference may have reflected the fact that Singapore
hosted the lowest number of refugees and Hong Kong the highest between
1985 and 1995 (see table 1).

Camp conditions also reflected the resettlement status of its residents—
a cruel ranking system that greatly affected the provision of resources necessary for maintaining human life in the camps. I differentiate between
two major types of refugee camps: the refugee processing centers that
focused on the micromanagement and rehabilitation of refugees bound

for resettlement, and the closed camps or detention centers that ware-housed rejected refugees and treated them as little more than the living dead. For the most part, refugees who arrived prior to the mid-1980s had a much higher chance of moving on to resettlement than those who came after. After 1980, these refugees transitioned through refugee processing centers in the Philippines and Indonesia that had considerably more amenities than most other refugee camps. By the mid-1980s, U.S. atten-tion had shifted from the plight of the boat people in Southeast Asia to the assimilability of its refugees in its neighborhoods—not only because the integration of refugees was an urgent domestic issue but also because the existence of long-term refugees in Southeast Asia undercut the U.S. claim that it had solved the Southeast Asian refugee crisis. As a result, these protracted refugees became, in Doan's words, "the forgotten ones."[44] Across Southeast Asia, the protracted refugees lived in prison-like camps, encircled by barbed wire and armed military guards.[45]

Refugee Processing Centers

With resettlement countries refusing to house refugee camps and first-asylum countries overburdened with refugee care, one of the compromises that emerged from the 1979 Geneva conference was the creation of refu-gee processing centers in the Philippines and Indonesia to help quicken resettlement. Established in 1980, the Philippines Refugee Processing Center (PRPC) on the Bataan Peninsula served as the most prominent transit center for almost all of the U.S.-bound refugees. Administered by the UNHCR, built on land donated by the Philippines, and funded mostly by the United States,[46] the PRPC had a capacity of 17,200 refugees; the goal was to resettle 3,000 refugees per month, replacing them with the same number from other first-asylum country camps.[47] In 1991, the PRPC was near maximum capacity, and 99 percent of the refugees were bound for the United States.[48] By the time it closed in 1995, more than 400,000 refugees had passed through its gates.[49]

Although refugee processing centers were formally established to relieve pressure on first-asylum countries, their unstated purpose was to transform refugees into good citizen subjects for resettlement countries.[50] Soon after the establishment of the PRPC, the United States shifted the resettlement tasks of language instruction, job training, and cultural orientation to the transit center.[51] Indeed, the existence of the PRPC made it possible for the Reagan administration to require every refugee to have a half-year course in English in the Philippines before coming to the United States.[52] In 1980, the UNHCR—using U.S. funds exclusively—contracted with the International Catholic Migration Commission (ICMC) for English as a Second Language/Cultural Orientation (ESL/CO) program. The program followed an established cycle: for those between the ages of seventeen and fifty-five, six months of ESL instruction, four days a week; cultural orientation twice weekly; work orientation six days a week; and two hours a day of work credit activities. Those between eleven and sixteen years of age attended Preparation for American Secondary Schools, which simulated U.S. school curricula and activities. According to the *ICMC Refugee Training Program* (1989), as many as six cycles of classes might take place at any one time, serving a total of 8,000–12,000 students.[53] The State Department reported that shifting the task of language training and cultural orientation to the PRPC represented "considerable savings" for the United States. In 1981, the ICMC paid its ESL teachers—188 Filipinos—an annual salary of just $3,376, and it relied largely on U.N. volunteers and international exchange students to teach cultural orientation classes.[54] It is important to note the neocolonial nature of the employment of Filipinos as ESL teachers: having acquired English as U.S. colonial subjects, Filipino ESL teachers were once again serving U.S. imperial needs by helping to transform Vietnamese refugees—another group of U.S. war spoils—into compliant U.S. subjects.

The work of PRPC personnel was biopolitical in nature: concerned with the welfare of the refugees, camp personnel provided food, clothing, and emergency shelter, and they developed projects that promoted and regulated the health, education, family, and social well-being of the refugees.[55] At the PRPC, refugee subjectivity was constituted not only through legal categories but also through cultural socialization, administered by an international network of relief workers, mainly from Western countries, which taught the refugees who they were expected to become in the West.[56] Besides tending to the needs of displaced persons, these aid workers introduced specific technologies of governing—concerning work, leisure, the use of time, and proper social behavior—that oriented and shaped the everyday behavior of refugees. The goal was not just to train refugees to qualify for asylum in the West or to teach them the skills needed to live in Western societies; it was also to persuade them to internalize the values and hierarchies of the United States and to "transform them into particular kinds of modern human beings (bound for Western liberal democracies)."[57] In this sense, the lives of refugees at the PRPC were mediated by humanitarian interventions that attempted to turn them into "good citizens," to instill in them American values and practices—all before they ever set foot on American soil.[58]

Closed Camps/Detention Centers

While those accepted for resettlement readied themselves in refugee processing centers for their new life in the United States, the "leftover" refugees—those who were screened out and/or rejected for resettlement—became stateless peoples who languished in closed camps or detention centers for extended periods of time without the juridical protection of citizenship.[59] In these detention centers, Vietnamese lives were *not* mediated by humanitarian interventions that attempted to turn them into good modern citizens; instead, they were routinely denied access to schools, health facilities, and most social services.[60] Detention centers were most numerous in Hong Kong, where thirteen prison-like camps detained thousands of Southeast Asian asylum seekers, sometimes for years. In Hong Kong, the refugee camps were tiered: Vietnamese who arrived prior to 1982 were housed in open camps while awaiting resettlement. In the mid-1980s, as Western countries reduced offers of permanent resettlement to Vietnamese refugees and as international pressure intensified against involuntary repatriation, increasing numbers of asylum seekers became "stranded" in Hong Kong. Subsequently, those who arrived between July 2, 1982, and June 15, 1988, were confined to closed camps, which segregated them from previous arrivals (sometimes even their own family members) and from the local community. After June 15, 1988, when Hong Kong had become the most popular destination for the boat people and the Comprehensive Plan of Action had been implemented, all new arrivals were held in detention centers until their refugee status was determined, with those found to be refugees (about 10 percent)

REFUGEE CAMPS AND THE POLITICS OF LIVING 61

moving to the closed camps and those determined not to be refugees remaining in detention awaiting repatriation.[61] In March 1993, 94 percent of the 44,301 Vietnamese in Hong Kong were either classified as or presumed to be illegal immigrants; all were held in detention centers indefinitely.[62]

What stands out among the reports on the detention centers and closed camps for protracted refugees is the constant theme of camp life as imprisonment. The comparison of refugee camps to prisons is not only figurative: in Hong Kong, the Correctional Services Department (CSD), which is part of the Prisons Department, ran the three closed camps at Chi Ma Wan, Cape Collision, and Hei Ling Chau.[63] Under the constant scrutiny of CSD guards, camp dwellers felt "like prisoners who are incarcerated without trial."[64] The closed camps and detention centers shared a common characteristic: immobilization—the constriction of daily life into a restricted space with multiple constraints.[65] In the closed camps at Hei Ling Chau and Chi Ma Wan, asylum seekers were packed in "something akin to industrial shelving":[66]

> The camps were composed of "huts" made out of metal containers. Each hut contained approximately 20 three-level bunk beds which were constructed using metal frames and thin plywood boards. Each level counted as a unit which was partitioned from its neighboring unit by a wooden board and drapes. The bottom levels were usually allocated to families, meaning that a family of three, four, or even five had to live in an 8' x 6' x 3' cubicle. The middle cubicles were usually allocated to couples, and the highest cubicles to single men or women.[67]

This system of human warehousing crammed internees into every inch of available space:

> These bed-spaces were made of re-enforced plywood stacked three high, each space being (at most) three square meters to accommodate two people. At Tai A Chau [in Hong Kong], for example, nearly 500 people lived in these spaces on one floor, and each building in turn had three floors. The top space was considered most desirable, as it had the greatest headroom; people could even stand up, and some had natural light from windows. However, it was also the hottest space. Climbing up was difficult for those who were disabled or elderly; hence the top spaces tended to be occupied by the young. The middle space suffered from noise and vibration from both

above and below, but at least had the benefit of natural light. The bottom spaces were considered least desirable. Although cooler in summer, and easier to access, they suffered from constant passing pedestrian traffic, and had little natural light.[68]

In camps where there were no triple decks, refugees were still subject to "tight packing." Hien V. Ho recalls that a communal building in Malaysia in which his family lived had "large cots made of wood planks [that] were used as living and sleeping quarters for a dozen families. Our family of five was allowed the space of about a king-size bed."[69] An ex-refugee succinctly describes this violent and dehumanizing cramming of "human cargo": "Behind the wire, inside a cage, within a hut, stuffed in a box."[70]

U.S. officials and news media were among the loudest critics of Hong Kong's (mis)treatment of refugees, especially its decision to repatriate them to Vietnam. Ayako Sahara has argued that, by pathologizing and sensationalizing Hong Kong (and other ASEAN nations) as an "inhumanitarian space" that mistreated Vietnamese refugees, the U.S. re-presented the refugees as victims of these countries' callous detention and repatriation policies rather than of U.S. brutal military and stringent resettlement policies. This re-presentation racialized first-asylum countries in Southeast Asia as morally inferior while casting the United States as an ideal(ized) refuge for the Vietnamese refugees. In this global racial order, the Vietnamese refugees became racially and culturally subordinate subjects to both first-asylum and resettlement countries.[71] Since the capacity to decide who will and will not be provided state protection is a key element of sovereign power, the refugee is never "forgotten" by the international community of nations because his or her fate is tied into the practices of exclusion and inclusion that constitute the very system of the nation-state.[72] In other words, the refugee is integral to the continued functioning of the nation-state system.

Although the United States roundly condemned the "sardine-like tiering of human cargo" in Southeast Asian camps, this system was not new: it shared a lineage with the Middle Passage imprisonment and the portable chain-gang camp of the U.S. postbellum period, among others.[73] According to Dennis Childs, the system of "tight-packing" was used from the early modern period through the nineteenth century aboard European slave vessels, in which the slave captives were packed "sometimes more than five feet high and sometimes less; and this height is divided toward the middle for the slaves lie in two rows [on platforms] one above the other, on each side of the ship, close to each other like books on a shelf."[74] During the Jim Crow apartheid period, the land-based moving prison, which housed black "criminals" who had been rounded up for such misdemeanor "crimes" as vagrancy and loitering, also used this "tier-style human cargoing":

> To fit so many prisoners into such a small space, the "cage" consisted of two parallel sections of three-tiered bunks with an access path running down the center and a hole cut in the middle of the walkway, through which prisoners were forced to urinate and defecate into a bucket placed on the ground below. The outer shell of these structures was either a lattice of wooden or metal bars that left the chain gang captive open to surveillance by camp guards and the public or four windowless wooden walls. This latter version of the rolling cage left prisoners with no view of the outside world and allowed them only a minuscule supply of breathable air through a narrow slit running along the top of the structure.[75]

These overlapping formations of imprisonment connect the racialized positionality of Vietnamese refugees to that of enslaved and criminalized blacks, not because these positionalities are identical and interchangeable but because mass human warehousing produces a shared "loss of status beyond which life ceases to be politically relevant." This dehumanization process projects the imprisoned as inhuman or subhuman and transmutes their personhood into objecthood.[76]

The thanato/necropolitics of the human warehousing of Vietnamese refugees—and of other racialized bodies, then and now—"made biological life tantamount to living death."[77] Living crammed together behind chain-link fences topped with barbed wire and patrolled by prison authorities, refugees in closed camps were not allowed to go beyond the boundaries set by the wired fences.[78] At the San Yick Closed Centre in Hong Kong, which the UNHCR consistently described as "unfit for human habitation," the residents, confined to the building, received no natural light for days on end. Each refugee was allowed an escorted outing from the building only once every thirty-three days.[79] Living in triple-decked cubicles the size of a twin bed, or on six- to eighteen-square-foot mats on the crowded floor, camp dwellers "[had] absolutely no privacy."[80] All daily activities,

even the most intimate, were conducted in public. Kept as virtual prisoners, camp dwellers were stripped of all decision making: "They are told
when to eat, when to sleep, and when to stay in their barracks in accord-
ance with the curfew."[81] Within their constricted world, they were depend-
ent on aid organizations for everything: their daily meals, building material, used clothing, and medical treatment.[82] After the adoption of the
Comprehensive Plan of Action in 1989, social and recreational activities at
the detention centers were suspended.[83] Perhaps the most dramatic of all
was the elimination of all educational programs above primary-school
level.[84] Inside the camps, adults had no jobs and children had no formal
school. Weekdays and weekends blended into each other—a series of rep-
etitious routines of waiting for meals, baths, and bedtime.[85] These abject
conditions devalued and dehumanized refugees, subjecting them to living
death with impunity.

"THE POLITICS OF LIVING"

This chapter is not only about the extreme situations of refugee camps but
also about the people who make their way in them. I am interested in
understanding not just how the refugee regime immobilizes bodies and
subjects but also how camp dwellers busily engage in daily life in order to
(re)produce security, community, and potency of place in displacement.
Attentive to what Ilana Feldman terms "the politics of living," I focus here
on everyday forms of human experience and adaptation: How do refugees
imagine and build a home—a refuge—in the midst of confinement? What
are the lifeworlds that can and do take shape within the space and conditions of the camps?[86]

As discussed in chapter 1, social scientists have largely reduced
Vietnamese refugees to mere victims, restricted in their capacity to act as
full subjects in their own right. Liisa Malkki and others have argued that it
is our attachment to the dominant framework of nation states and our own
rootedness that blind us to the lived meanings that exists in the in-between
social world that refugees-in-transit inhabit.[87] Against this overemphasis
on the rupture of forced migration, I look for the multiple, albeit fleeting,
ways through which Vietnamese refugees sought to make the refuge

camp a "home" via material forms, physical objects, and domestic and ritual spaces.[88] I *look for* rather than *document* these place-making practices
because they are seldom officially archived, not because they do not exist
but because refugee life has too often been described only in terms of loss,
dormancy, and inactivity. Below, I cull from disparate sources—mainly
oral histories, blogs, commentaries, and memoirs, most of which come
from Internet sources—to sketch how lives and relationships were being
(re)built, however haltingly, in these camps. The majority of the oral histories referred to in this chapter are from the digital Vietnamese American
Oral History Project at the University of California, Irvine. Of the 101 oral
histories available in April 2013, thirty-two profiles were selected because
they include details on refugee camp life.[89] Of course, these oral histories,
by their very nature, capture only the lives of those Vietnamese who made
it to the United States; unarchived are the stories of the protracted refugees warehoused for years in the closed camps and detention centers in
Southeast Asia and of those who had been repatriated to Vietnam. For
those stories, I rely on more transitory sources such as photographs and
paintings, newspaper reports, and humanitarian workers' accounts.

Dis/Emplacement

The song "Biển Nhớ" that opens this chapter is not only about the people
that stay behind but also about the *place* they leave behind. Even as it bids
farewell to the leaver, its lyrics emplace the departing person in the local
landscape—the beckoning sea, mountains, sandy beach, rocks, and drooping willows. Here is a sample lyric: "Tomorrow, you leave. Missing you, the
sea will whisper your name. Whispering to the soul of the drooping willows and the late night's white sandy beach."[90] The allusion to water in the
song title is significant because, in the Vietnamese language, "the word for
water and the word for *a nation, a country,* and *a homeland* are one and
the same: *nước.*"[91] The repeated references to sea, ocean, and water
throughout the song also evoke the imagery of the "boat people," thus
ensconcing their experiences in Vietnamese diasporic lore, even as the literature on diaspora rarely deals with them or with refugee camps. As
such, the song that bid farewell to the departing refugees simultaneously
anchored them in Vietnamese landscape, history, and social relations.

As the refugees' stay lengthened, they erected physical structures to mark the rituals of their day-to-day life. Religious structures were found in almost all of the camps. Vietnamese refugees at the PRPC in Bataan who arrived in 1986 built a monument that showcased the influence of the three great religions—Buddhism, Confucianism, and Taoism—on Vietnamese culture.[92] They also constructed two Buddhist temples, one guarded by a huge image of the Buddha and the other by a meditating Buddha and a female Bodhisattva or saint, which became a favorite "meditation corner" for many of the Vietnamese (and later Lao and Khmer refugees).[93] Like their Buddhist compatriots, Vietnamese Catholics at the PRPC and at Palawan in the Philippines also erected religious monuments—a Virgin Mary statue and a Virgin Mary grotto, respectively, to thank her for their safe arrival in the country.[94] Even on their crammed bedspaces, refugees recreated the traditional Vietnamese custom of keeping an altar, where they prayed and burned incense and offered rice, water, and fruits to their ancestors.[95] For example, at the height of the boat refugee exodus in 1979, at the Kai Tak camp in Hong Kong, where some 14,000 people were housed at two-and-a-half people to a bunk and where the bunks were stacked three-high from floor to ceiling, some refugees still managed to give their living areas—their bed-spaces—"a touchingly warm and homey atmosphere."[96] Photos of the camp, snapped by Project Ngoc[97] student activists in the late 1980s and 1990s, show refugees hanging material from the steel framework of the shelving to delineate and act as curtains around their spaces—an often-futile effort to create some semblance of privacy. On these bedspaces, where all their possessions were also kept, people would spend much of their lives: sleeping, talking with neighbors, eating meals, and worshipping.[98] Given their meager resources and dilapidated living conditions, these attempts to be "creative and alive . . . [were] both moving and sad" since they represented not only the refugees' attempt to create a liveable space for themselves but also their resignation to the fact that they may never leave the camps.[99]

Displaced from Vietnam and treated primarily as victims devoid of historical subjectivities, refugees also reclaimed their stolen histories—and their *place*—by literally carving them into the ground of the camps. At the Palawan camp in the Philippines, the only home that thousands of Vietnamese refugees knew for over two decades (from 1979 to 1997), some refugees carved their stories of escape from Vietnam and other confidences on large sections of concrete scabs scattered over the grounds of the camp; others etched their names on the walls of several wells dug for fresh water.[100] On one wall at the camp, an anonymous Vietnamese refugee penned a short poem lamenting their stateless conditions: "Where can a refugee find happiness? Which country will record my footprint?"[101] Other short poems or aphorisms were also carved into rocks strewn along the seashore.[102] In several camps, such as the PRPC in Bataan in the Philippines and the Galang Island refugee camp in Indonesia, boats that had been used in the escape from Vietnam were enshrined as memorials.[103] On Galang Island, refugees also erected the Statue of Humanity, depicting the figure of a woman named Tinh Loai Han, who had committed suicide after being raped by a fellow refugee, and the Three Ladies shrine as a tribute to three other young Vietnamese women, Thai pirates' rape victims, who were shamed by fellow refugees into taking their own lives.[104] These public "archives," ensconced in the camp's natural environment, emplaced the refugees—the "unwanteds," "leftovers," and "forgotten ones" of the exodus from Vietnam—into the foreign landscape, proclaiming their presence and preserving their history for posterity. It is significant that these archives, which emphasize loss, escape, and survival, memorialize the refugees' lives *in transit,* suggesting that Vietnamese subjectivities materialize not only in relation to a prewar Vietnamese homeland or the U.S. nation-state but also in the space *between* nation states. I contend that these public archives do more than preserve individual refugee stories; their very presence constitutes material evidence of the longer history of U.S. wars in Asia and the massive loss of human lives that characterized the resultant refugee crisis.

Finally, Vietnamese literally emplaced themselves in the new landscape as they buried hundreds of their fellow compatriots who had died in the camps while waiting for resettlement.[105] As a Bataan refugee camp website states, "There were others, too, who never left the Camp, but were resettled, sooner than they expected or wanted, in what came to be known as Neighborhood 11: the cemetery."[106]

Making a Life

For Vietnamese refugees, what was set into motion by the Vietnam War, the Fall of Saigon, and their boat journey was not only the loss of land, property, and position but also an entire social fabric—the dense network of social relations and one's location within it. Refugee life stories are replete with frantic attempts to reconnect with lost family members. For example, in 1976, a news reporter found a left-behind letter in a refugee camp in Guam, stamped by the U.S. postal service, "return to sender service indefinitely suspended," addressed to Vo Thi at this long address: My Hoang, Ninh Than, Ning Hoa, Khang Hao, South Vietnam. Dated September 2, 1975, the letter indicated that the writer, Vo Tinh, was writing for the fourth time to his parents and grandparents but had not received any responses from his family. On October 16, 1975, Vo Tinh sailed for Vietnam aboard the Thuong Tin I, along with other Vietnamese who had demanded to be repatriated to Vietnam in large part to locate missing family members.[107] Others, like thirty-year-old Loc Nam Nguyen, spent years abroad searching for lost family members. In 1975, Nguyen escaped Vietnam on a C-130 plane with no possessions aside from old family photos. During his stay at Camp Pendleton in California, every day, Nguyen would search bulletin boards with lists of refugee names hoping for signs of his parents and ten siblings, from whom he had been separated during the escape. It would be years before his entire family was reunited in the United States.

The refugee camp environment also inflicted serious and often lasting wounds on Vietnamese family life. Like Japanese American families in internment camps during World War II, Vietnamese families in refugee camps struggled to recreate family life under very trying conditions: lack of privacy, mass meals, regimented routines, uncertain future, and changing gender and generational dynamics.[108] For young women without families, sexual harassment was rampant, made worse by the close living quarters and lack of privacy. Refugee studies scholars have long recorded the sexual violence that women in refugee camps endure and whose concerns are often left unaddressed by overwhelmed camp personnel and by the largely male representatives designated as the community liaisons to U.N. official authorities.[109] Suzie Xuyen Dong Matsuda remembered that, as a young woman without family, she was subject to sexual harassment and sexual abuse in the camp: "There's several incidents but I am not going to share here. I overcome that, but it ... really did take a toll on me."[110] Young women also had to fend off sexual assault from local police and officials. Duc Huu Nguyen, who stayed at Camp Laem Sing in Thailand for one year, remembered that the men in the camp had to chase off the lecherous Thai police: "The Thai police would . . . get drunk and come down and try to rape girls, you know, in the camp and when that happened most of the men in the camp would come out and bang on the pot and start screaming, bring out a stick or something like that trying to scare them away, because you don't want to get in the physical fight with them because, you know, we were just refugees living there. We have no rights or anything."[111]

Yet even in this very space of despair and chaos, refugees managed to create new and meaningful social relations. Bound by their shared fate, confined in a crammed environment, and with ample time to spare, refugees often developed intense kin-like relationships with each other. The significance of camp life in Vietnamese diasporic lives is evident in the pilgrimages that resettled refugees later organized to revisit their former refugee camps. In March 2005, an Australian organization based in Melbourne called Archive of Vietnamese People (Văn Khố Thuyền Nhân Việt Nam) organized a pilgrimage to the former refugee camps Pulau Bidong and Pulau Galang in Malaysia; it drew a group of 142 self-funded former boat refugees who had since resettled in Australia, the United States, Canada, France, England, and Denmark, some thirty Buddhist monks and nuns from Australia and the United States, and a Catholic priest and three Catholic nuns from Australia. At the former refugee camps, the group commemorated their exodus by dedicating two memorials to honor those who had perished in the camp and in the South China Sea.[112] At Pulau Bidong, at the dedication of the memorial, Reverend Anthony Nguyễn Hữu Quảng, a Catholic priest from Sydney and a former Galang refugee, referred to the camp as a "sacred territory . . . built not only by the sweat and tears of the Vietnamese refugees, but also by the bones and blood of the hundreds of thousands of Vietnamese who had died on their quest for freedom" and vowed that the memories of Bidong camp "will never be erased from the memories and souls of us Vietnamese refugees."[113] These declarations, and the former Vietnamese refugees' collective and public act of self-mourning, elevated the meanings of refugee camps like Pulau Bidong and Pulau Galang beyond mere transient sites of refuge—a place en route to the idealized and coveted West—and instead marked them as sacred, moral, and significant spaces in the formation of Vietnamese subjectivities.[114] As Quan Tue Tran concludes, by commemorating the boat refugee exodus, the Bidong and Galang memorials "offered a quintessential origin narrative of the contemporary Vietnamese diaspora, one that was born from a massive refugee movement out of the Socialist Republic of Vietnam in the post-1975 era."[115]

A quick Internet search for "Southeast Asian refugee camps" also produces numerous photographs of camp inhabitants of all ages posing with large groups of friends or families. Eyes bright, smiles wide, arms linked, their warm intimacy radiates from the computer screen. These pictures can be found on official refugee camp websites or sometimes on personal flickr accounts. As an example, Diem Chau's flickr account includes a handful of pictures taken at the PRPC in Bataan, where she and her family lived for close to a year in the mid-1980s. In one photo, with the accompanying caption "Boogie in the Classroom," Chau's father dances merrily with a colleague at an ESL class graduation party; just behind them, a table laden with food and a cake awaits. Such images of fleeting friendships constitute evidence of the cultural and social activities that refugees organized to shield themselves against the camp's dehumanizing environment. Mary Hoang Long, who spent fifteen months at Phanat Nikkhom camp in Thailand, described how camp living broke down regional divisions among her camp mates: "When they lived in my country, they all lived in different cities and they have different foods, different culture. Food and something, clothes, and anything were a little bit different, but when we lived in the camp, every people go together. . . . Before, we South, we don't like people of North, and the Middle they don't like North or South. When we lived in the camp and the life was very difficult and poor, so every people very good together."[116] At Songkhla refugee camp in Thailand, whenever camp residents spotted a refugee boat in the open sea, practically the whole camp would rush toward it, waving and yelling, with some attempting to swim out to the boat to welcome the newcomers.[117] These examples suggest that Vietnamese refugees were bound as much by their shared fate as an imperiled people-in-transit as by their shared origin in Vietnam.

By most accounts, children like Chau, ignorant of the worries that plagued adults and freed from most schoolwork and household responsibilities, delighted in cavorting with readymade playmates in the camps.

Oral histories suggest that children were free to spend most of the days unsupervised, either because parents had perceived the camp as a safe place and/or because they had lost the ability to discipline their children. As Dan Nguyen, who was a young mother during her ten-month stay in Camp Galang in 1984, recounted, "While I was in [English] class at school, [my daughter] played with the crowd close to home or the kids in the same age range. Back then I didn't think about the kidnapping problem, did not think of the problem at all, just said: 'Well, stay home, I'm leaving.' It was very comfortable. Went to school from 8 a.m to 11 a.m, then went home and cooked meals."[118] Paul Chi Hoang recalled that, as a nine-year-old boy, he reveled in exploring Camp Galang in Indonesia with his sister: "I was in school. I was supposed to be learning English but I don't remember learning anything, just remember having fun and doing a lot of things there [that] was fun, playing with kids, going around. I remember at night time my sister and I go bother kids with somebody, go into the field to catch frogs so that we can cook and eat, and then we would go and try kill the komodo dragon."[119] For Chau, her favorite memories involve simple childhood frolics such as harvesting mangoes with other children:

> OMG! Being a kid there was the best thing ever. . . . We lived next door to a grove of mango trees. . . . Occasionally a few ripe ones would fall off, but during the monsoons with heavy wind branches will break off and tons of green mangoes will be shaken off. The kids made a game of gathering mangoes in the storm. Yeah . . . dangerous, but we didn't know any better.[120]

Chau's mango story, posted on the PRPC website, elicited this reply from another camp alumni: "I used to live in this camp back in 1990, cycle 141, Vung 9 or Section 9. Filled with memories back in those days. I'm still looking for my friends who used to go to school with me. Hope I will. Mangoes!!! After school, I used to climb up to the top of the mango tree to pick mangoes. Lots of fun."[121]

Even though Chau was a young child when she lived in Bataan, she still cherishes the "intense friendships and bonds" that she experienced at the camp:

> You get to know people intimately at the refugee camp, but we're all just passing through. It's a funny relationship, you can easily pour your heart and soul out, some of the most intense friendships and bonds were formed

there. Then only months later you have to say goodbye. Most people have no idea where they will be going, they have no address, no phone number. There's no way to keep in touch. Like sand running through your fingers, you just have this one moment so you learn how to cherish it.[122]

She explains that these "intense friendships" made camp life tolerable and even enjoyable:

It was hard, but most look back on it fondly. It reminds me a lot of the movie *Stand By Me*,[123] a short journey taken by a group of friends. :) I really miss it. . . . It's the interrelations between the residents that was cut short. The idea that we were all strangers stranded in the same place made it easier for us to bond.

On the PRPC alumni website, which Chau started, she has written: "The PRPC was unforgettable and played a highly influential role in my life. Although I was there as a child and only for a brief time the people and stories will always live with me."[124] Often, these bonds assumed the form of kinship—"camp families"—and endured long after departure from the camps. In Chau's case, her family of three shared their living unit at the Bataan camp with another family of four, with whom they still keep in touch some thirty years later.[125]

Music was key to the social life in refugee camps. According to ethnomusicologist Adelaida Reyes, music making, especially singing, was central to the construction of Vietnamese refugee identity and community, a means to look back nostalgically to pre-1975 South Vietnam as well as forward to new identities and lives.[126] In camps across Southeast Asia, such as Northwest W9 camp in Thailand, refugees would gather at night and sing Vietnamese and Western songs and Christian hymns.[127] At Bataan camp, some refugees' apartments would be transformed nightly into makeshift cafés featuring entertainment from the local talents.[128] In the late 1980s, at Pulau Bidong refugee camp in Malaysia, where most Vietnamese refugees stayed up to ten months awaiting resettlement, a musical stage was set up that hosted regular music festivals performed by the refugees and Malaysian musicians as well as U.N., Malaysian Red Crescent Society, and Police Task Force personnel.[129] Vietnamese refugees also actively participated in sports, especially soccer. According to Reyes, in the 1980s and early 1990s, about 40 percent of the camp population at

Palawan participated in organized sports and cultural activities.[130] At one time, Pulau Bidong camp had up to twenty-four competing soccer teams, with both adult and youth divisions. The Boy Scouts organization, which had been active in refugee camps across the world since World War I, had a prominent presence in camps in Southeast Asia, engaging children in all kinds of outdoor activities.[131]

Camp dwellers also marked the passage of time by organizing annual holiday celebrations, often with improvised props. A letter-writer named Thien, who referred to his two-year stay at Galang refugee camp in Indonesia as "the best years of my life," remembered fondly that "we kept our tradition: for example, our New Year, in Vietnam, we normally make fireworks. In Galang, we searched for wood and we made a big fire and we made a lot of noise with pots, pans, with everything we could find."[132] Amid the shabbiness of their living quarters, the refugees celebrated Vietnamese New Year with gusto, replete with "fake fire-crackers" and "fake Vietnamese cherry trees":

> [A] fine moment was the celebration of the Viet New Year. We had a fair where fake fire-crackers were hung from fake Vietnamese cherry trees. The pagoda was decorated with look-alike Chinese characters welcoming Tet [Vietnamese New Year]. . . . That night, we had a large bonfire that burned until the wee hours. . . . One of my favorite pictures shows my wife in front of our apartment. Above her hangs a five-pointed, star-shaped lantern that I made myself from bamboo rods and paper for my children. It is a Vietnamese tradition to hang that kind of paper lantern during holidays like Christmas or Mid-Autumn festival.[133]

Festive celebrations took place even in the most depressed refugee camps. When photographer Brian Doan arrived in Palawan in January 2004, the remaining boat people, some of whom had spent close to three decades in the camp, were preparing for Tet, the traditional Lunar New Year celebration. As the "forgotten ones," these refugees "[were] stuck in a backwater, forced to live as outcasts, far away from any place where they could lead normal lives," yet they still greeted with anticipation the dawn of a new year, belting out songs about their life in exile and the fate of the diaspora. But the time warp was evident: these still-favored songs, prevalent some twenty years ago when the refugees first entered the camp, were already disappearing from popular Vietnamese music in the diaspora.[134]

Pictures and blogs posted online by former Vietnamese refugees capture other festivities: young children dancing with their daycare friends; children welcoming First Lady of the Philippines, Imelda Marcos, to the camp;[135] and students dancing at a party celebrating the end of the ESL/CO classes.[136] Mary Hoang Long described a typical day's activities for her family at Phanat Nikhom refugee camp: "On the day, like me, I volunteer, I work for the office for interview with new people come to the camp. My sister, she volunteers to teach at the preschool. My cousin, he volunteers and teach soccer and table tennis for the minor kids. On the night, we go to two theaters. In the camp, there are two theaters. One theater always had ghost movies and one theater for the drama movies and we can go to the movies in the night or we can dance. Yeah, and so fun."[137] Other, more quiet rituals punctuated the passing of each day of camp life: "After a hard day at work, women usually get together in the shade of trees near their home. Talking about the past and sharing their dreams of resettlement in a third country are favorite social habits of the stateless Vietnamese in the Philippines."[138] These celebrations, both the boisterous and the quiet ones, are testaments to the depth of the refugee spirit—to their ability to tap out a rhythm of life to interrupt, however briefly, the monotony of their suspended existence.[139] As Thien professed, "It wasn't luxurious but we were happy. Everybody helped each other. It was very social. . . . There are a lot of good memories there. . . . God, I miss those days!"[140] In some camps, refugees also established a number of micro-businesses to serve the camp population, including bakery shops, tailor shops, fruit stands, small markets, and even discos and bars.[141]

In the camps that housed long-stayers, refugees out of necessity institutionalized many aspects of their daily life. The Vietnamese Refugee Center in Palawan in the Philippines is a good example. Built in 1979, the center was intended to accommodate 2,000 people but had housed as many as 7,000, many of whom had been rejected by one or more resettlement countries. Houses of worship, schools, libraries, restaurants, and other micro-businesses such as tailoring, manicuring, and photo studios sprang up over the years to accommodate the long-stayers' growing needs. Some refugees raised pigs and poultry and planted flowerbeds and vegetable gardens to supplement their income and food needs.[142] Palawan camp residents also established a governing body, the Vietnamese Refugee Council, which had jurisdiction over the internal affairs of the camp. The principal goal of the council was to create a "small Vietnam" *in situ*; a unique ritual was "the weekly flag ceremony at which the flag of the former Republic of South Vietnam was raised, the old national anthem was sung, and the chairman of the VR Council spoke to the gathered camp population to make announcements and to exhort the Vietnamese to uphold Vietnamese values."[143] This nation-building ritual was gendered, since most members of the council were former officers of the South Vietnamese military who, in diaspora, embodied the fallen nation and the opposition to communism professed by the majority of the refugees. Moreover, though many displaced Vietnamese disliked the label *refugee* as an ascribed identity, former military men embraced the fact that they were refugees: "The tremendous loss of pride that was suffered at the time of surrender . . . is partially restored within the camp where it is possible for them to construe the label 'refugee' as a badge of defiance."[144] To counterbalance the effects of cultural orientation and English-language classes that prepared refugees for eventual resettlement, the council also instituted educational programs to provide the young with regular instruction in Vietnamese history, geography, culture, and language.[145]

Palawan occupants' active participation in shaping communal life was not a Vietnamese cultural trait; rather, it was the result of the indeterminate period of waiting that suffused life in Palawan. Some refugees spent close to three decades there. In contrast, Vietnamese refugees at the PRPC in Bataan, who had been accepted for resettlement in the United States and who anticipated a brief camp stay, appeared to display "a pronounced disinterest" in getting involved in aspects of camp life.[146] Another difference between the two groups was that refugees in Palawan resisted whenever they could the camp's organizational discipline, engaging in such subversive activity as black market dealings, whereas refugees in Bataan exhibited an "unquestioning acceptance of the routines and procedures imposed from the outside," lest they jeopardize their imminent resettlement in the United States.

Organizing against Detention

Thus far, I have shown that refugee camps, however bleak, also constituted meaningful lifeworlds for Vietnamese refugees who managed to build family and community within them. However, it is important to note that these place-making practices occurred primarily in refugee processing centers and open camps in which most refugees had some access to the outside world and a decent chance at resettlement. In contrast, in detention centers and closed camps, where dwellers were segregated from the local community, held in a state of legal limbo, and prevented from exercising or making claims to rights, refugees were reduced to "bare life" literally and metaphorically.[147] In his highly influential text *Homo Sacer*, Giorgio Agamben draws from descriptions of Nazi concentration camps to theorize "the camp" as a space where camp dwellers are placed in a lingering state of "bare life," stripped of juridical protections and reduced to a biological minimum but not declared dead or outside the rule of law.[148] Expanding on Agamben, scholars of refugees and refugee camps have argued that, by containing refugees within an unlivable space and in a suspended state of noncitizenship, host states are in effect treating long-term refugees as bare life.[149] Agamben's "camp" thus provides a compelling framework for refugee camp studies because it calls attention to the space outside the normal juridical order where refugees who lack institutional or political recourse to citizenship are reduced to the depoliticized state of bare life.[150] However, Agamben, like many other refugee camp studies scholars, tends to treat the camp as a unified and monolithic type of space rather than explaining how different types of camps rely on different logics and daily material practices.[151] Agamben's "camp" is thus a more apt descriptor of detention centers and closed camps, in which protracted refugees become constituted as "no longer human,"[152] than of refugee processing centers and open camps, in which refugees are converted into modern human beings bound for the modern West. Although markedly different in practice, both types of camp racially marked refugees as people needing to be transformed.[153]

Agamben's concept of *homo sacer* turns refugees into abject subjects and essentializes camp into a space of victimization. But as other scholars have shown, abject spaces can also become "spaces of politics" when camp dwellers enact themselves "as political by exercising rights that they do not have"; in so doing, they turn bare life into political life.[154] Examples of political interventions staged by refugees that counter the state of abjection range from public and collective demonstrations against deportation and repatriation to setting boats afire to avoid being transferred to off-shore detention centers to suturing mouths closed to protest against stringent state asylum laws.[155] Through these political stagings, refugees enact the politics of their own liberation, defying the image of camp as bodies of victims. Peter Nyers refers to these political practices as "abject cosmopolitanism": efforts by refugee (and immigrant) groups to resist their targeted exclusion by disrupting the camp's administrative routines and day-to-day perceptions and constructions of normality.[156] These radical political acts imply that being reduced to a condition of rightlessness does not negate one's desire or capacity to act as a political subject. As Engin Isin and Kim Rygiel have argued, "It is in the very claiming of rights—the rights that one does not have—where one enacts one's political existence."[157] In this way, spaces of "abjection" are always contested spaces where resistance from a position of assumed equality can and does take place.[158]

Vietnamese detainees' political stagings in Hong Kong throughout the 1990s confirm that detention centers, however austere, are never only spaces where people are rendered incoherent, invisible, and inconsequential. In the 1990s, sparked by the overcrowded, prison-like conditions, reductions in services and employment opportunities, the indeterminate duration of their stay, and their fear of repatriation, Vietnamese detainees in Hong Kong detention centers vented their anger and distress over their bleak future through a series of riots, with some resulting in serious injuries and deaths.[159] In early May 1991, a riot took place at Whitehead Detention Centre, a steel and barbed-wire cage in the middle of one of Hong Kong's wealthiest enclaves; 1,200 policemen and Civil Service Department staff used tear gas to subdue the detainees.[160] In 1992, when Hong Kong cut basic services, a massive riot left twenty-four Vietnamese dead at Sek Kong camp.[161] A massive riot at Whitehead in May 1996 was ignited when police and prison guards tried to repatriate hundreds of boat people; detainees torched the administrative building and huts, injuring forty-seven policemen and staff members of the Correctional Service Department and seven boat people. Over a hundred detainees fled the camp, many of whom were later recaptured and imprisoned. Protesters left behind at the camp, wielding clubs and hurling makeshift spears and rocks, battled nearly 2,000 security forces who tried to subdue them with

240 rounds of tear gas. On the second day of the riot, about 200 detainees staged protests atop the camp's residential barracks, waving banners and chanting slogans about freedom and democracy. In all, the rioters destroyed seventeen buildings, set fifty-two vehicles ablaze, and briefly held fifteen camp officers hostage. They also burned down a building that housed their personal records in an effort to slow down the repatriation process. Widely covered in the local news media, the riots became front-page news, with photos of a series of huts on fire and accompanying captions that racialized the refugees as "beast-like creatures who started the fire" and whose "brutal nature" led to the "ruthless killing."[162]

Detainees in Hong Kong detention centers also protested through their artwork. A collection of over 200 pieces of art, part of the Project Ngoc Collection at U.C. Irvine, invokes the imagery of a prison, with many oversize paintings depicting the camps encircled by tall fences and barbed wire. According to Daniel Tsang, these detention camp artworks share a stark similarity to the "Visions from Prison" (1990) art produced by inmates in the California State Prison System's Art in Corrections program and to a collection of Vietnamese artists' depiction of incarceration in Vietnam. Yet these artworks also hint at human bright spots amid the regimented gloom. For example, in a painting entitled "Barbed Wire," several children are crouched on the ground, playing marbles or some other popular children's game. Their colorful clothes, in vivid red and blue with some white, constitute a defiant sign of life in this very zone of indistinction. A graphic design from the covers of the periodical *Tự Do* (Freedom), published monthly at the Whitehead Detention Centre, also highlights imprisonment. In a sign of agency and defiance, however, its one-year commemorative issue depicted barbed wire in the foreground with the silhouettes of a man and a woman with arms raised, propping up the periodical that they have created.[163]

•   •   •   •   •

In this chapter, I have extended my argument begun in chapter 2 that the humanitarian idea of "refuge" follows on the heels and smooths over the damage wrought by military intervention in parts of the world racialized to be always-already "violent-prone." As Michel Agier succinctly states: it is about "striking with one hand, healing with the other."[164] The literature on refugee camps has often paired the construct of Vietnamese refugees as passive objects of sympathy with a plea for the West to "assume an *active* role in caring, counseling, or intervening."[165] Such calls to action naturalize and buttress the U.S. self-appointed role as rescuers, whose magnanimity promises swift deliverance from a bleak life of "no exit" to one of boundless possibilities. The prevalent narrative of refugees coming from the poor Third World, obligatorily passing through first-asylum countries in Asia, and ending up happily in the First World, if left uninterrogated, repeats a racial lexicon that depicts Vietnam and other Asian countries as a global region to which freedom is a foreign principle, and the United States as that to which freedom is an indigenous property. This construct represents the Vietnamese as only passive recipients of U.S. "generosity" and Asian countries as inadequate substitutes for the West, thereby precluding any critical examination of U.S. military interventionism in Asia in inducing this forced migration in the first place.

In this chapter, I have intervened in this literature on refugee camps by exposing the role that first-asylum countries played in constituting the United States (and other Western resettlement countries) as the benevolent refuge, thereby calling attention to the unequal international division of labor and hierarchies of refuge that replicate First and Third World distinctions. I have also called attention to the *life* that existed in these camps. At the nexus of the charitable power wielded by Western refugee aid organizations, the local politics of the first-asylum camps, and the lived experience of hope and hopelessness that took place within the refugee camps, Vietnamese refugees developed new subjectivities and new social relations "in this time out of life."[166] With camp life stripped of the social and reduced to the barest functions of maintenance, Vietnamese refugees worked to create a new social fabric out of the hardship. These place-making structures were monuments to the refugee presence and the history that brought them to the camps but also marked the refugees' resignation to their extended stay at the camps.

In addition, I have differentiated between at least two different types of refugee camps: the refugee processing centers and open camps that transformed Vietnam's runaways into acceptable refugee subjects, and the detention centers and closed camps that incarcerated the asylum seekers into something similar to industrial shelving. Together, these different camp spaces tell the story of a displaced people in transit—of lives that could or would have been, as well as lives that did emerge from the ruins of war and its aftermath. This sense of "in-betweenness"—of living between languages, homes, and countries—suggests that, for Vietnamese refugees, "peace" became a de facto "war without end" as they continued to bear the lifelong costs of one of the most brutal and destructive wars of the twentieth century.

4 The "Good Warriors" and the "Good Refugee"

For the past twenty-two years, I have been searching to find some reference in mainstream journalism or scholarship to an American invasion of South Vietnam in 1962 (or ever), or an American attack against South Vietnam, or American aggression in Indochina—without success. There is no such event in history. Rather, there is an American defense of South Vietnam against terrorists supported from the outside (namely from Vietnam).

Noam Chomsky, *The Chomsky Reader*

There is no such event in history. Noam Chomsky's admonition[1] underscores the fact that much of official U.S. history about the Vietnam War is based on organized forgetting. Thirty years (1945–75) of warfare destruction, coupled with another twenty years of postwar U.S. trade and aid economic embargo, shattered Vietnam's economy and society, leaving the country among the poorest in the world and its people scattered to all corners of the globe.[2] By most accounts, the Vietnam War was one of the most brutal and destructive wars between Western imperial powers and the people of Asia, Africa, and Latin America. Yet post-1975 public discussions of the Vietnam War in the United States often skip over this devastating history. This chapter originates from my concern that, at the milestone twenty-fifth anniversary of the Fall of Saigon (hereafter, twenty-fifth anniversary), a "determined incomprehension"[3] remained the dominant U.S. public stance on the history of the Vietnam War. Instead of using the occasion of the twenty-fifth anniversary to critically analyze and assess the political reasons for and ongoing consequences of the war, U.S. print media have opted to present a personalist, ahistorical, and ultimately "we-win-even-when-we-lose" account of the war and its aftermath. This "skipping over" of the devastation of the Vietnam War, especially the costs borne by the Vietnamese, constitutes an organized and strategic forgetting that has enabled "patriotic" Americans to continue to push military interventions as key in America's self-appointed role as liberators—protectors of democracy, liberty, and equality, both at home and abroad.

Through detailed analyses of U.S. mainstream press coverage of the twenty-fifth anniversary in April 2000, I identify two overarching and overlapping narratives: one that centers on innocent and heroic Vietnam warriors, and the other on liberated and successful Vietnamese refugees. It was not inevitable that the media coverage of the twenty-fifth anniversary would focus on the veterans and the refugees. At the end of the Vietnam War in 1975, both groups were unwanted and even despised by the American public. Ambivalent about the reasons for war, horrified by reports of war crimes, and humiliated and emasculated by defeat, many Americans shunned the veterans—the visible symbol of America's failure—upon their return from the battlefront. In no other war were Americans who fought in it so scorned by their fellow Americans. A 1973 Harris poll revealed that the American public ranked the military only above sanitation workers in relative order of respect.[4] Similarly, in May 1975, a Harris poll found that the majority of Americans did not welcome the refugees: more than 50 percent of those polled felt that Southeast Asian refugees should be excluded; only 26 percent favored their entry.[5] This pairing of the Vietnam veterans and the Vietnamese refugees in 2000 was unexpected. As Marita Sturken observes, in most public depictions of the Vietnam War, the Vietnam veteran displaces the Vietnamese as "the central figure for whom the war is mourned."[6] Because warfare is ultimately a conflict over which warring nations' cultural constructs will prevail, the production of postwar memories often relies on the material reality of the soldier's dead body to make the nation's cultural claims "real." As Viet Thanh Nguyen argues, "From the American perspective, the Vietnamese bodies must be dehumanized, de-realized, in order to allow for the humanization of the American soldier and the substantiation of *his* body and, through it, of American ideology and culture."[7] Thus the prominence and the pairing of stories on the veterans and refugees in 2000 have to be understood as highly organized and strategic—an attempt to recuperate U.S. status as the world's mighty yet moral leader.

In themselves, the narratives of noble U.S. veterans and Vietnamese American model minorities are not new. What is new is my insistence that we critically juxtapose these two narratives and that we analyze them in relationship to the U.S. cultural legitimation of the Vietnam War. Many American studies scholars have detailed how the recuperation of the Vietnam veterans has been central to the ongoing renovation of U.S. mythic innocence.[8] This chapter adds to this discussion by showing how popular narratives of *Vietnamese refugees* have also been deployed to rescue the Vietnam War for Americans. Although most scholars have separated Vietnam veterans and Vietnamese refugees into different fields of study, I show how they are necessarily joined: as the purported rescuers and rescued, respectively, they *together* re-position the United States as the ideal refuge for Vietnam's "runaways" and thus as the ultimate victor of the Vietnam War. I contend that it is this seeming victory—the "we-win-even-when-we-lose" certainty—that undergirds U.S. remembrance of Vietnam's "collateral damage" as historically necessary for the progress of freedom and democracy.[9] It is this ability to conjure triumph from defeat that has energized and emboldened the perpetuation of U.S. militarism in the post-9/11 era. By critically juxtaposing the constructions of the Vietnam veterans and the Vietnamese refugees together and *in relation* to continued U.S. militarism, I draw on and bring into conversation three often-distinct fields: American studies, refugee/immigration studies, and war/international studies.

ABOUT THE TWENTY-FIFTH ANNIVERSARY

I focus here on the U.S. media commemoration of the twenty-fifth anniversary because of its symbolic significance as a milestone—an occasion for the retelling, reenacting, and reimagining of the war a quarter of a century later.[10] Beyond its symbolic significance, the twenty-fifth anniversary is noteworthy because it took place in a moment of full restoration of U.S. world power. Since World War II, U.S. popular culture has attempted to present the United States as the leader of the "free" world, often recasting its history of imperialism and racial exclusion into triumphant stories of Western benevolence and racial democracy. However, the Vietnam Syndrome—national malaise over the U.S. humiliating defeat in Vietnam, widely understood as a "profound failure of nerve" and a "weakness of resolve"[11]—disrupted the insistent and ongoing memorialization of World War II triumphs.[12] The Vietnam War was so divisive and exhausting that, in its aftermath, Americans of different political convictions forged an uneasy truce that there would be "No More Vietnams."[13] Indeed, after the war, the United States decreased the number of its overseas bases, with the sharpest declines in Southeast Asia and the Pacific, from 183 bases in 1975 to 121 in 1988.[14] During the 1980s, in response to the widespread fear of repeating a national mistake, the United States sent combat troops to back up its Cold War policy only once—in its 1984 invasion of Grenada. However, this anti-interventionist mood was short-lived. By the end of the 1980s, the U.S. had "won" the Cold War, making it the world's sole military power.[15] Soon after, the media spectacularized the 1991 Persian Gulf War victory as the ending of the Vietnam Syndrome, featuring a gleeful President George H. W. Bush declaring, "By God we've kicked the Vietnam Syndrome once and for all." The 1994 lifting of U.S. trade embargos against Vietnam, which the media narrated as Vietnam "opening up" to the West, constituted an important milestone in U.S.-Vietnam relations. In the next five years, the two countries hammered out a major trade agreement, signed on July 13, 2000, that formalized their ties as trade partners. In sum, by 2000, the United States had won the Cold War and the Persian Gulf War, and Vietnam (as well as China) had begun to "open up" to the West. With these military and economic "successes," the United States appeared to have left behind the Vietnam Syndrome as it confidently reasserted its world power, calling for a "New World Order" under its management.[16]

By the thirtieth anniversary of the "Fall of Saigon," almost four years after the attacks of 9/11, the U.S. military had metamorphosed into a "global calvary," threatening to launch preemptive wars against "rogue states," "bad guys," and "evil doers" in the so-called "arc of instability," which runs from the Andean region of South America through North Africa, across the Middle East to the Philippines and Indonesia.[17] Since 1990, the size and geographic spread of U.S. military bases had increased greatly. In 2002, the size of the U.S. "military empire" was estimated to be between 750 and 1,000 different bases in almost sixty countries and separate territories, with many of the new bases located in the "arc of instability."[18] Coverage of the thirtieth anniversary seemed to shift accordingly. Although a detailed study of the press treatment of the thirtieth anniversary is beyond the scope of this chapter, a comparison of the *Los Angeles Times* coverage of the twenty-fifth and thirtieth anniversaries suggests that the United States no longer felt hampered by its loss in Vietnam. In 2000, given its proximity to Orange County's Little Saigon, the largest Vietnamese community outside of Vietnam, the *Los Angeles Times* published twenty-five articles on the twenty-fifth anniversary, the most of all the major periodicals, detailing the war's many "lessons and legacies."[19] In contrast, in 2005, it printed only four stories on the thirtieth anniversary, none of which scrutinized the impact of the war on U.S. society, culture, and institutions.[20] Two of those four articles focused on Vietnam's commemoration of the anniversary and stressed that country's flourishing economy and its "deep ties with the United States." Less than a week later, the newspaper publicized the pending visit of Vietnamese prime minister Phan Van Khai to the United States—the first such visit by a Vietnamese leader since the war's end.[21] During Phan's visit, the two countries pledged to work together to strengthen security and anti-terror cooperation in Southeast Asia.[22] As widely anticipated, Phan's visit prompted vigorous protests by Vietnamese living in the United States, with many carrying signs likening Phan to Saddam Hussein—the face of the current enemy— in the hope of goading Washington into rejecting Hanoi's overtures for closer U.S.-Vietnam relations. However, except for a few obligatory remarks regarding Vietnam's human rights record, President George W. Bush mainly ignored the protesters' pleas. Most tellingly, Bush rejected the protestors' effort to link Vietnam and Iraq, and communism and terrorism, stating instead that the two nations would work together in the "global fight on terrorism."[23] In other words, thirty years after the war's end, from the U.S. perspective, Vietnam appeared to be well on its way to becoming yet another "satellite regime" of the ever-expanding American empire.[24] In this "New World Order," Vietnamese refugees, and their insistent demand for *history*, were cast aside yet again.

In short, juxtaposed with the daily reporting on the "crisis" in Iraq, the comparatively sparse thirtieth anniversary coverage and the focus on Vietnam's "deep ties" to the United States implied that the United States had by then *won* the Vietnam War, which could be read as an encouraging sign of what was to come in Iraq. Thus the specificity of the twenty-fifth anniversary: it took place at the height of the U.S. final recovery from the Vietnam Syndrome and the full restoration of its global power. In what follows, I show that the media's substitution of the Vietnam Syndrome with the we-win-even-when-we-lose syndrome provides the crucial ideological support for continued U.S. militaristic intervention around the world.

DOCUMENTING THE PRODUCTION OF WAR MEMORIES

In my examination of U.S. press coverage of the twenty-fifth anniversary, I am interested in understanding cultural memory's role in naturalizing certain understandings of the past, in interpellating and producing subjects, and in reinforcing specific concepts of the U.S. nation. Cultural memory, as a "field of cultural negotiation through which different stories vie for a place in history,"[25] is one of the primary means by which a nation's "collective desires, needs, and self-definitions" are revealed.[26] Since memory activities are always mediated by relations of power and accompanied by elements of repression, it is necessary to identify "what is at stake in remembering and forgetting past events in certain ways and not in others."[27] Scholars have underscored the centrality of the *anniversary* in the making and unmaking of war memories, as the annual commemoration provides a familiar yet always-fresh terrain to "variously sustain, erase, and transform memories of past events" for present purposes.[28] In the context of a historical anniversary, we need to be especially attentive to the "forgetting of forgetfulness"[29]—in this case, to how the process of remembering the Vietnam War as an eventual success entails the forgetting of U.S. military aggression and destructiveness in Vietnam. As Lisa Yoneyama writes, "the ongoing reformulation of knowledge about the nation's past is a process of amnes(t)ic remembering whereby the past is tamed through the reinscription of memories."[30]

Table 2   Media Stories on the Twenty-fifth Anniversary of the "Fall of Saigon"

News Source	Number of Articles in 2000
Los Angeles Times	25
New York Times	10
Washington Post	16
Orange County Register	14
San Diego Union Tribune	13
San Jose Mercury News	19
Time Magazine	1
Newsweek	2
Miscellaneous (from Internet sources)	12
Total	112

In this chapter, I focus on U.S. mainstream press outlets because I am interested in the most widely circulated and therefore dominant remembrances of the Vietnam War and in how these narratives are linked to U.S. global designs. In the next chapter, I will examine Vietnamese American memory-making practices, paying particular attention to how Vietnamese in the diaspora have used online memorials and commemorative street names to literally write their histories into the American landscape.

Media scholars have long established that mainstream media invariably reinforce prevailing social arrangements because they operate within and reproduce the dominant discursive-ideological frameworks.[31] In my analysis, I pay close attention to the various "textual structures and strategies"[32] by which the press deployed the twenty-fifth anniversary to naturalize the U.S. display of political, military, and economic power. The analysis that follows is based on a total of 112 articles (see table 2). About half came from three major U.S. newspapers (*Los Angeles Times, New York Times,* and *Washington Post*). I also included three California newspapers from communities with the highest concentrations of Vietnamese Americans (*Orange County Register, San Diego Union Tribune,* and *San Jose Mercury News*) and two from the nation's leading weeklies (*Time Magazine* and *Newsweek*). Finally, twelve articles came from various

Internet sources. Because 70 percent of the articles covered either the U.S. veterans (30 percent) or the Vietnamese refugees (40 percent), I focus on the comparative and relational depiction of these two groups.[33]

THE RECUPERATION OF THE WARRIORS: THE INNOCENT AND MIGHTY HEROES

The defeat in Vietnam battered U.S. masculinity, signifying, in Melani McAlister's words, "failure of will, sexual failure, and . . . military failure."[34] A revitalization of U.S. masculinity thus necessarily involves the recuperation of its veterans' masculinity. Robin Wagner-Pacifici and Barry Schwartz identify the Vietnam Veterans Memorial, erected in 1982, as a watershed: it reconciled the conflicting memories of the divisive war by celebrating the traditional virtues of courage, self-sacrifice, and honor of the veteran *but* without reference to his cause.[35] By 1989, a Harris survey found that Americans ranked their trust in the military above big business, organized labor, the medical community, banks, newspapers, Congress, television, newspapers, and even the Supreme Court.[36] A 1990 Gallup poll showed that 69 percent of those surveyed believed that Americans had not treated Vietnam veterans well; this figure climbed to 72 percent in 2000.[37] Already in 1991, the U.S. military had appeared "inviolable" in public discussions of the Gulf War. As McAlister reports, even the most vocal opponents of Desert Storm "found it inappropriate to criticize the troops or their conduct."[38] By 2000, the press depiction of U.S. Vietnam veterans seemed to be a consolidation of these earlier trends, with the majority of the articles emphasizing the veterans' personal sacrifices and their roles as friends and rescuers of the Vietnamese. Below, I show how this strategic repackaging of U.S. veterans was central to the cultural transformation of the Vietnam War into a "good war."

"Loss of Innocence"

"Loss of innocence" was how many journalists described the U.S. soldiers' experience in Vietnam: "You were an American boy, whose innocence was lost here in the war"; the Vietnam War "was about a forced and painful loss of American innocence"; a CIA agent who helped evacuate South Vietnamese out of Saigon later "wrote an angry book about his loss of innocence in Vietnam"; and a Vietnam War film's "grim depiction of young Americans' loss of innocence stirred raw emotion in audiences in 1978."[39] Besides depoliticizing the war and its conduct, this "lost boys" motif immediately places the United States and its warriors squarely within the territory of modernity; it is they who purportedly inhabit the moral domain of innocence. In contrast, Vietnam and its people are seen to occupy the other side of universality—a place where violence is indigenous.[40] This narrative is thus fundamentally about race, space, and time: American soldiers travelling to Southeast Asia is figured as a journey backward in time to an anachronistic moment of prehistory—from orderliness to chaos, from innocence to violence. In numerous news accounts, journalists projected Vietnam, "a tiny tinhorn country half way around the world," onto anachronistic space, depicting it as "exotic," "sensual," "alien," and infected with "sweltering, insect-ridden jungles," a place of "horror," "madness," and "violence," replete with snipers, drugs and prostitutes—in short, "hell."[41] In a story on the death of U.S. serviceman Darwin Judge, reporter Elsa Arnett established the discursive distance between the two countries by describing Judge's hometown as a place where residents baked cherry pies, tended vegetable gardens, lived in cozy ranch houses, and lazed at "a quiet park with a butterfly garden bordered by rolling soybean fields." In contrast, Arnett depicted Vietnam as a "steamy, mysterious jungle" 10,000 miles away—a place where innocent boys, "raised on snow cones, Little League and Eagle Scouts" were sent only to return home "in polished steel coffins."[42]

A standard representation of U.S. warriors stressed the soldiers' innocence by locating them in the private sphere of family, emotions, and domesticity. In a generative analysis of U.S. media representation of the Iran hostage crisis (1979–80), McAlister argues that the location of the hostages in the world of "private life" is "the guarantee of 'innocence'"; it is what constitutes the hostages as virtuous victims, "allied with family, emotions, and domesticity, rather than diplomacy, officialdom, or politics."[43] The focus on emotion is most evident in news stories on the Vietnam Veterans Memorial (and its replicas), with reporters itemizing and sentimentalizing the personal artifacts left at the wall(s) by the deads' loved ones: a handwritten note from a little sister; a "black paper flower attached to a snapshot of a young man"; a high school yearbook; a "wallet-sized hospital photograph of a newborn girl"; a marriage license; a set of plastic toy soldiers; an aunt's poem that implores "What would Jimmy do? What would Jimmy be?"[44] These sentimentalized stories invite the reader to mourn the innocent (American) dead alongside their loved ones, and in so doing to become a member of the family nation. By consistently representing the veterans as private individuals identified by their relationship to home, and not as official Americans identified by their positions in the U.S. military, the media effectively foreclosed any critical discussion of the actions in, reasons for, and ongoing consequences of the war.

A prominent example of the privatization of the Vietnam War is the story on William Benedict Nolde, the last official U.S. casualty of the Vietnam War, killed just eleven hours before the cease-fire took effect.[45] An ambitious, "fast-rising Army lieutenant colonel," Nolde had returned to Vietnam for a second tour with hopes of getting his first general's star. Reporter Elizabeth Jensen introduced the reader to Nolde as a loving husband, doting father, popular teacher, loyal friend, and active member in the Lions Club and Boy Scouts. We learned that Nolde's first son, Blaire, was only ten days old when Nolde left for Korea; that daughter Kimberly "totally lost it" the day she learned of his death; that his wife never wanted to remarry because "[she] had the best"; and that son Bart "has built his life around his father's last words to him." A 1966 family photo showed a beaming Nolde flanked by his family—all smiles and in their Sunday best. In contrast, this was all we glimpsed of Nolde's duties in Vietnam: "Nolde visited orphans and refugees in An Loc, the South Vietnamese village where he died, and worked with a local priest on rebuilding efforts." This brief glance of Nolde's Vietnam tour presented Nolde as a model American who "was in the Army to spread good." By consistently identifying Nolde in relation to his family, his friends, and his hometown, rather than by his position and duties as a U.S. Army lieutenant colonel, reporter Jensen repeats the common practice of honoring the war dead but without reference to his cause, thereby recasting the story of the "last man down" as one about human tragedy and suffering rather than about war and international politics.

Although a significant number of those killed in Vietnam were working-class and poor infantrymen, many of whom were men of color,[46] the press

Hypocritical — isn't she doing the same w/ vietnamese refugees?

coverage of the twenty-fifth anniversary presented Nolde, a white male career officer, and others like him as virtuous warriors tragically killed while "spread[ing] good." Nolde's ideal(ized) family further reinforced an ideology of the white heterosexual family as fundamentally committed to the well-being of nonwhite families around the globe.[47] The media's hyper-investment in figures like Nolde bespeaks the ongoing need to reinscribe American manhood and exposes the centrality of white heterosexual masculinity to the national sense of self.[48] In the past fifty years, the cumulative effects of anticolonial struggles and emancipation, feminism and women's political activism, and ethnic and racial power movements have challenged the dominant narratives of U.S. global power and opened up new possibilities for "critical re-membering."[49] As such, the proliferation of narratives on white manhood, recuperated to represent "the Just, the Legal, and the Good,"[50] works to uphold the dual image of U.S. innocence and potency, both of which undergird the current "War on Terrorism."   WTF does any of that mean?

Friends and Enemies

Cast in the mainstream media as "innocent" and "benevolent," the United States and its warriors are positioned as friends and rescuers who are committed to ensuring the well-being of nonwhites around the world. On the twenty-fifth anniversary, the U.S. war in Vietnam was re-narrated as a noble and moral mission in defense of freedom and democracy, rather than as an attempt to secure U.S. geopolitical hegemony in Southeast Asia and, by extension, in Asia. Thus, in numerous news accounts, we read that U.S. soldiers "went [to Vietnam] to fight for freedom"; that "America entered Vietnam with noble intentions—to stanch the spread of communism"; that "U.S. armed forces had performed heroically"; and that Americans need to honor the "selfless contributions" of soldiers "who died attempting to preserve freedom in a far-away country."[51] Convinced that they were there to "save" the Vietnamese, some veterans still flinched at what they perceived to be Vietnamese ingratitude toward Americans: "The Vietnamese didn't see us as liberators. . . . And I'd think, 'Excuse me. I've just come 10,000 miles to save you from communism. So what's with this attitude you've got?'"[52]

News reporters even managed to turn U.S. defeat—the Fall of Saigon—into a feat of heroism by extolling U.S. last-ditch efforts to evacuate Americans and Vietnamese allies out of Saigon in late April 1975. A *Washington Post* story recorded this glowing assessment from a veteran pilot: "Never in the annals of flying and I am including all U.S. combat air operations of any war, have a group of pilots performed as magnificently as the helicopter pilots who extracted these folks out of Saigon."[53] Whereas the American pilots were "superb" and "magnificent," willingly risking their lives "to save more people," the South Vietnamese were "desperate" and "frantic," wailing with pain, grief, and terror at the prospect of being left behind.[54] Some Marine pilots were reported to be "full of pride" for having snatched "8,000 lives out of the jaws of the dragon in a matter of 20 hours"; others lived with guilt for years for having abandoned the "masses we had come to save so many years earlier."[55] In either case, news reporters repositioned the U.S military as a valiant rescuer of fleeing Vietnamese, all the while ignoring the military's role in bringing about this last-ditch evacuation and the ensuing "refugee crisis" in the first place.

News accounts of the postwar period emphasized reconciliation, depicting American veterans as *friends* of Vietnam and its people. Several news stories stressed the refugees' gratitude to the United States for "sacrificing 58,000 Americans ... in South Vietnam" and for "help[ing] Vietnamese refugees resettle in the United States."[56] The theme of friendship also framed stories about Vietnam's attitude toward the United States: "We are ready to move on, to be friends with America"; "Vietnam has forgotten about the war, adoring Americans, 'You say you're American and they clasp you to their bosom.'"[57] Consistently, reporters represented Vietnam as a nation in crisis, imploring its former enemy to "inject much-needed foreign currency into the economy."[58] In one story, American veterans returned to Saigon to build low-income housing units because they "want[ed] to do some good for the people who our country sent us over there to help 30 years ago."[59] Reporters even turned a story on Agent Orange, a highly toxic herbicide that the U.S. military sprayed on Vietnam in order to defoliate the trees for military objectives,[60] into a story about U.S. riches and magnanimity, concluding that the Socialist Republic of Vietnam "ultimately ... depends on American help" to care for the approximately 2.5 to 4.8 million Vietnamese who were exposed to the dangerous chemical.[61]

These nested narratives, of the United States as a nation of innocents and do-gooders, mobilize beliefs in the fundamental decency of Americans and in their ability to promote democracy and freedom worldwide, while directing attention away from the geopolitical, military, and economic causes and the ongoing devastation of the Vietnam War for the majority of Vietnamese people, both in Vietnam and in the diaspora. Certainly, this "good war" narrative is not new; these stories draw their power in part by referencing the mythologized World War II, whose fiftieth anniversary in 1995 occasioned a flurry of widely reported commemoratives and the outpouring of new books, television specials, and big-budget movies inspired by nostalgia for what has been dubbed "the last good war."[62] What is new, however, is the fact that, by 2000, reporters were able to rescript the Vietnam War, the war with the "difficult memory," within this master narrative of World War II. This masculinist "America-wins-even-when-it-loses" rhetoric is evident in commentator Stanley Karnow's slant on the war's legacy: "The fall of Saigon was a debacle but it wasn't a disaster. . . . Since then, America has become probably the most popular country in the world. . . . It's almost chic to be an American in many places"[63]—a claim that has become more dubious in the post-9/11 context. Other writers were blunter: the paradox of Vietnam is that "the loser has returned to instruct the winner. A quarter of a century after the end of the war, mostly everyone wants the same thing: American-style prosperity"; and "An impoverished nation with a shrunken army, Vietnam needs the access Washington could give it to the modern training and equipment that would put it on an equal footing with its more prosperous neighbors in Southeast Asia."[64] As proof of America's eternal appeal, and thus ultimate victory over Vietnam, commentator Richard Cohen cited the mass exodus of Vietnam's people for America: "Their children want to learn English, live in the States, surf the Web. Even the son of a war hero has left the country" for the United States.[65] This reductive version of history—that Vietnamese communists create refugees while Americans save them—reflects the "willed forgetfulness of the American imaginary" that attempts to naturalize the great disparity in level of development between Vietnam and the United States.[66] Given the ideological importance of Vietnamese "runaways" in the construction of a benevolent and victorious United States, I turn my attention next to the twenty-fifth-anniversary representation of Vietnamese refugees in the United States.

VIETNAMESE REFUGEES: THE ANTICOMMUNIST
MODEL MINORITIES

Thus far, I have shown that the making of "good war" narratives requires the production of "good warriors": the triumphant do-gooders. But to be truly effective, the "rescue and liberation" narrative also needs the figure of the rescued. On the twenty-fifth anniversary in 2000, the majority of articles on the refugees focused on their rags-to-riches accomplishments and on their "fanatical" anticommunist stance. Juxtaposed with the recuperated Vietnam veterans, the freed and indebted Vietnamese refugees remake the case for the appropriateness of U.S. war in Vietnam. In many ways, these refugee narratives resemble those told about other racialized immigrants and refugees in the United States: both groups are regularly cast as exiles from the indigenous space of un-free, violence, backwardness, and nonindividuality—all of which help to authenticate the United States as the site of freedom, modernity, and progress.[67] However, I believe the "good refugee" narrative does something else: it enables the United States to chart a lineage of war triumphs directly from the mid- to late twentieth century. Indeed, in a 2003 speech promoting the U.S. occupation of Iraq, President Bush seamlessly inserted Vietnam into his list of "rescue and liberation" missions: "In the trenches of World War I, through a two-front war in the 1940s, the difficult battles of Korea and Vietnam, and in missions of rescue and liberation on nearly every continent, Americans have amply displayed our willingness to sacrifice for liberty."[68]

As discussed in chapter 1, social scientists have participated in the construction of the "good refugee" by closely charting Vietnamese economic adaptation and celebrating successful adjustment as the attainment of the "American dream." In the early 1980s, scholars, along with the mass media and policy makers, began to depict the newly arrived Vietnamese as the desperate-turned-successful—that is, as the newest "model minority." Since World War II, social citizenship in the United States has been defined as "the civic duty of the individual to reduce his or her burden on society."[69] By the 1960s, two racial categories had emerged—"model minority" and "underclass"—to refer to nonwhite groups who were deemed independent of or reliant on the state, respectively. In the midst of the civil rights movement and race rebellions in cities across the United States, the popular press and social scientists began to publicize the alleged economic success of Asian Americans in part to delegitimize black and brown demands for economic equity and formal political claims.[70] In other words, Asian Americans who heretofore had been conspicuously absent from public racial discourse suddenly became highly visible as the model of successful ethnic assimilation—"as embodying the human capital of diligence, docility, self-sufficiency and productivity."[71]

Refugee studies authors were particularly effusive about the "legendary" academic accomplishments of Vietnamese refugees' children.[72] For the most part, this literature promotes cultural essentialism: Vietnamese American achievement is said to be rooted in their culture of strong work ethic, high regard for education, and family values.[73] Nathan Caplan and his colleagues report that, when asked to explain their children's "startling and extraordinary progress," the parents "imply that there is something intrinsically gratifying in learning, carrying with it the motivational reinforcement to continue learning independently."[74] In a later case study of Vietnamese youth in New Orleans, Min Zhou and Carl Bankston likewise claim that students who have strong adherence to traditional family values, strong commitment to a work ethic, and a high degree of personal involvement in the ethnic community tend disproportionally to receive high grades, to have definite college plans, and to score high on academic orientation.[75] Cumulatively, these studies suggest that, like other Asian Americans, Vietnamese rely on their "core cultural values" to overcome racial barriers to gain access to the opportunities readily available in the United States. In other words, it is their cultural traditions—that is, their "difference"—that underpin their accomplishments.

It is important to note that Vietnamese Americans themselves have participated in the making of the "good refugee" narrative in U.S. mainstream presses. Most concretely, Vietnamese American reporters penned approximately 20 percent of the 112 articles on the twenty-fifth anniversary, most of which represented Vietnamese refugees as successful, assimilated, and anticommunist newcomers to the American "melting pot."[76] Undoubtedly, the reporters' perceived Vietnamese-ness enhanced the "authenticity" of these stories. Vietnamese Americans also contributed first-person accounts and interview materials that buttressed the media's cultural legitimation of the Vietnam War. As an example, the *Orange County Register* featured editorials penned by Vietnamese community contributors who regularly intoned that "the United States is a free country where freedom is not forgotten. Vietnam is a communist country where freedom is forgotten."[77] Given the innumerable losses suffered by Vietnamese in the diaspora, and the ongoing erasure of *South* Vietnamese accounts of the war not only in the United States but also in Vietnam,[78] the refugees' public denouncement of the current government of Vietnam is understandable, even expected—a necessary retelling of their history, lest it be further forgotten by the American public and/or the next generation of Vietnamese Americans.[79] Yet we need to recognize that this "anticommunist" stance is also a narrative, adopted in part because it is the primary political language with which Vietnamese refugees, as objects of U.S. rescue fantasies, could tell their history and be understood from within the U.S. social and political landscape. As discussed in chapter 3, Vietnamese seeking asylum in the United States had to prove beyond a shadow of a doubt that they were fleeing communism. Thus, at the very beginning of their incorporation into the U.S. nation, Vietnamese refugees were interpellated chiefly as anticommunist subjects. However, by reducing the multifaceted histories of the Vietnam War and of their lives into a single story about communist persecution, Vietnamese Americans may have unwittingly allowed themselves "to be used in justifications of empire by those who claim to have fought for [their] freedom."[80]

Liberated and Grateful Refugees

The refugee success story is deceptively simple. Its bare structure—flight, adjustment, and assimilation—is evident in this typical sample: "Over the years, desperate to flee communism, 1 million refugees have streamed into America. . . . Most, after a period of adjustment, have been succeeding in business and a wide range of professions, while their children assimilate at a dizzying pace."[81] Like other "rescue" narratives, most refugee stories inevitably follow the common formula of the "before" and "after" photographs—a staple since Victorian times to visually depict the often-complete transformation of the socially stigmatized (the "before") into the socially recognized (the "after") primarily due to white benevolent intervention.[82] As Laura Wexler reminds us, although the socially stigmatized—in this case, the refugees—are the subjects of the photos, they do not play the leading roles; instead, they constitute the human scenery deployed to confirm the superiority of the white American middle-class way of life and the righteousness of "rescuing" projects.[83]

Most refugee stories discursively feature a "before" (shot) of the refugees languishing in backward and destitute Vietnam, and an "after" (shot) of them flourishing in the cosmopolitan and affluent United States. Often, the description of the "before" draws on established and naturalized notions of Third World poverty, hunger, or need, with the soon-to-be-rescued Vietnamese living in decidedly premodern conditions; the "after" relies on accepted knowledge of U.S. democracy and freedom, with the now-assimilated refugees touting access to private property and economic mobility. This example is from a story entitled "The Boat People":[84]

> **Before:** Born in 1976, Tran grew up in rural villages off the coast in the south, living in thatched huts. While she romped barefoot in mud puddles and made bracelets from palm leaves, her parents were trying to find ways to get to the United States.

> **After:** She thrived in her new world. After only two years in a Sunnyvale elementary school, she was earning straight A's. She chose the University of California–Berkeley over Yale so she could be close to her parents. Married last year, she is now director of marketing at a local San Jose company. She weaves her shiny black Mercedes through traffic . . . .

The transformation brought about by life in the United States is unmistakable: from the "thatched huts" of her rural village, Tran has transformed into a successful professional woman, with a black Mercedes to boot. Lest the reader miss Tran's "makeover" depicted by the "before" and "after" (shots), reporter Arnett deployed another trope: the "would have been"—a postulation of how different the refugees' life and life chances would have been had they stayed in Vietnam:

> **Would-Have-Been:** If they stayed in Vietnam, they knew, their daughter's life would not be much different from their own. At 8, Tran had never stepped inside a school. She didn't know how to read. She didn't even know how to add two plus two. In America, . . . things would be better.[85]

In many ways, the "would-have-beens" are the most powerful in communicating the allures of the United States because they assume the form of a testimonial—a looking back from individuals who have tasted life on the "other side." They are powerful because they make the case that *this* life—of education, opportunities, and social mobility—would be unimaginable in Vietnam, and thus could only be had *here* in the United States. Most often, these "would-have-beens" are mere speculation, as in the following statement attributed to a Vietnamese man who "owns a $419,000 home and a metal-coating business, and drives a Mercedes-Benz": "If I were still in Vietnam, I wouldn't have the business. . . . My children would not have succeeded. They would be working in the rice paddies."[86] This statement is mere speculation because, of course, there could be no tangible evidence of what his life would have been like had he stayed. The fact that these uncorroborated statements graced so many of the refugee stories testifies to the journalists' confidence in the readers' ability to fill in the "evidence" with their learned cultural knowledge about the differential quality of life in the United States and Vietnam.

On rare occasions, the "would-have-been" stories are fleshed out with lurid "evidence" of life in Vietnam. In a four-page spread in the *Los Angeles Times Magazine*, reporters Scott Gold and Mai Tran tracked the divergent lives of a divided family, juxtaposing the relatively comfortable lifestyle of the father, mother, and three younger children in the United States with the squalid existence of the two older children left behind in Vietnam.[87] Five years into their new lives in the United States, the Trans were reportedly "now nestled in Southern California suburbia," their life "a mosaic of frozen pizzas, skateboards and well-kept lawns." Against this image of orderliness and abundance, the reporters stressed the "hand-to-mouth lives" of those "left behind": "They have never ridden in an airplane, stayed in a hotel or eaten chocolate. They do not have a car or TV"; "The family's address is Alley 116, and the home is a mishmash of corrugated tin and plywood. . . . The home's shower doubles as the dishwasher, but at least the family has running water and electricity, unlike many in Vietnam"; and "The older children left behind make about a dollar a day. At times, they cannot afford salt, much less meat. . . . His tiny 5-year-old daughter has a persistent cough. Her front teeth are black, and no one is sure why." The reporters also projected that divergent lives begot divergent futures by contrasting the bright prospect of the American-raised teenager who "wants to be a pediatrician" to the already-doomed future of the granddaughter in Vietnam who "probably won't finish middle school."

In the following segment, the article's "would-have-been" trope is unambiguous:

Contrasting Routines: Daughter Be Ba Tran . . . can earn 50 cents a day by doing other families' laundry. The plank she walks on behind her home serves as a bridge over a polluted creek. Children sometimes play there, and the fat rats don't bother to scurry out of the way when people pass by. On the other side of the world, her sister, Kieu Tien Tran, 17, returns to her parents' modest two-bedroom apartment in Stanton with a load of family laundry.

The message is clear: but for the opportunity provided by being "on the other side of the world," Kieu Tien Tran's life would have been as miserable as that of Be Ba Tran; she would have had to do other families' laundry instead of her own, walking over "polluted creek[s]" instead of "well-kept lawns." The appeal of the United States was reportedly so self-evident that, when faced with the choice of staying in Vietnam or leaving behind a daughter and son (who could not emigrate with their parents because they were already married), the family "decided to separate in the hope that at least one faction would find freedom, if not happiness." Whereas many Vietnam War stories invite the reader to mourn the war-induced separation of American families, this story prods the reader to mourn *not* the separation of the Vietnamese family but the misfortune of those who were forced to stay behind—and even to celebrate this family separation, for it is only in leaving Vietnam that the Trans could partake in modern life. Indeed, the pain of being forced to live in Vietnam, the other side of modernity, was so devastating that the older son reportedly would rage against his wife, "If it weren't for you, I'd be gone!" This ahistorical juxtaposition of life in Vietnam and in the United States naturalizes the great economic disparity between the two countries, depicting the two economies as unconnected rather than relationally constituted.

The overrepresentation of "rags-to-riches" refugee stories is misleading because the economic status of many Vietnamese Americans is characterized by unstable, minimum-wage employment, welfare dependency, and participation in the informal economy.[88] To be sure, some news reports featured both successful and unsuccessful refugees. In "3 Roads from Vietnam," reporters Philip Pan and Phuong Ly tracked the lives of three friends who were fellow military academy graduates and officers in the South Vietnamese Air Force: Xuan Pham, Hai Van Chu, and Giau Nguyen.[89] Once peers, their lives in the United States diverged considerably, with Pham now a prosperous research engineer, Chu a comfortable computer programmer, and Nguyen a struggling dishwasher. Although the story is purportedly about the men's divergent lives in the United States, the authors said little about how U.S. conditions had affected the men's life chances. Instead, the story is about *luck*: the lucky Pham, who "had the opportunity to escape the country" on the day Saigon fell; the lucky Chu, who left relatively soon after; and the unlucky Nguyen, who endured twenty years in Vietnam before he could "get out." The reporters attributed the men's divergent lives solely to their fate on April 30, 1975: "Today, their lives continue to be influenced by what transpired *on a single day*, by the happenstance that determined who made it out and who didn't." Once again, the point is simple: only by "mak[ing] it out" could Vietnamese partake in the good life. By reducing Vietnamese's life chances to circumstances "on a single day," the reporters "skipped over" the long war that preceded that "single day" and discounted the power structures that continue to constrain the life chances of even the "lucky" ones who made it to the United States.

Vietnamese in "The Land of the Free"

On the twenty-fifth anniversary of the Fall of Saigon, reporters assured American readers that all Vietnamese refugees ever wanted was *freedom* and that this freedom could be found only in the United States. This rhetoric of liberation and emancipation, so crucial for U.S. world domination since World War II, was what transformed the Vietnamese from "enemies" to "liberated" (from foes to lovers of freedom) and the United States from "war aggressor" to "freedom protector." By treating the United States as self-evidently "*the* Democratic nation par excellence,"[90] reporters (re) deployed a racial lexicon that depicts Vietnam as a global region to which freedom is a foreign principle and the United States as that to which freedom is an indigenous property.[91] For instance, a *Los Angeles Times* article stated that Vietnamese refugees have a "love and hate relationship" with freedom: while the refugees "treasure the freedoms of their new home" and are "amazed by the freedom they see [here]," they also "have less tolerance for . . . freedom than the average American population" because "they came from a country that didn't have freedom."[92]

Constituted as existing on the other side of freedom, Vietnamese could only be incorporated into modern subjecthood as the *good refugee*—that is, only when they reject the purported anti-democratic, anti-capitalist (and thus anti-free) communist Vietnam and embrace the "free world." Otherwise absent in U.S. public discussions on Vietnam, Vietnamese refugees become most visible and intelligible to Americans as anticommunist witnesses, testifying to the communist Vietnamese government's atrocities and failings. Repeatedly, we read accounts of Vietnamese boycotting Vietnam-produced books, magazines, videos, and television broadcasts, waving American flags while shouting anticommunist slogans, denouncing human rights violations committed by the "corrupt" and "heartless rulers of Vietnam," and plotting the overthrow of the communist government.[93] As discussed earlier, in the post–Cold War and especially post-9/11 era, the refugees' reliance on old Cold War rhetoric to *remember* their history alongside that of U.S. nationalist history has become increasingly futile.

Most often, news reporters deploy the anticommunist trope to valorize capitalism, equating "freedom" with economic access and choice, upward social mobility, and free enterprise. As U.S. Representative Dana Rohrabacher (R-Calif.) opined in a press release on the twenty-fifth anniversary, "The compelling difference between [Vietnamese American] success and the poverty and under-development in their homeland is democracy and freedom."[94] By many news accounts, Vietnamese refugees who "arrived in the United States with little more than the shirts on their back" are "living the American dream, a dream unimaginable 25 years ago."[95] This narrative of opportunities bolsters the myth of "private property as fundamental to human development" and promotes "freemarket/capitalist and procedural notions" of freedom, citizenship, and democracy rather than the more radicalized social transformations.[96] As John Fiske suggests, a standard way of marking the difference between capitalist and communist societies is through the language of commodities. According to this capitalist myth, consumer choice promotes individual "freedom," enabling individuals to have control over their social relations and their points of entry into the social order.[97] This narrative is evident in commentator Karnow's glowing assessment of the post-Vietnam United States: the United States has emerged from the war "as the world's sole superpower, inspiring people everywhere to clamor for free enterprise, consumer products, the unbridled flow of information and, above all, a greater measure of democracy."[98] It is this collapsing of capitalism into freedom and democracy that discursively distances "the free world" from "communism" and more recently from "terrorism"; it is this alleged distance that justifies continued militaristic intervention in the service of defending and bestowing freedom. It is no wonder that President George W. Bush regularly evoked past war "successes" and the rhetoric of freedom to sanctify U.S. military conduct in the Middle East: "The United States has adopted a new policy, a forward strategy of freedom in the Middle East. This strategy requires the same persistence and energy and idealism we have shown before. And it will yield the same results."[99]

Vietnamese refugees are also pivotal to the U.S. construction of itself as multiculturalist, pluralist, and open-minded. Since World War II and the subsequent civil rights, ethnic identity, and racial liberation movements, U.S. authority both at home and abroad has rested precisely on the official disavowal of racism and the promise of equality among multiple cultures.[100] Accordingly, media representations of the Vietnam War promoted the theme of "military multiculturalism," depicting the war as a redeeming site where U.S. race relations were transcended—where, at a time of increasing racial tensions in the homefront, soldiers of all colors embraced each other as equals on the battlefront.[101] On the twenty-fifth anniversary, reporters heralded the arrival of the Vietnamese refugees as yet another sign of the nation as racially tolerant, inhabited by a population *free* to insist on and delight in its own diversity. In an article entitled "The Melting Pot Is Seasoned Anew," reporter Don Sevrens informed readers that the Vietnamese arrival, depoliticized as yet another "new wave of immigration," has "brought peoples, cultures, and religions previously only lightly sprinkled into the melting pot called America." He further praised the group's "success" as proof that "the melting pot is clearly at work, with the passing of time, the passing of generations."[102] After 9/11, the Bush administration expanded its narrative of multiculturalism to include religious diversity even while initiating "an unrelenting, multivalent assault on the bodies, psyches, and rights" of "Muslim-looking" individuals.[103]

The vision of a pluralist American society is also gendered, formulated around a discourse of consensual heterosexuality and marriage in which women can *freely* choose their partner, regardless of race and often in defiance of their parents' restrictions. In an article on Vietnamese American Janet Lightfoot, who left Vietnam as a baby in 1975, reporter Michael Leahy described Lightfoot as being "in love with the concept of mixed breed, thinking how exotically American it sounds."[104] Lightfoot, who was married to a "German, Irish, black, Cherokee, but 'light skinned'" man and expecting her first baby, gushed over her American multiracial family: "I'm having an American baby—a mixed breed baby.... That's interesting to me.... Life here is *so* different than what it might have been." In this account, the United States became "a country where anything seems possible ... even the most unlikely romantic pairings" and Vietnam a place where one is born into families "whose ethnicity had been an unbroken chain for feudal centuries." Since Vietnam and its people were represented as untouched by time, having changed little "for feudal centuries," Janet's freedom to "discover" herself, to choose her own husband, and to carry "the new face of America in her belly" could only be realizable in the United States. This gendered narrative of multicultural inclusion is unmistakable in the story's summation: "Twenty five years after Vietnam, Janet's story is the oldest of American tales, in a society increasingly filled with mixed breeds." This depiction of the U.S. nation as a multicultural family is not only about domestic racial politics, meant to ease racial tensions at home but is also about U.S. international politics, meant to promote the moral authority of U.S. leadership on the world stage. That is, the narrative of a Vietnamese woman's freedom to have a mixed-race baby in the United States is simultaneously a narrative about the appropriateness of U.S. global reach: U.S. hegemony in the world is proper and just precisely because a liberal multicultural America is morally superior to the putatively more stifling and repressive "regimes" of the "unfree" regions of the world.

.   .   .   .   .

As the only war that the United States had ever lost, the Vietnam War has the potential to upset the well-worn narrative of "rescue and liberation" and refocus attention on the troubling record of U.S. military aggression. Despite important antiwar efforts, both in the United States and globally, the U.S. loss in Vietnam did not curb the American crusade to remake the world by military force. Instead, the United States appears to have been able to fold the Vietnam War into its list of "good wars"—military operations waged against "enemies of freedom" and on behalf of all "who believe in progress and pluralism, tolerance, and freedom."[105] On the milestone twenty-fifth anniversary of the Fall of Saigon, U.S. mainstream press coverage of the anniversary privileged personal stories of suffering, tragedy, and success, thereby naturalizing Vietnam's neediness and America's riches and producing a powerful narrative of America(ns) rescuing and caring for Vietnam's "runaways" that erased the role played by U.S. interventionist foreign policy and war in inducing this forced migration. As adoptees of the "world's sole superpower," Vietnamese refugees reportedly gained much more than they ever lost from the war, suggesting that the United States had to take everything away from the Vietnamese in order to "give them everything."[106] Yoneyama has argued that it is this "we-need-to-destroy-it-in-order-to-save-it" mentality that allows the nation "to at once anticipate and explain that the enemy can be freed and reformed through U.S. military interventions and territorial takeovers"—a common refrain, too, in the subsequent war in Iraq.[107]

If, as Sturken suggests, "the way a nation remembers a war and constructs its history is directly related to how that nation further propagates war," then this selective retelling of the Vietnam War builds support for and emboldens U.S. military interventionism in the world.[108] Although routinely "forgotten" in most U.S. public discussions of the Vietnam War, Vietnamese refugees became the featured evidence of the appropriateness and even necessity of U.S. world hegemony on the twenty-fifth anniversary of the Fall of Saigon. The refugees—constructed as successful and anticommunist—recuperated the veterans' and thus U.S. failure of masculinity and re-made the case for U.S. war in Vietnam: that the war, no matter the costs, was ultimately necessary, moral, and successful. Together, the themes of rescue, anticommunism, freedom, and multiculturalism present the United States as having a right and even an obligation to consolidate its political, military, and economic power—that is, a right to hegemony—in all parts of the world that are deemed "enemies to freedom."

5 Refugee Remembering—and Remembrance

It should not surprise anyone that Vietnamese Americans would want to remember amidst all that forgetting. One does not become recognizably human until one acts in one's history. And for that, one needs to have history.

Nguyên-Vo Thu Huong, "Forking Paths"

Đại Tá [Colonel] *Hồ Ngọc Cẩn.* I stared at the Vietnamese name on my computer screen, startled. I was searching online for stories on South Vietnamese soldiers when the name of my *cậu hai* (oldest maternal uncle) and a headshot of him in full military gear popped up on my screen—an unexpected sight(ing) from the past. When I was a child in Saigon, my uncle was seldom around, but his presence loomed over our extended family. We were at war, and worries about my uncle's safety hovered uneasily as we went about our daily lives. His rapid rise through the ranks of the Republic of Vietnam Army Rangers was the stuff of family lore—a source of unabashed pride for our economically struggling extended family, especially for my maternal grandparents who had toiled all their lives to provide for their ten children. After graduating from the Armed Forces of the Republic of Vietnam (ARVN) Junior Military Academy and Đồng Đế Officer Military Academy, my uncle, who had only a primary education, rose quickly from platoon leader to captain in 1965, to major in 1968, to lieutenant colonel in 1971, and to full colonel in 1974. Also in 1974, as the most decorated battalion commander, he was appointed province chief of Chương Thiện Province, in Vietnam's southern Cà Mau Peninsula—a Viet Cong stronghold. My connection to my uncle—indeed, to my whole extended family—ended abruptly when my mother and I left Vietnam in April 1975.

I do not remember exactly when my mother told me that my uncle had been publicly executed by a Communist firing squad—the only known execution of a captured high-ranking ARVN officer. I know that the news of his death did not reach us until months after the actual dates of his capture and execution: May 1, 1975, and August 14, 1975, respectively. By the time the news reached me, I had become immersed in my life as an English-learning teenager in an economically depressed Latino-majority town in Southern California. There had been other war-related deaths in our family, and I viewed my uncle's death as yet another senseless but not out-of-the-ordinary casualty. Even once we made regular visits to Vietnam beginning in the mid-1990s, I would spot his picture on the family altar at my aunt's house but did not think to ask more about him and his death. It was not until much later that I realized that, in the Socialist Republic of Vietnam, it was not possible to publicly mourn or even to speak of men like my uncle who had fought and died in the Armed Forces of the Republic.[1] As Hue-Tam Ho Tai tells us, in that context, "southern dead, absent from national commemoration, often go unmentioned in the collective narratives of their extended families."[2] Even now, more than three decades later, my family in Vietnam still shies away from talking about my uncle, either out of habit or lingering fear of reprisal.

As stated in chapter 1, amid all the forgetting, this book is an act of remembering—and remembrance. The current chapter is concerned with the ways that the ARVN dead—and their families' grief—went officially unacknowledged, not only in the United States but also in Vietnam.[3] Following Judith Butler, I conceptualize grief not as a private or depoliticized sentiment but as a resource for enacting a politics that confronts the conditions under which "certain human lives are more grievable than others."[4] Commemorating the South's war dead is not the same as valorizing them; rather, it is acknowledging that they are worthy of remembrance. As Tai exhorts, any study of the Vietnam War would need to include the dead of South Vietnam, lest we risk "turning them into the scholarly equivalents of the wandering ghosts of those who, dying unmourned, constantly haunt the living in an attempt to force their way into the consciousness of the community, to be acknowledged as worthy of being remembered if only because they once walked the earth."[5] This chapter thus does more than document how the dead of South Vietnam had been disappeared; it also shows how they have "force[d] their way into the consciousness of the community,"[6] refusing "to be unmourned."[7]

In chapter 4, I showed how the U.S. press media, by way of remaking the Vietnam War into a just and successful war, depicted Vietnamese in the United States as the "good refugee," the purported fanatical anticommunist model minorities. In this chapter, I tell the Vietnamese refugee version of this story, not simply to correct representational mistakes or to fill in the backstory but to steer attention toward quotidian memory places—the places where ghosts reside. According to Avery Gordon, "The ghost or the apparition is the principal form by which something lost or invisible or seemingly not there makes itself known or apparent to us."[8] Thus, to write from this haunted position is to look for the living effects of what seems to be over and done with. As such, the ghost is important not as a dead figure but as a sign of what is missing—or, more accurately, of what has been disappeared.[9] Since South Vietnamese history intersects, and not just coincides, with American nationalist history, recovering the ghosts of the former would simultaneously reveal those of the latter; such is the goal of this chapter.[10]

A few words about methodology. Below, I look for "what is missing" by paying attention to how and why South Vietnam's war dead—like my uncle—have become so central to the refugees' retellings of South Vietnamese losses in the United States. As tellers of ghost stories, these aging refugees bring into being the seething presence of the things that appear to be not there. To follow these ghosts, then, is to shift the gaze from officially sanctioned and bounded sites of commemoration to more fluid and shifting social memories—the types that *appear* (as in *apparition*) "throughout society at different scales and in mundane, everyday places."[11] Accordingly, I intentionally look for the wider production of social memory by focusing on two quotidian memory places—Internet memorials and commemorative street names—that Vietnamese Americans have improvised in order to remember their dead. In this chapter, I also write more about my family experiences with the war than in the rest of the book. This is so because the public erasure of Vietnamese American history necessitates a different methodology, one deploying personal affect, in order to expose and reclaim "the something else" that resides at the intersection between private loss and public commemoration. Following Slavoj Zizek's insight that the parallax—the space or "gap" between two irreconcilable perspectives—is a productive site that enables a different way of seeing, I argue in what follows that a critical rereading of refugee remembering emerges at the very points where public and private memories intertwine parallactically.[12]

"GHOST SOLDIERS": THE "DISAPPEARED" OF SOUTH VIETNAM

Writing about the approximately 30,000 people who had been disappeared during Argentina's military government of 1976–83, Gordon contends that disappearance is "a complex system of repression" that involves "controlling the meaning of death" and "enforced absence and fearful silence."[13] In this section, I conceptualize the organized forgetting of the more than 200,000 ARVN dead as a form of forced *disappearance*.[14] As scholars have documented, the state is eager to control the cultural production of war memories.[15] Although this section focuses on U.S. memory-making practices, it is important to note that, in the postwar years, the Socialist Republic of Vietnam controlled the production of war memories by literally razing the dead ARVN soldiers from the landscape, demolishing the many monuments and national cemeteries that had been dedicated to them.[16] In the United States, the ARVN soldier was also erased from almost all historical accounts of the war. According to Philip Beidler, a Vietnam veteran turned English professor, "The ARVN soldier remains at best a creature of scattered references, hand-me-down scholarship, supplementary statistics squirreled away in the odd military history archive or document collection."[17] In short, in the United States, the life of South Vietnam's dead fails to become a "publicly grievable life."[18]

To invoke the ARVN in the United States would be to recall American war failure: "They died for a nation called the Republic of Vietnam. And in so doing, they became the image of [American] failure."[19] Beidler argues that the American vilification of the ARVN as corrupt, cowardly, and incompetent—and the (mis)treatment of them as nonexistent "ghost soldiers," both during and after the war—became necessary because "it reinforced our eventual mythologizing of our own army of Vietnam as betrayed, sacrificed, used up, hung out to dry."[20] In other words, the ARVN became the scapegoat for America's defeat in Vietnam.[21] Even those on the American Left have reduced South Vietnamese fighters into mere puppets of U.S. imperialism, thereby erasing any legitimate position or human agency for South Vietnamese acting in contradictory ways in extremely complex realities of what was also a civil war in Vietnam.[22]

The forced disappearance of South Vietnam's soldiers is also evident in the steep opposition directed against Vietnamese American attempts to monumentalize their status as America's allies and collaborators. In 2009, Vietnamese Americans in Wichita, Kansas, raised funds to erect a monument in the Veterans Memorial Park of that city. They had envisioned a modest-sized bronze statue depicting an American service member with his arm "protectively" around the shoulder of a South Vietnamese comrade, with a plaque expressing their gratitude to their American allies and friends. To their surprise, American veterans objected to the proposed placement of the monument, insisting that Memorial Park was reserved for "America's veterans who fought America's wars for America's armed forces." A compromise was struck: the monument would be placed on city-owned land *adjacent* to but *separated* from Memorial Park by an earthen wall, referred to by one offended Vietnamese-American as "the Berlin Wall."[23]

In another case, the original design of the Texas Capitol Vietnam War Monument, approved in 2005, featured four American servicemen representing different ethnic groups and a soldier of the Republic of Vietnam being treated by a U.S. medic. However, in July 2012, without consulting the local Vietnamese American community or the steering committee, the executive committee changed the name of the monument to the Texas Capitol Vietnam *Veterans* Monument and replaced the South Vietnamese soldier with an Asian Texan soldier—a belated and insulting attempt at "completing the ethnic diversity by adding the Asian American."[24] Although the figure of the South Vietnamese soldier was depicted as an *object* of U.S. rescuing mission, and its inclusion would have fortified the narrative of the "grateful refugee," its removal angered the local Vietnamese American community, for whom the ARVN figure represented "an important symbolic element concerning the suffering of the Vietnamese."[25] An online petition requesting that Governor Rick Perry restore the original design, published by Vietnamese veteran Michael Do on October 6, 2012, characterized the decision as "an insult to many Vietnamese American veterans and people in the Vietnamese American community."[26] These protests notwithstanding, the revised version of the monument, with the South Vietnamese soldier omitted, celebrated its ground breaking in March 2013. In an effort to appease the Vietnamese American community, the executive committee pointed to a panel on the monument's pedestal that features three South Vietnamese soldiers: a wounded soldier being cared for by his two comrades. Not surprisingly, for Vietnamese Americans, the placement of the panel, on the monument's pedestal, undercuts the message of South Vietnamese soldiers serving as allies *alongside* U.S. troops.[27]

The first successful attempt to erect a monument commemorating South Vietnamese soldiers took place in 2003 in Westminster, California— home of the largest Vietnamese community outside of Vietnam. However, it is instructive to review the staunch opposition that the community faced along the way.[28] Unable to secure public funding, the $1,000,000 statue was financed almost entirely with donations from the Vietnamese community. Even once the money was raised, most city officials and about 70 percent of non-Vietnamese residents in Westminster continued to oppose the project.[29] As in the Wichita case, Westminster city officials and residents wrangled over the *location* of the memorial, with some balking at the initial proposal to place it at the Civic Center, complaining that it would be "too visible" there and that a "*private* memorial" was inappropriate for city property.[30] Angering the Vietnamese community, council members ultimately relocated the project away from City Hall to a vacant lot on the far side of the Westminster Civic Center—a decision that required the community to raise an extra $500,000 to improve the site, which was "full of potholes and in need of leveling," for the statue installation.[31] The term "private memorial" is telling, because city officials and news reporters consistently referred to the memorial as a mourning place for only the Westminster Vietnamese community and Little Saigon visitors.[32] In other words, the Westminster Vietnam War Memorial, even when explicitly designed to honor the bond between South Vietnamese and American soldiers, could neither be designated nor perceived as deserving a place within America.[33]

The memorial design—a pair of fifteen-foot, three-ton somber-looking bronze soldiers, one white American and one South Vietnamese, standing side by side flanked by flags of the United States and the former Republic of Vietnam (figure 3)—also provoked resident ire. In an interview published in the *Los Angeles Times*, Westminster's then-mayor Frank Fry intimated that "his council colleagues and other civic leaders always had a problem with the notion that the statue would show the Vietnamese and American together."[34] Some residents wanted to remove the South Vietnamese figure altogether; others suggested that it might be more appropriate to replace the South Vietnamese soldier with a refugee family "to convey the message that America freed them ... and they are here now"[35]—an insidious attempt to sanitize the Vietnamese war experiences and to assimilate them into the benign narrative of immigration and multiculturalism. In 2003, after seven years of bitter struggle and twenty-eight years after the Fall of Saigon, the Vietnamese community in Little Saigon, California, was finally able to unveil the Vietnam War Memorial, the first memorial in the world to commemorate South Vietnamese soldiers.[36] Although the memorial can be read as a Vietnamese American attempt to feature the intertwined histories of the United States and the Republic of Vietnam, artist Tuan Nguyen reveals that he designed the memorial, which features the American GI carrying an M-16 rifle, with his helmet off, and the South Vietnamese soldier carrying a similar rifle but with his helmet on, "to show that for the American the war is ending and he's ready to go, but for the South Vietnamese the war is still going on. We lost our country."[37] In other words, even though Westminster's Vietnam War Memorial features an American soldier and is erected on American soil, it is fundamentally a monument created by, about, and for South Vietnamese refugees.

INTERNET MEMORIALS: "AN ACT OF SEDITION"

In recent years, scholars have noted the increasing importance of new electronic media in shaping our contemporary remembrance practices,

Figure 3. Vietnam War Memorial, Westminster, California. (Photo by author.)

particularly the web memorials that have begun to appear in cyberspace. In the United States, Internet memorials have been set up, often spontaneously, to commemorate such nationwide tragedies as the 1999 Columbine High School massacre and the September 11, 2001, attacks.[38] Entrepreneurs have also launched online memorial websites for private individuals to allow families and friends to mourn and celebrate the life of a lost loved one by penning biographies, sharing stories and photos, and leaving tributes and videos in their memory.[39] Internet memorials, hosted either by private individuals or by for-profit groups, have become popular virtual gravesites—"'resting places' for the dead that can be visited with ease by the bodyless and faceless bereaved."[40] Highly interactive, online memorials entice because of their capacity to collect, preserve, sort, and display a theoretically infinite amount of "texts, drawings, photography, video, and audio recordings" and to hyperlink to different sources, producing an evolving and ephemeral patchwork of private and collective memories.[41]

The Internet has changed the power dynamics of representation for traditionally marginalized groups. Because digital technology allows users to "route around" the traditional gatekeepers and express themselves in ways that previous generations could not, it has enabled the instant circulation of sensitive or even censored materials to potentially millions of viewers.[42] As Mike Featherstone contends, with the Internet, "informational control and formation ceases to be in the form of the panopticon with its bureaucratic forms of control and surveillance" and the "knowledge becomes freer to flow through decentered networks."[43] Bereft of onsite memorials to honor the now-defunct ARVN, the Vietnamese diasporic community has taken to cyberspace to create what Evyn Lê Espiritu has termed a "subaltern digital archive" to preserve in perpetuity the stories of ARVN heroes, including that of my uncle, in blogs, on websites, and in YouTube videos.[44] Although these Internet sites that commemorate South Vietnam's war dead are not technically online memorials, I argue that, collectively, they constitute a repertoire of counter-memorials, part of an uncoordinated online movement to puncture the silence about South Vietnam's war dead and, by extension, its haunting history. Their virtual existence indicates that the dead—in this case, the ARVN soldiers—can never be completely managed and disappeared. As Gordon reminds us, the ghosts always return, "demanding a different kind of knowledge, a different kind of acknowledgement."[45] To be a writer of ghost stories, to fight for a past that has been repressed, to make this past come alive in the present, my task—our task—is, in Gordon's words, "to follow the scrambled trail the ghost leaves, picking up its pieces, setting them down elsewhere."[46] That is what I have attempted to do in this chapter: my methodology has been to follow the virtual trail that my uncle's photos and stories have traveled, in the belief that a great deal—not everything, but still a great deal—of what can be known is tied to the doing of the search. Because these online memorials exist outside the sites of hegemonic official memory, because these dead are not expected to *appear*, and because they appear nonetheless, an encounter with them is a disturbing confrontation. As in the case of the Mothers of Argentina who defiantly displayed photographs of their disappeared children in the Plaza de Mayo, the very center of state authority in Argentina, the public display of South Vietnam's war dead on the Internet is itself "an instance of an oppositional political imaginary at work, an act of sedition."[47]

More so than onsite memorials, online memorials collapse the distinction between public and private: a private personal grief becomes, sometimes instantaneously, part of a collective loss.[48] In my case, the public and private confrontation proceeds in the other direction: the collective grief that I discovered on the ARVN online memorials belatedly became my own. Until then, like other 1.5 generation Vietnamese Americans who came to the United States immediately after the Fall of Saigon, which I will discuss in greater detail in chapter 6, I had limited knowledge of the Vietnam War and did not think to mourn the passing of the forgotten soldiers of the South Vietnamese Army, including that of my uncle. But the self-mourning aspect of these memorials crystallized for me the forced disappearance of South Vietnam's history and its war dead. As Nguyên-Vo Thu Huong writes, Vietnamese American refugees "mourn to let the dead live on in us, speak in us, because they no longer can exist outside of us, because they would otherwise be silent."[49]

FOLLOWING THE PHOTOGRAPH TO THE REQUIEM

In *Camera Lucida*, Roland Barthes probes the emotional effect of the photograph on the viewer, declaring that "the photograph itself is in no

Figure 4. Colonel Hồ Ngọc Cẩn, ca. 1968–70.
(Author's family photo collection.)

way animated ... but it animates me: this is what creates every adven-
ture."[50] Barthes thus steers our attention to what he calls *punctum:* that
aspect of a photograph, often a personally touching detail, "that rises from
the scene, shoots out of it like an arrow, and pierces [the viewer]."[51] When
I first stumbled unintentionally onto my uncle's headshot some thirty
years after his death, I was startled by the online display and circulation of
what I thought was a private photo—the very photo that graces the family
altar at my aunt's house in Saigon. In it, my uncle, in full military uniform,
bedecked with medals, stares at the camera, intently, unflinchingly—his
celebrated bravery so evident in his forthright manner (figure 4). As I
study the photograph, his brooding eyes, almost the exact shape, color,

and intensity as my son's eyes, constitute the touching detail that "bring[s] to life the life external to the photo."[52] In Barthes' conceptualization, this detail, the eyes, works as "an interference, as a wound, prick, mark" that conveys the existence of and furnishes a type of evidence for the profound loss that has not been registered as such until then. In truth, I had not intended to write this chapter, or even to write about photographs, until I happened upon my uncle's headshot and experienced what Gordon calls a "moment of affective recognition."[53] I would like to think that this unexpected "reunion," after all these years, was an invitation to trace an "absent presence." I have accepted this invitation to follow the photograph, not knowing where it might lead, but trusting the journey.

With my uncle's photograph as my guide and my starting point, I was led to other photographs and other ARVN heroes. With these discoveries came the hard truths: the details of his public execution, which I had known before only in the most general terms. I first sighted my uncle's "other photograph" in April 2011 on the website vnafmamn.com, which was established in 2005 by Timothy Pham, a former ARVN officer who came to the United States soon after the Fall of Saigon in April 1975, "to pay tribute to all US and Vietnamese airmen who flew the wings of freedom over the sky of Vietnam and never returned." As I scrolled down a page entitled "April 30th, 1975: betrayed and abandoned," under the heading "Requiem," I came across a grainy, black-and-white photograph of my uncle that I had not seen before: hands bound, surrounded by uniformed gunmen, standing on a chair with a banner behind him that announces his captors' "resolve to punish" those like him who served the defeated Republic of South Vietnam (figure 5). This photo was apparently taken at a public denunciation session, or what the vnafmamn website calls "the Communist Kangaroo martial court"; my uncle was apparently "publicly executed by the Communist firing squad" soon after this photograph was taken. No high-resolution reproduction of the photograph exists; this gritty image, circulated on the Internet and in real space, is *the* one used in all commemoration events. I found the grainy quality of the image poignant, haunting even—an apt illustration of the barely there existence of the South Vietnamese dead.

The Requiem also includes photographs of six other celebrated ARVN high-ranking officers—Major Dang Si Vinh, Brigadier General Le Van

Figure 5. The public execution of Colonel Hồ Ngọc Cẩn in Cần Thơ, ca. August 1975. (Photo in public domain.)

Hung, Brigadier General Le Nguyen Vy, Major General Nguyen Khoa Nam, Brigadier General Tran Van Hai, and General Pham Van Phu—all of whom famously committed suicide on April 30, 1975, rather than surrender to the encroaching communist forces. In the Requiem, each photograph becomes a memorial: the South Vietnam flag adorns the photo corner; the military insignia signifies the deceased's achievements; and the tributes highlight the heart-rending circumstances of death. Celebrating heroism, martyrdom, and sacrifice, these memorials express a *belated* collective grief over the demised ARVN officers and soldiers, both those named and unnamed, whose death coincided with the death of South Vietnam and thus had gone largely unmourned. In an interview over email, Pham explains his reasons for constructing this online tribute:

> The deaths of other generals and Colonel Ho Ngoc Can were very much well known among the former members of ARVN after April 30, 1975. I decided to feature their sacrifices on my webpage because they are the symbols of Patriotism, Honor, and Duty that all ARVN soldiers had been taught and kept for their conducts during the time they were trained at any ARVN military school in South Vietnam. They also mirrored the images of uncounted numbers of lower ranking ARVN Officers and soldiers who had given their lives in the same circumstance on April 30, 1975 or on the days after.[54]

The tribute that accompanies each man's photograph serves as an epitaph, which might have been inscribed on their tombs had the circumstances been different. Although epitaphs are generally inscribed to honor the deceased, providing a brief record of their personal and professional accomplishments, these online epitaphs double as history lessons not only about the Republic of Vietnam but also about the evils of communism.

Although the date of the collective suicides—April 30, 1975—speaks volumes about the officers' antipathy toward communism, the epitaphs still include explicit anticommunist references. As an example, the online tribute for Major Dang Si Vinh includes excerpts from his suicide note, in which he exclaims: "Because our family would not live under the Communist regime, we have to end our lives this way." For Brigadier General Le Van Hung, his decision to kill himself stemmed from his refusal to surrender to the ruthless communist forces who "would spare nobody in Can Tho in order to win [and who] would not hesitate to shell Can Tho into rubble." In my uncle's case, his death has become a *cause célèbre* in the Vietnamese diasporic community not only because of his great courage in the face of death but also because his public execution provides a potent symbol and proof of communist atrocities. His epitaph thus reads:

> On April 30, 1975, [Can] refused to surrender to the enemy. Along with His troops, Can was fighting with all his might, holding the provincial headquarters until 11:00 PM on May 1, when his forces were out of ammunition. In the last minutes, he ordered the soldiers to leave the headquarters for safety while he and a faithful Popular Force militiaman covered them with a machine gun. He fell into the hands of the Communist force after he failed an attempt to kill himself. He told the enemy that he wouldn't surrender, and asked them to let him salute the ARVN colors with his uniform on before the execution.

Just as soldiers' bodies are often used for the consolidation of the nation,[55] the Requiem, in commemorating the lives and deaths of the ARVN officers, simultaneously mourns another death: that of the nation of the Republic of Vietnam, which ceased to exist when the South surrendered to the North on April 30, 1975. The photos of the ARVN dead, adorned with the yellow-and-three-red-stripes South Vietnam flag, affirm the continuance of the Republic of Vietnam in the diaspora and extol its status as a beloved nation worthy of being fought for and grieved over by its people.

In many ways, the hagiographic Requiem, which exalts flags, soldiers' bodies, and militarism, is a nationalist project, one that singles out male war heroes to represent the defunct Republic of Vietnam to the exclusion of "the women, the children, and the men without ranks or guns."[56] As

Cynthia Enloe reminds us, "nationalism typically has sprung from masculinized memory, masculinized humiliation, and masculinized hope."[57] Yet even as we remain critical of nationalism, particularly its masculinist glorification of the defunct nation-state and its insistence on a homogeneous national culture and history, it is important not to minimize the meanings, symbols, emotions, and memories that these online memorials evoke for many Vietnamese in the diaspora. As I perused the "Guest Book" pages of the vnafmamn website, which had logged close to 200 messages as of March 2013, I was struck by the heartfelt and at times anguished posts thanking Pham for creating this website—for providing a virtual space for diasporic Vietnamese to mourn their dead and, in turn, their country and former way of life:

> Thank-you for creating this website. What these men had done for their country and for their people should never be forgotten. I, myself thankful daily for them. And I hope that I am worthy of their sacrifices.
>
> Nguyen Thi Loan, USA, August 16, 2010
>
> Republic Of Vietnam, ARVN and VNAF forever. Hope your website will have one new section in the near future: Fall of Hanoi.
>
> Vu Dinh, USA May 25, 2006
>
> Thank you for creating this website, for the benefit of those who served our country under the flag of VNAF, their families, for perpetuating the ideals of patriotism, liberty, democracy among the younger generation, and to offer tribute to our fallen heroes.
>
> Nguyen Tan-Hong (VNAF Medical Service), December 5, 2005

In a touching gesture, Trong D. Nguyen of Houston, Texas, asks the webmaster to add his father's photo, "the only photo I have of him while in uniform," to the online memorial, so that he too may be celebrated and memorialized. In short, the Requiem enables Vietnamese in the diaspora to narrate a heroic story of war and flight from Vietnam and to write themselves into national memory and history.

The Requiem's prominent display of South Vietnam's war dead, particularly of my uncle's public execution, provides a virtual and *visual* critique of the Socialist Republic of Vietnam's erasure of the violence inflicted on South Vietnamese by northern troops and their allied forces in the South during the war and by the government in the form of postwar policies.[58] However, in promoting an anticommunist nationalist version of South Vietnam's history, the Requiem risks being assimilated into the U.S. "we-win-even-when-we-lose" narrative, as discussed in the previous chapter. However, the Requiem does more than mourn the demise of the Republic of Vietnam and castigate the current Vietnamese government; it also pointedly critiques American imperial practices of war and abandonment of Vietnamese allies. As mentioned earlier, the Requiem is part of a larger page entitled "April 30th, 1975: betrayed and abandoned," whose stated purpose is to make visible the U.S. "sellout of South Vietnam." The page begins with this strongly worded and italicized preamble about U.S. abandonment and betrayal of its South Vietnamese allies:

> *Whenever talking about Vietnam War, most of the US politicians, officials, journalists, or political pundits would mention it in a way the war is their own, the South Vietnamese at that moment seem to be invisible or just the bystanders, bearing no brunt of the war effort. But there was one day, only one single day in which all of them would shy away from that claim. The day they have nothing to do with that war. The day they return the outcome back to the South Vietnamese: The APRIL 30th 1975.*
>
> *For that reason, one has heard some very familiar words like "The Fall of Saigon," "Evacuation," "Frequent Wind Operation," etc. Those technical terms and euphemism are conveniently served just like the toilet papers to cover somebody's own mistakes and to wipe out his embarrassing accident. So let's tell straight out what it is on that day: Cut-and-run.*
>
> *April 30th, 1975: The day South Vietnam is delivered to Evil due to betrayal and abandonment.*

It then proceeds to display and describe a series of photos of the atrocities endured by and committed against the South Vietnamese on "that fatal day," clearly insinuating that Americans were responsible for the fate of "the innocent civilians, the abandoned plain soldiers, and the deads!" At about the mid-way point, the page features a dozen or so of the now-iconic photos of U.S. last-ditch efforts by helicopters and Navy ships to evacuate fleeing Vietnamese out of the country (see chapter 2) but headlines them with these unexpected words: "When the Ally Cuts and Runs." In so doing, it refuses to celebrate U.S. rescuing efforts, which have been key to U.S. attempts to re-narrate national glory in the aftermath of the Vietnam War, insisting instead that we critically evaluate the role that U.S. military and government policies played in bringing about the demise of South Vietnam and the subsequent refugee outpour. To underscore that point, right below the U.S. rescuing photos is an excerpt from Quang X. Pham's *A Sense of Duty, My Father, My American Journey,* which likens U.S. abandonment of South Vietnam to his family's desertion of their dog as they fled Saigon: "We lost him in the dust cloud kicked up by the scooter. We abandoned him, the same way the United States left South Vietnam, like a dog that just didn't fit into its plans." This Requiem thus encapsulates the complex political subjectivity of Vietnamese refugees in the diaspora: a tangle of nostalgia for the former Republic of Vietnam, antipathy for the current government of Vietnam, and resentment of America's "abandonment" of its South Vietnamese allies.

AROUND THE WEB: "MOVING" MEMORIALS

In the mid-1980s, Vietnam veteran John Devitt of Stockton, California, created a transportable half-size replica of the Vietnam Veterans Memorial, named it the Moving Wall, and toured it across the country so that people who were unable to travel to Washington, D.C., might be able to access the wall and honor the American fallen men and women of the Vietnam War. First displayed to the public in Tyler, Texas, in 1984, the Moving Wall has visited more than a thousand towns and cities and been viewed by millions of people. As it has moved across the country, the Moving Wall has reached a cross-section of Americans, creating a temporary site of memory for diverse groups of people—from grieving family members to proud veterans to sympathetic bystanders—to either hold silent vigil or come together with others to pay homage to the dead.[59] In this section, I examine how Vietnamese online memorials also *move*, in this case around the web, as users and webmasters circulate and repost photos, images, and tributes and/or provide hyperlinks to re-direct traffic to various memorials. Like the Moving Wall, these Moving Memorials travel around the web, reaching a cross section of Vietnamese in the diaspora. However, unlike the Moving Wall, online encounters are not scheduled months in advance through an application process; rather, they are chance meetings with the disappeared of the Republic of Vietnam, which often lead to encounters with other ghostly aspects of Vietnam history.

An Internet search of my uncle's story, using primarily Google but also other popular search engines,[60] yielded thirty-two websites that feature articles and/or videos that commemorate his life and death. In many ways, my uncle's life is significant precisely because of its end—his refusal to surrender and his public execution at the hands of his North Vietnamese captors. I discovered that these different sites reference and borrow from each other, circulating roughly—sometimes exactly—the same biographies of my uncle's military accomplishments and public execution and the two photographs of him discussed above. According to Timothy Pham, webmaster of the vnafmamn website, the biographies of the ARVN officers had been retrieved from an English-language website hosted by a group of Việt Quốc members. Short for Việt Nam Quốc Dân Đảng (VNQDD),[61] the Vietnamese Nationalist Party, Việt Quốc exists today only outside Vietnam and is recognized among some sections of the overseas Vietnamese community as Vietnam's leading anticommunist organization.[62] On the Việt Quốc homepage, one can click on the Vietnam War section and then on "The Suicides on April 30, 1975" tab to assess the biographies of these deceased officers.[63] The page contains neither photographs of the men nor the yellow-with-red-stripes flag of the Republic of Vietnam; it presents just facts about their military lives and the known circumstances of their deaths. Thus unadorned, the page appears more as a somber history lesson than a hagiographic requiem, as presented on the vnafmamn website. In turn, the spruced-up content and photos of the latter site, replete with the South Vietnam flag, are reposted on other Vietnamese websites such as Michael Do's under the heading "In Honor of the Memory of Our National Heroes." A former Vietnam Air Force (VNAF) combat infantryman who spent "10 years of hard labor, starvation and torture in Communist concentration camps (1975–1985)," Do has maintained an active bilingual English-Vietnamese website since 2002, and his objective is to "contribute positively to the struggle of our Vietnamese people to overthrow Communist regime for a free and democratic Vietnam."[64]

As the Moving Memorials travel around cyberspace and land on various websites, they assume the form and purpose of each website, thus reaching a wide swath of people. Of the thirty-two websites that com-memorate my uncle, twenty-nine are exclusively in Vietnamese, and almost all of them have been established by ARVN veteran organizations to pay tribute to the military heroes of the Republic of Vietnam. The three other websites—vnafmamn, Việt Quốc, and Michael Do—deliberately use English in order to attract young, English-speaking Vietnamese in the diaspora. As Pham explains:

> My website is aiming at the young Vietnamese Americans who could read English only (there are tons of websites on Vietnam war subject, or ARVN military associations' website, etc. but most in Vietnamese). As a Vietnamese vet, I used to hear so many war stories from former comrades or friends at the coffee shops' table whenever we had a chance to get together. The stories we (the Vets) already knew, but after the coffee was over, we went home. No one else would know the stories, but us, the old Vets only! To young Vietnamese-Americans, I would like them to know the true history of Vietnam War that they wouldn't be able to find in U.S. media common sources. The good deeds and sacrifices of their fathers, uncles, grandfathers and countless unknown ARVN private soldiers (most finished only elemen-tary school, or due to poverty never had a chance to go to school), who are the stepstones for their existence in America.[65]

Judging from the Guest Book posts, it seems that the vnafmamn website is reaching its intended audience, not only in the United States but also in Australia and Canada. Here is a sample of posts from young Vietnamese:

> Thank you for creating such a resourceful and unique website. For the first generations of Vietnamese born overseas, it sheds light on our parents' untold stories and repressed memories. Please keep up your website so we can continue to learn more.
>
> P. Nguyen, Sydney, Australia, May 30, 2010

> Thanks again for maintaining such an incredible website! I'm so inspired and touched by all the sacrifices of your generation for our country.
>
> T. Pham, Northern CA, March 1, 2009

> You have made an excellent website about the Vietnam War. It's a great change from reading biased websites that mock the South Vietnamese. Thanks to you, I'm able to do a year long school project which consists of a sci-fi miniature army inspired from the ARVN.
>
> Huynh Kinh-Luyên, Laval Quebec, March 13, 2010

The website also reaches young people in Vietnam, as indicated in the poignant post below:

> Hi! I'm a 21 year old born and growing up in Da Lat. I came to this site hours ago through some old pictures of Da Lat on the Internet. When I saw the whole collection it almost brought tears to my eyes. You have no idea how much this means to me. Thank you for creating this site. Please keep it alive forever. And long live VNAF!
>
> An Duy, Da Lat, September 16, 2011

An Duy's comments suggests that the online Requiem, whose primary purpose is to pay tribute to South Vietnamese war heroes, also has the potential to disrupt the self-legitimation of the postwar nation of Vietnam.[66] Parents also write in to thank Pham for creating the website for the younger generations. Here is an example of parental gratitude: "I'm very happy that the younger generation will have the opportunity to learn about the sacrifices that the older generation of the South Vietnamese Air Force has made to preserve our homeland."[67]

In the same way, the primary objective of the Việt Quốc website is to provide English-speaking "young Vietnamese outside Vietnam" with "profound insights into the true situation in Vietnam and the conflict between the communists and the non-communists" in the hope that they would "establish strong bases for the democracy movement outside Vietnam against any kind of dictatorship today or in the future in their Fatherland."[68] And Michael Do posts this on his home page: "All 'the Right Stuff' soon will be passed to the Vietnamese younger generations so that all the priceless lessons of Vietnam War won't be lost in vain." Chapter 6 will discuss in greater detail the war "memories" of the post-1975 generation: the generation of young Vietnamese who were born after the official end of the Vietnam War.

These websites are not designed specifically as Internet memorials, but they resemble other websites in that their main function is to disseminate information, in this case, about the "lost nation"—its history, politics, culture, art, people, and heroes. However incompletely, these websites offer a panaromic view of the defunct Republic of Vietnam through their stories, images, and political views, publicly displaying and virtually circulating a record not only of national loss and death but also of the *presence* of the disappeared but beloved Republic of Vietnam and its people. For example, blogger Nam Ròm's website, which includes a prominent tribute to ARVN war heroes, showcases past as well as contemporary images of Vietnam, pictures of prisoners of war, and in-depth biographies of important historical figures in the old Republic of Vietnam.[69] In short, these online memorials do more than honor the dead; they also represent the Vietnamese refugees' desire to retrieve unspeakable absences and create presences in their place.[70] As Beidler muses, "getting sculpted or painted or photographed, written down in a documentary, a novel, or a movie" cannot get you unwounded or unkilled, "but it does in its strange, haunting, even horrific way, at least get you remembered."[71]

Nation, in Benedict Anderson's often-quoted words, is imagined.[72] However, the process of imagining a nation is always contested and in formation. The Moving Memorials, which circulate a record of South Vietnamese male warriors, retell a masculinist narrative of nation and nationalism. However, amid all the organized forgetting both in Vietnam and in the United States, these online memorials constitute an alternative meeting place for the Vietnamese diaspora from which to transmit traumatic memory, forge cultural identity, and re-narrate national history—all of which have the potential to challenge the historical amnesias here and elsewhere that treat the Vietnamese wandering ghosts, both the dead and the living dead, as natural products of exile and migration, rather than historically produced byproducts of war and forced disappearance. Moreover, the always-in-progress character of online memorials, its life and live quality, means that the history lessons that emerge from these unplanned encounters with South Vietnam's ghosts, however poignant and unsettling, remain both unfinished and fragmented. Therein lies the ever-present possibility of "brush[ing] history against the grain" in order to explore and illuminate the promises and possibilities for change.[73]

[handwritten marginal note: Feminist critiques throughout seem like an after-thought]

"SCRIPTORIAL LANDSCAPE": COMMEMORATIVE STREET NAMES

The impetus for this section also begins with a photograph: four aging Vietnamese men in crisp white military uniforms and red berets, apparent holdovers from the era of French colonialism, stand at attention by a street

sign bearing my uncle's name: Hồ Ngọc Cẩn (figure 6). The uniforms sig-
nify that they are graduates of the Thiếu Sinh Quân Việt Nam Cộng Hoà
(the ARVN Junior Military Academy), from which my uncle also graduated,
and the street sign is located in Eden Center, the thriving Vietnamese shopping center in Falls Church, Virginia. The juxtaposition is jarring: ghosts of
the Republic of Vietnam's defunct ARVN *appearing* amid the hustle and
bustle of an American mall. When my aunt sent my mother a copy of the
photograph, about five years ago, all my mother knew was that the street
was somewhere near Washington, which she translated to mean that it was
in Oregon, adjacent to the state of Washington, rather than Virginia, bor-
dering Washington, D.C. I mention my mother's geography error in order
to comment on the spatialities of memory for immigrants: the ways that
their memories become materialized in place but also the ways that U.S.
geography remains incomprehensible to many first-generation Vietnamese
Americans, even as they toil to emplace themselves into its landscapes.

Focusing on the practice of street naming as part of the Vietnamese
refugees' quotidian memory practices, this section examines how the retelling of the past often happens in and through places and landscapes.[74]
Recent literature in geography conceptualizes streets as important cultural
and political arenas, and street naming as a highly contested and politicized practice.[75] Heeding Henri Lefebvre's insight that space is a social
product and an important medium for storytelling, geographers have
focused on how memories become materialized in place, documenting the
politics behind the production and manipulation of memorial landscapes.[76]
Daniel Gade argues that "scriptorial landscapes"—publicly visible inscrip-
tions such as signs, banners, graffiti, and street markers—are important
social and cultural indicators despite their seemingly ordinary nature and
utilitarian function, and Maoz Azaryahu shows how street names, in addition to their role in the spatial organization and semiotic construction of
the city, participate in the cultural production of the past.[77] As part of landscape communication, street names are embedded in larger systems of
meaning and ideology that passerbys read, interpret, and act upon.

A fundamental feature of modern political culture, commemorative
street names are utilized most often to shore up the national narrative of
the past and subsequently to legitimize the sociopolitical order. The power
and politics of street naming thus lie in its ability to determine the appro-

Figure 6. ARVN veterans standing by the street sign bearing the name of Colonel Hồ Ngọc Cẩn in Eden Center, Virginia, April 30, 2006. (Author's family photo collection.)

priateness of remembering the past in certain ways and not others. As Derek Alderman tells us, "Commemorative street naming is a powerful and controversial practice because it not only participates in the construction and reification of a selective version of the past but also incorporates that version of history into the spatial practices of everyday life."[78] In postwar

Vietnam, the Vietnamese government attempted to erase South Vietnam history by renaming streets in southern cities and neighborhoods with a new and unfamiliar pantheon of martyrs. Saigon itself, a designation that predated even Vietnamese settlement there, was reinscribed Ho Chi Minh City.[79]

Shifting the gaze from officially sanctioned street names, I focus here on street names that have been emplaced by marginalized communities in an effort to rewrite landscapes of public memory. In 1993, Native Hawaiian leaders petitioned the Honolulu City Council to change Thurston Avenue to Kamakaeha Avenue, based on Queen Lili'uokalani's birth name, Lili'u Kamakaeha. The resolution charged that, since Lorrin A. Thurston was the early leading force behind the 1893 overthrow of Queen Lili'uokalani, continuing to have a street named after him was "especially anachronistic."[80] In the same way, Brenda Yeoh argues that the renaming of streets in postcolonial Singapore helped to divest the landscape of its colonial past.[81] Below, I examine how the commemorative street names in Eden Center, honoring my uncle and other deceased ARVN generals, constitute memorials that have been topographically incorporated into the refugees' living spaces. The weaving of the dead into the refugees' everyday places and practices suggests that, in the absence of resources and lack of control over commemorative infrastructures, the political history of South Vietnam(ese) in the United States has been sedimented not in officially commissioned monuments and cemeteries but in quotidian memory places scattered throughout the diaspora.

Eden Center: Making Place, Making Memory

As the largest commercial center for Vietnamese goods and services on the East Coast, Eden Center has become the cultural and economic anchor for Vietnamese in the Virginia, North Carolina, Maryland, Washington, D.C., and Pennsylvania areas. Founded in 1984 on the corner of Wilson Boulevard at Seven Corners in Falls Church, Virginia, Eden Center is a 20,000-square-foot mall arcade, providing space for over 100 stores hawking products and services that are not easily found anywhere else in the eastern United States.[82] Designed to serve as a reminder of urban southern Vietnam, the complex derives its name from the 1960s Saigon district Eden, and it features a replica of a clock tower modeled on one at a market in downtown Saigon (now Ho Chi Minh City).[83] The flag of the former Republic of Vietnam—yellow with red stripes—also flies boldly over the center, urging patrons to continue to identify with the lost nation.

Considered the premier tourist destination in the city of Falls Church, Eden Center has expanded along with the region's growing Vietnamese population. According to the 2010 census, 28,770 Vietnamese persons live in Fairfax County, which represents 2.7 percent of the county's total population.[84] The Vietnamese population around the Washington, D.C., metropolitan area is the fourth largest in the United States—after Orange County, California, San Jose, California, and Houston, Texas—and it is the largest in the eastern United States.[85] Vietnamese constituted the largest Asian immigrant group and were second only to Salvadorans in the number of immigrants entering the metropolitan region. Vietnamese who first came to Washington, D.C., and its northern Virginia suburbs had connections to, and in some cases were sponsored by, U.S. governmental organizations as former members of the ARVN and as diplomats or State Department officials. This has made Arlington, Virginia, one of the most heavily impacted refugee regions in the United States. Moreover, in the 1960s, Arlington had a Vietnamese language school that employed dozens of Vietnamese instructors, many of whom returned to Arlington in 1975.

Because of their military backgrounds, Pentagon connections, and relationships with and proximity to U.S. governmental organizations, the region's Vietnamese Americans, like their compatriots elsewhere in the diaspora, have been staunchly anticommunist.[86] As the self-proclaimed "heart and soul" of the East Coast Vietnamese community, Eden Center has become "the ultimate memorial to the Vietnam War."[87] The center's patrons, many of whom are veterans of the war and of postwar reeducation camps, regularly assemble at the complex to protest U.S. recognition of the Hanoi government, denounce perceived humans rights abuses in Vietnam, and mark the anniversaries of the Fall of Saigon every April.[88] As Gene Nguyen, president of the area's Vietnamese-American Chamber of Commerce, exclaimed at a Moon Festival event held at Eden Center, "This place is a landmark—it's a symbol of freedom."[89] A Vietnamese patron concurred, declaring with certainty that "Nobody [at Eden Center] believes in Communism."[90] Joseph Wood, a long-time researcher of Eden Center, concluded, "Eden Center is a refuge, a place where Vietnamese Americans can be Vietnamese and where many can express political opposition to the present government in Vietnam."[91]

Taking It to the Streets: Honoring ARVN War Heroes

Since its founding in 1984, Eden Center, which has more Vietnamese-owned stores than any other single shopping center in the United States,[92] has been hailed in local media and scholarly publications as a representation of Vietnamese economic success in the United States. With ethnic entrepreneurship proffered as evidence of the soundness of the American dream and the free-enterprise system, Vietnamese small business owners ideologically constitute the "good refugees" who "embody success stories of freedom gained and good work rewarded."[93] Nevertheless, the ghosts have followed the refugees here, dragging the Republic of Vietnam's unfinished history and discarded people into this very space of perceived cultural assimilation and economic integration. Since April 30, 2006, the drive aisles of Eden Center have been named after ARVN war heroes—an affirmation for those Vietnamese who recognize the war dead, but disorientation for those who know neither Vietnamese history nor its writing. For most visitors to Eden Center, the complex is simply a booming economic center for ethnic foods and services, but for many others it is also a somber *memorial* that honors the Republic of Vietnam and its dead. There is something subversive about this "un-visibility": the fact that the names of the ARVN war heroes are there, visible to all, but understood only by some. In many ways, the un-visibility of these honorary street names mirrors that of the Republic of Vietnam history, which is always present and yet has been rendered ghostly—as the thing that is seemingly not there, or barely there.

In her work on Palestinian refugee camps in Lebanon, Laleh Khalili argues that the significance of quotidian memory places—"alleyways where a loved one fell to a missile or a mortar, cellars where shelter was sought during Israeli bombing campaigns, or even lonely water taps at the edges of the camp, where women queuing for hours were exposed to sniper fire"—rests in their incorporation into the daily lives and routines of the Palestinians in the camp.[94] It is their accessibility that enables these memory places to have the widest possible range of meanings to the refugees. Like these quotidian memory places, the names of the ARVN war heroes in Eden Center are woven into the shopping and eating places and practices of Vietnamese refugees, inscribing the space with potential stories and invocations of the past.

Street naming involves struggles not only over which memory to preserve but also over where best to locate or place that memory within the cultural landscape. The selection of suitable locales to honor historical figures is a carefully negotiated and politicized process aimed at ensuring that the importance of the chosen street is commensurate with the esteem due to the honored person.[95] In an example of how street naming is enmeshed in larger issues of race and power, African Americans have frequently protested the attachment of Dr. Martin Luther King, Jr.'s name onto what they perceive to be relatively minor streets, or portions of roads located entirely within poor and predominately African American neighborhoods, or—as in the case in Brent, Alabama—a road leading to a garbage dump.[96] Moreover, African American activists negotiate among themselves between exterior and interior uses of memory: an external mode of commemoration would use King's image to challenge race-bounded views within the larger society, whereas an internal mode would deploy it to inspire fellow blacks to take pride in their own heritage and history. These perspectives lead to different ideas about the appropriate scale on which to memoralize King: the "exterior" view would construct his commemoration at a geographically expansive scale, whereas an "interior" view would emphasize the importance of spatially locating King's commemoration within the geographic confines of the black community.[97]

Vietnamese Americans interested in commemorative street names also have had to gauge the desirability and feasibility of an external versus an internal mode of commemoration. According to Trinh Nguyen,[98] an active member of the Vietnamese Community of DC, MD, and VA, the street names in honor of the ARVN war heroes were added to Eden Center on April 30, 2006, on the thirty-first anniversary of the Fall of Saigon. The street names are those of the Vietnamese generals who committed suicide rather than surrender at the end of the Vietnam War—the same men listed in the online memorials. Mr. Nguyen added that, though my uncle was not a general and died by execution rather than by suicide, the group unanimously agreed to add his name to the list of proposed honorees. According to Mr. Nguyen, the organization wanted to put up the street names in order to honor the fallen military heroes and to remind people of the men's bravery and sacrifice. He indicated that, since it is difficult for the older generation to "sit down and preach to the young people," the visibility of the street names could serve as a conversation starter that will spur the younger generation's interest in the history of the Republic of Vietnam.

After researching the process of how to petition for a public street name and concluding that the process was too long, difficult, and bureaucratic, the organization decided that it would be more feasible to put up the street signs on the drive aisles in Eden Center. Since the drive aisles are on private property, it would only require the consent of the property owner. According to Alan Frank,[99] general counsel and senior vice-president of Eden Center, when the Vietnamese Community of DC, MD, and VA approached Eden Center for permission to name the drive aisles after prominent military persons that served in the South Vietnamese Army in the 1970s, the center readily agreed to accommodate the request, in part because it made good business sense: "We have always had a good working relationship with the community. We did not have to get any specific approvals from the City of Falls Church. We researched the history of each person before allowing the signs to be installed and knew it was a good idea. Visitors take pictures of the signs and they are reminders of the great leaders of South Vietnam."

The naming of the drive aisles after ARVN generals at Eden Center suggests that commemorative Vietnamese street names have largely been forced out of public space and onto private property—yet another public erasure of Vietnamese American history. According to Mr. Nguyen, Vietnamese communities across the United States have mostly erected Vietnamese street names on private property due to the difficulty of gaining city approval for (re)naming public streets. Although he said that he hoped "someday we can do it," he anticipated that it would be hard for the Vietnamese community to have the political clout needed to push through a public street name because of its status as a "minority in society." Mr. Nguyen also voiced concerns about offending city officials and residents: while Vietnamese need to "try to get our own people not to forget," they also need to "keep to ourselves, try to not offend other people." In the end, for Mr. Nguyen, an internal mode of commemoration is more important: the organization is less concerned about whether or not the street names are understood by other Americans; their main goal is to invite the Vietnamese community, especially the young U.S.-born generation, "to pay tribute to their fallen heroes and to remember the history of the war."

For first-generation Vietnamese visitors to Eden Center, the commemorative street names evoke deep emotions. As one Vietnamese American man explained, "You'll notice the honorary street names here—they're named after our generals who fought the communists. That's what our fathers fought for, so we can be here today, so this is a special place for us."[100] For another local resident, John Tran, who has been getting his hair cut at Eden Center for more than twenty years, "Eden Center, with its traditional foods and streets named for South Vietnamese leaders, such as Major General Nguyen Khoa Nam, offers a place of comfort where he and other expatriates can share memories." It was at the center that Tran, who escaped from Vietnam by boat in 1980, unexpectedly reunited with a friend "he had made on the boat leaving Vietnam, and they had a chance to relive their rescue at sea and their arrival at a refugee camp in Malaysia."[101] However, for second-generation Vietnamese visitors, the center does not appear to invoke the same fervor. For many, it is a "nice stop . . . to load up on Vietnamese food necessities" and to "chow down on Vietnamese food." One second-generation Vietnamese American blogger posts a picture of the street names on her website but appears oblivous to their historical significance: "It was funny how they named the lanes in the parking lot with Vietnamese street names."[102] Tellingly, this picture is displayed alongside other pictures of "ethnic" artifacts sold in Eden Center, such as Vietnamese plants, fruits, and foods—reverence for the war dead nonexistent.

For non-Vietnamese visitors, the street names appear to be no more than markers of Vietnamese authenticity, adding to the "ethnic charm" of Eden Center. The following remarks come primarily from food and vacation bloggers who regard Eden Center as "an exotic locale":

> I go to Eden Center when I feel in need of a cheap vacation to an exotic locale. I love the street names that reflect the ethnicity of the center, which serves the 80,000 Vietnamese living in this area—a small city unto itself.[103]

Located in Falls Church, the Eden Center and surrounding environs are an international mash up of Vietnam (Eden Center), pan-Asian vegetarian (Sunflower Café) and the Grand International Mart (everything you need for Asian cooking). The signs of the Eden Center, even those that demarcate the parking lot (the lanes have street names), are in Vietnamese.[104]

The first thing one notices upon entering Eden Center is that you feel like you're in a foreign land. . . . The community feeling is evident in the Vietnamese street names assigned to the parking lot rows, and the seemingly endless array of restaurants and cafes.[105]

So Eden Center is an area like China Town, it's basically Little Saigon/ Viet Town. Instead of being blocks and streets in an urban area, it's located by Seven Corners in a little shopping center complete with the cultural arches and Vietnamese characters (Along with English ones) for store names. The rows for parking lanes even have Vietnamese street names.[106]

Not all bloggers appreciate the "ethnic" character of Eden Center. One writer ends his travelogue on the Chesapeake Region with this:

Finally, this oddity. The Eden Center mall in Arlington, Va., is totally Vietnamese-run shops. Even the mall parking lanes have Saigon street names. They fly the old South Vietnam flag next to and on equal height with Old Glory. Isn't that a violation of flag protocol?[107]

Finally, I found a photo of the street name bearing my uncle's name on a flickr account, with the photographer's caption: "Parking Lot Sign. To remember where I parked"—implying that the Vietnamese street names, complete with diacritical marks, make it impossible to remember them outright—thus the photo.[108] The caption suggests that, even when the refugee community has been able to inscribe their memory into a public space, those who do not have access to that memory will continue to literally "forget" this history.

"GHOSTS ARE NEVER INNOCENT": WHO OWN THE DEAD?

In her generative work on "ghostly matters," Gordon reminds us that "ghosts are never innocent: the unhallowed dead of the modern project drag in the pathos of their loss and the violence of the force that made them, their sheets and chains."[109] In this section, I want to think about how the Vietnamese refugees' deployment of ghosts is never innocent. First, as discussed above, both the Internet memorials and the honorary street names commemorate only "fathers" of the lost nation, imposing the names of "Great Men" on the Vietnamese cultural landscape. This nationalist version of history thus mourns some but not all the dead in the war and its aftermath: "There was no mention of those who died fighting in the National Liberation Front or the People's Army of the northern Democratic Republic of Vietnam. Women and children on either side did not make it to the altar."[110]

As widely reported in the media, in Vietnamese communities across the United States the practice of "mourning the dead" has also allowed Vietnamese Americans who espouse anticommunism to accuse and attack the living, often in harsh and unforgiving terms. An incident at Eden Center in 2000 provides a deadly example. On the twenty-fifth anniversary of the Fall of Saigon, about 300 people, "including aging Vietnamese veterans in army fatigues," had assembled in the center's parking lot for a solemn ceremony. Two drunken Vietnamese American men, Mai Thai Nguyen and Nelson Du, allegedly questioned why the older generation could not just forget the war, and one or both men then urinated near an altar honoring the war's victims. According to the *Washington Post*, a brawl ensued, and Nguyen, who was a high school student when Saigon fell in 1975, died a few days later from head injuries he suffered that night. In the aftermath, the Nguyen case became an emotional symbol of a "war that still evokes anger, tension, and suspicion" among the Vietnamese community in the D.C. region. To a number of first-generation Vietnamese refugees, the deadly brawl at Eden Center was in fact a battle against communism, with some accusing Nguyen and Du of having been hired by "communists" to desecrate the ceremony. As Viet Nguyen, one of the ceremony's organizers and a former member of South Vietnam's airborne division who spent nine years in communist labor camps, told a *Washington Post* reporter, "I felt sorry that it happened, but it was a very heavy insult to the souls of our war heroes. . . . You may ask what they would do if someone peed in Arlington Cemetery. They would kill them on the spot."[111]

This practice of attacking others in the name of the dead has long plagued the Vietnamese diasporic community. In 1990, in Fairfax, Virginia,

Vietnamese magazine columnist Triet Le, who wrote critically about anti-communists as well as communists, was gunned down—along with his wife—outside their home.[112] In Little Saigon in Westminster, California, virulent protests against any perceived display of sympathy toward communist Vietnam have been unrelenting.[113] As Nhu-Ngoc Ong and David Meyer explain, for the Vietnamese American protestors, the protested "are proxies for the Vietnamese government and the Communist Party."[114] As Vietnamese American feminist scholars Lan Duong and Isabelle Thuy Pelaud argue, even when anticommunist activists intend their protests to be pedagogical, to remind future generations of past and ongoing abuses of power by the Vietnamese government, these masculinist efforts nevertheless construct a monolithic discourse about cultural citizenship that relies on the false binary of being "with" or "against" one's community. Such gendered discourses end up silencing other kinds of critiques such as those "dealing with sexual abuse, domestic violence, and corruption, which attack the sanctity of the family and its hierarchical nature."[115]

Finally, who own the dead? What is the line between private grief and public memory? Are the dead considered lost kin or sacrificed heroes—private losses mourned by individual families or public deaths claimed by the nation?[116] In August 2010, in its Vietnamese-language section, *Viễn Đông* newspaper, based in Orange County's Little Saigon, published an article on my uncle's wife, detailing her opposition to an open invitation to visit my uncle's grave on the thirty-fifth anniversary of his death, issued and signed by a group of his former military comrades.[117] In the transcribed telephone conversation, my aunt insisted that the group did not have her permission to hold a commemoration in her husband's name. In the following excerpts, my aunt attempted to wrest control over her husband's body from those who wanted to claim his death solely for the lost nation:[118]

> I have kept my silence. My husband is dead, and his grave had been moved from one place to another. Now that I have been able to bring his body here, I don't want to do anything at all with it, so that he can rest in peace.[119]

> My husband has been dead for 35 years now. That's my own personal life. I don't want it to become a big public event. . . . If I wanted to do anything, it would be just with my son and me.

I am the head of the household, and I didn't make any announcement. Who is
he to issue invitation, to make announcement, and to invite me? And he didn't
just invite a few people, he invited the military, the civil, the political people.

My aunt's attempt to distinguish private grief from public use, and to
reclaim the mantle of "the head of the household," calls attention to the
critical insights that can materialize at the intersection of personal grief
and public remembrance. As I have shown, this intersection makes visible
critiques of U.S. imperial war and abandonment of allies as well as
Vietnam's maltreatment of those in the South after the war. Yet my aunt's
claim to private grief, when juxtaposed against the ARVN veterans' desire
for postwar public recognition, reminds us that refugee remembrance,
however critical, becomes problematic when it elicits a nationalism that
replicates patriarchal control as a means to buttress lost status and identities in the postwar diaspora.

.   .   .   .   .

In this chapter, I have critically juxtaposed private loss with public commemoration and shown how this intersection has allowed me to reread
Vietnamese refugee commemoration practices in the United States as
critical disruptions to the hegemonic American discourse on the war and
its refugees. Exploring the link between space, identity, and collective
memory, and the process and politics of remembering from the vantage
point of the Vietnamese diasporic community, I have shown how
Vietnamese Americans have used Internet memorials and commemorative street names to interrupt quotidian time and space in order to literally
write their histories into the American landscape. I have intended this
chapter to be a rejoinder to the "good refugee" narrative, discussed in
chapter 4, to show that anticommunist practices are not necessarily or
only about propping up U.S. ideas of assimilation and empire. Instead, I
have shown that they constitute highly complex and contingent commemoration efforts to counter an erasure of the history of the Republic of
Vietnam while denouncing the U.S. betrayal of its former allies as well as
the failure of Vietnamese communism. I have also pointed out that the
blind spots of this practice can and do lead to harsh and unrelenting

attacks against the living, especially those who harbor more critical visions of the diasporic community.

Vietnamese refugees are, according to lê thi diem thúy, a "people larger than their situation."[120] It is thus imperative that we capture this "complex personhood"—the "complex and oftentimes contradictory humanity and subjectivity" of the Vietnamese people, here and elsewhere.[121] In part, this means that we need to think carefully about how to critique Vietnamese mourning practices—which often remember the Republic of Vietnam as only free and democratic, North Vietnam as only ruthless and communist, and the United States as only benevolent and powerful—and yet still bear witness to the "other truths" behind these retellings. There is no way to close off new readings of old stories, and, indeed, it is precisely through the retellings and rereadings of these stories that people negotiate, forge, and live with their version of history, however fragmented and contested.

6 Refugee Postmemories: The "Generation After"

> I began searching for a history, my own history, because I had known all along that the stories I had heard were not true and parts had been left out. I remember having this feeling growing up that I was haunted by something, that I was living within a family full of ghosts. There was this place that they knew about. I had never been there. We had been moved, uprooted. We had lived with a lot of pain. I had no idea where these memories came from, yet I knew the place.
>
> From Rea Tajiri's film, *History and Memory*

One day, in a class on U.S. wars in Asia, I lectured on the spraying of chemical defoliation on Vietnamese soil by the U.S. military during the Vietnam War, which killed or maimed an estimated 400,000 people and poisoned the country's water, land, and air. That night, a young Vietnamese student in the class dreamed that her body was covered with the toxic Agent Orange. Like many U.S.-born Vietnamese Americans of her generation, she knew little about the details of the war prior to taking the class. Yet, in her nightmare, her body somehow "recalled" the physical pain endured by older generations of Vietnamese during the war. This chapter analyzes the experiences of the post-1975 generation: the young Vietnamese who were born in Vietnam or in the United States after the official end of the Vietnam War. How do young Vietnamese Americans, born and/or raised in the United States, create "memories" of a war that preceded their births or their consciousness? How are these memories mediated by their parents' direct experiences with and recollections of the war, by the politics of war commemoration practiced in the home, and by both Vietnam and the United States?

This book, and this chapter in particular, arises from a set of concerns that revolve around silences and silencing and their relation to structures of power. In the previous chapters, I have discussed the silence of history, both in the United States and in Vietnam, on the ongoing costs of the war borne by the South Vietnamese. In this chapter, I am interested in the silences that prevail within refugee families and that arbitrate interpersonal relations, paying particular attention to their capacity to index structures of power, violence, and identity.[1] Over the past few decades, feminist scholars have shown that war is not exclusively a matter for men, or a masculine domain. Instead, it is a complex process that transforms not only public institutions and national economies but also intimate relationships.[2] Adopting this feminist approach, I pay particular attention to what British cultural materialist Raymond Williams terms the "structure of feeling": social experiences that are often not "recognized as social but taken to be private, idiosyncratic, and even isolating."[3] As such, feelings, though "actively lived and felt," are "elusive, impalpable forms of social consciousness" and thus tend to disappear from social analysis altogether.[4] Since the most common modes of social analysis define the social as the known and reduce it to fixed forms, they tend to miss the "complexities, the experienced tensions, shifts, and uncertainties, the intricate forms of unevenness and confusion" that constitute the living present.[5] However, Williams argues that the alternative to these analytical reductions is not the silencing or disappearance of these complexities and tensions but "a kind of feeling and thinking which is indeed social and material."[6]

The process of generational transmission of war memory is complex and difficult, not only for the survivors but also for their children, as the latter move between honoring their elders' memory and constructing their own relation to this contentious legacy.[7] In a lucid account of the intergenerational legacy of the Holocaust, Marianne Hirsch argues that shards of memories of traumatic events persist to mark the lives of children of survivors. Although separated in time and space from the devastating histories, the postwar generation "remembers" these powerful experiences by means of the fractured images, stories, behaviors, and affects transmitted,

Grandma Puwki

sometimes indirectly and wordlessly, within the family and the culture at large.[8] Hirsch has called this memory of the "generation after" *postmemory*: "the experience of being separated in time and space from the war being remembered, yet of living with the eyewitness memory."[9] According to Hirsch, postmemory—a secondary, mediated, and inherited memory of a lost past—is not the same as memory in that it does not recall but rather imagines, projects, and creates the past, yet it can be just as weighty because it "approximates memory in its affective force."[10]

"postmemory"

As discussed in chapter 5, Vietnam, both the war and the country, continues to be a site of contradictions and ambivalence for the first generation. How are these layered memories, which contain both "nostalgic longing as well as negative critical recollection," transmitted to and understood by the postwar generation?[11] How has this "grip of the bequeathed trauma" manifested, not only psychically but also materially, in the lives of young Vietnamese Americans?[12] Although this grip is powerful, it is difficult to say precisely what it is or what it does. As I detail below, the war appears to have no consistent meaning for young Vietnamese Americans; rather, it is a shifting specter that hovers over personal heartaches, family tensions and dissolution, and/or economic insecurities.

The information in this chapter comes primarily from in-depth tape-recorded interviews that my then-research assistant, Thúy Võ Đặng, and I conducted with sixty Vietnamese Americans—thirty men and thirty women—in Southern California between 2005 and 2010.[13] All of the respondents belong to the postwar generation: the majority (57 percent) were born between 1981 and 1985; 26 percent between 1975 and 1980; and 17 percent between 1986 and 1990. Over half of the respondents (55 percent) were born in Vietnam; 38 percent in the United States; and 7 percent in a refugee camp. In-depth interviews are valuable because they allow us to listen to individuals' own interpretations, definitions, and perceptions of their experiences. As Irving Seidman suggests, "At the root of in-depth interviewing is an interest in understanding the lived experience of other people and the meaning they make of that experience . . . because [their stories] are of worth."[14] Yet we now know that interview data, especially about a topic as fraught as that of war memories, are full of gaps. It is true that people lie or evade, but it is also the case that, by their very nature, war-related stories contain many uncertainties and projections.

As Grace Cho insists in her work on Korean trauma memories, the point is not to smooth over or fill in the gaps but "to enter these empty spaces to find out what emerges, what one can learn from listening to silence." Like Cho, I believe that the interweaving threads that cover up the traumas of war "are not so tightly woven that [they] cannot come undone."[15] Thus, in what follows, my aim is not to cross-check the oral stories against documented histories but rather to point out the suggestive and productive nature of the gaps, cracks, and uncertainties that are part and parcel of the (re)tellings of Vietnamese lives.

"THEY CERTAINLY DON'T TEACH IT IN SCHOOL!"

Writing on the postmemory of the children of Holocaust survivors, Hirsch contends that even "the most intimate familial knowledge of the past is *mediated* by broadly available public images and narratives."[16] However, whereas the descendants of Holocaust refugees have access to the multitude of Holocaust memorials, both material and cultural, and live within an American public history and a culture that acknowledges, commemorates, and mourns their losses, Vietnamese refugee children have to come to terms with their family histories of war, loss, and displacement amid the representational emptiness and the deliberate concealment of the war's costs borne by their parents' generation.[17] For the most part, all that the children of Vietnam War refugees have is a "wayward archive, a grasping at the ineffable, a dialogue with ghosts."[18] Amid this organized forgetting, how do young Vietnamese acquire, sustain, erase, and/or transform *their* understanding of the Vietnam War?

For young Vietnamese Americans, the continuing U.S. ambivalence about the Vietnam War means that their relationship with American history and their ability to claim a Vietnamese American identity is tenuous at best. In particular, the absence of Vietnamese perspective(s) of the war in public education has affected Vietnamese youths' identity and well-being. A Southern California task force—formed in the late 1990s to investigate troubling patterns of gang membership, school drop-outs, relatively high rates of suicide, and intergenerational conflicts among Southeast Asian youth—concluded that "the sense of not belonging and not knowing their roots intensified the identity crisis that normal adolescents experience."[19] As an example, a Vietnamese American high school student told a task force interviewer that his involvement in gang activities stemmed from "this emptiness and void" that he longed to fill: "What good is it to earn straight A's and receiving all these accolades when you don't know who you are?"[20] Another frustrated student ranted about the lack of access to Vietnamese history and culture, both at home and in school:

> I grew up in a low-income neighborhood. I was never a whiz, never a valedictorian. I was constantly criticized. Vietnamese youth are constantly criticized by elders. They say we don't know, don't understand, our history and culture. But where do we go to learn this? They don't talk about it at home and they certainly don't teach it in school![21]

Given the lack of meaningful Vietnam War curricula in U.S. schools, especially ones that incorporate Vietnamese history, culture, and experience, it is not surprising that many of the U.S.-born Vietnamese we interviewed possessed incomplete knowledge of the war. Embarrassed and apologetic, these young people insisted that, as Vietnamese, they should have known more—somehow. In the excerpt below, Mimi Lâm,[22] who was born in the United States and raised by a single mother, was clearly flustered when she could not provide a coherent synopsis of the war:

> Urgh! I sound so stupid. I don't think I learned about the Vietnam War anywhere, even in college. Besides the few movies I've watched. I took two Asian Pacific American studies classes [in college] and we didn't talk about the Vietnam War. I think I even read the books thoroughly but there just wasn't anything. The war was in the seventies, right? So why were they fighting? I honestly don't know why. Something about the Communists, I don't know. I know the Việt Cộng tried to fight because they wanted Communism and the U.S. didn't want Communism. I'm really bad . . . I'm horrible. . . . I feel dumb. I just don't know much about it. I'm sorry!

Mimi's butchering of even the most basic facts of the war is not typical. The majority of the U.S.-born Vietnamese we interviewed were able to name some of the war's key timelines, concepts, and events—information that they had gathered, often in snatches, from high school or college history courses. But what they uniformly lacked, and wanted, was a coherent framework that explains the whys of the war from a Vietnamese stand-point. Minh Nguyễn, whose family came to the United States via a peril-ous boat journey and prolonged stays in two refugee camps, expressed this ambivalence when he said, "We were taught that the war was America's first mistake and they shouldn't have gone in there to help the people. And a lot of people died. . . . But then it seems like America did help, since the Vietnamese people are now in America. But I really don't know. . . . I don't know how to view the war. . . . I just want to know how to feel about things."

In many ways, Vietnamese American ambivalence about the Vietnam War mirrors that of the larger American society. As discussed earlier, the United States has solidified the master narratives of World War II around the myth of American benevolence and racial democracy, but it has still not been able to resolve the conflicting memories of the Vietnam War—a war that deeply divided the country and called into question its national image and international reputation. As a visible reminder of the war, Vietnamese in the United States have had to bear the brunt of these irres-olutions. Ngọc Liên Nguyễn recounted that her mother, who came to the United States at the age of twenty-three in 1977, faced the hostility of a country still reeling from the recent loss in Vietnam, which affected her job prospects: "She came here to California. She tried to get a job and she got turned down because she didn't know how to speak English yet. But she said that a lot of the people that she went to for jobs looked at her like she was part of the problem, like she was the cause of the whole war. That's what she interpreted it as. She said that her last name is Nguyễn, so people knew that she was Vietnamese." As a consequence, some young Vietnamese Americans avoided the topic of the war altogether for fear that they would be mistaken for America's war enemies rather than its allies. As Hùng Phạm, who came to the United States in 1979 at the age of two, explained:

> It's kind of sad that I know nothing about the war, but in school, I would kind of feel a little awkward when they would talk about the Vietnam War. So maybe for some reason I blocked it out of my head because of that, just because . . . obviously I'm from *there*. For the longest time, when I was grow-ing up, I kind of felt like the white people didn't really like us too much because maybe the families they lost or whatever . . . because of the war.

Ngọc Châu Hồ, who was just two months old when her extended family of eighteen set out on what would become a two-year journey to the United States, concurred: "I think it's still a very touchy subject. In my high school, no one really knew how to teach it or talk about it. I didn't want to talk about it either. I didn't want to say that my family is Vietnamese and have to deal with all of that and all the questions that I couldn't answer." Tina Ngọc Đặng, a twenty-two-year-old college student at the time of the interview, did have "to deal with all of that" the summer she graduated from high school, when she was aboard a tour bus heading to the Vietnam Veterans Memorial in Washington, D.C. Already feeling vulnerable in such a setting, Tina was startled when an older white man paused in front of her and spit out, "My brother died in your jungle," before proceeding to the back of the bus. Shaken, Tina got off at the next stop and never made it to the memorial. These incidents of racial lumping shape young Vietnamese Americans' postmemory of the Vietnam War, instructing them that their place in the United States is intimately, and at times violently, related to Americans' racialized understanding of "Vietnam" and its people.

Vietnamese media, especially the wildly popular Vietnamese musical variety series *Paris By Night*, fill in some of the missing history for young Vietnamese Americans. Since 1983, the Thúy Nga Production Company has produced and distributed over a hundred *Paris By Night* episodes that feature Vietnamese-language musical performances, one-act plays, and comedy skits. With a huge and loyal following, *Paris By Night* has become a leading cultural and political voice of and for the Vietnamese diaspora— a ubiquitous presence in Vietnamese homes and Vietnamese-run businesses such as restaurants and nail and hair salons.[23] *Paris By Night 77* was the episode that my interviewees referenced the most: produced in 2005, it commemorated the thirtieth anniversary of the Fall of Saigon. The show interspersed three prominent themes: the cruelty and corruption of communist rule, the flight and plight of Vietnamese refugees, and the progress of Vietnamese communities in the United States. Most compelling for my interviewees were the montages of frantic Vietnamese fleeing Saigon, perishing at sea, and languishing in overcrowded refugee camps. Twenty-year-old Lisa Vũ, a third-year college student majoring in political science, explained how *Paris By Night 77* helped her to "create" memories of the war: "The images that I have [of the war] are created from *Paris By Night*: the mother holding her children and running . . . bombings . . . jungle warfare. I have this image of a family just running in the dark. It's always at night. Oh, and the raidings and people hiding from the Communists so that they don't get shot."

Many of the young Vietnamese whom I interviewed, like Hắng Võ, connected viscerally to the searing images of anguished Vietnamese on their screen:

> It's just so emotional for me to watch what happened during the war and postwar and how people died. Even though I can't relate to what my parents went though, I can feel it through those videos and have an idea of how difficult it was. I don't know why it's so emotional, but whenever I watch, it always brings tears to my eyes. . . . Just seeing people running for their lives and running to try to get to the U.S. makes me imagine that those people are my parents and that was what they went through. All of my aunts that came over here were boat people. I see how the boat people go through all of that and I would think, oh my gosh, that's what they went through. When I watch *Paris By Night* or *Asia* [another musical variety series] and when it gets to that part, I can't watch and I just walk away because I get so emotional that I can't sit there without crying.

For these young viewers, the emotional quality of the *Paris By Night* thirtieth anniversary show contrasted sharply with the objectification of Vietnamese often found in American media. As twenty-two-year-old Hân Trần, a psychology student, explained:

> I think from the American media, it's a war that the U.S. lost. The U.S. came in as the heroes, helping these poor and ignorant Vietnamese people. We are always shown as peasants or hookers. So we were objects. From the Vietnamese perspective, there has much more emotion attached. This is the war that *we* lost. We fought and we fought but we still lost. It's more personal I think, hearing and seeing the Vietnamese perspective. The 30-year anniversary show was very moving. It was from the Vietnamese perspective and it allowed me to see the whole perspective.

On occasion, these Vietnamese-language media act as a prop and a prompt for parents to begin disclosing their war experiences. As Hân elaborated, "One thing that would bring up communism and the war would be when we watch *Paris By Night*. They would sometimes have shows on the war. That's probably the only time when I would hear [my parents] talk about it. They would watch it and sometimes casually mention something that they could relate to or something that they don't agree with." For some parents, no shows could ever capture the reality of war as they experienced it. As Lisa Vũ recounted, "We saw the *Paris By Night* video when they commemorated the 30 years, and my stepfather was like, they should have shown more footage of the war and this and that. He's never happy with those things. They are never warlike enough for him and it's never real enough for him. That's because it's still so real in his mind."

THE SOUNDS OF SILENCE: "THEY DON'T WANT TO TALK ABOUT IT"

As complex and subtle as spoken language, silence, as a language of family, can protect and cherish and/or deny and control.[24] Writing on the cross-generational transmission of historical trauma, scholars have noted that, in many families, silence prevails and that children of survivors experience family history as one of "untold stories."[25] In her important film *History and Memory*, third-generation Japanese American filmmaker Rea Tajiri discloses that she was haunted by her parents' silence about their internment camp experience: "I was living within a family full of ghosts."[26] In the same way, Vietnamese refugee families wrap their war memories in a shroud of silence and forgetting. When asked to recount what their parents had told them about their war experiences, the respondents' most common answer was: "They don't want to talk about it." Nancy Thúy Trần, whose parents came to the United States in 1976 as boat people, exclaimed that "they tell me straight up that they don't want to tell me." Even when she needed the details for a homework assignment, her parents were still hesitant: "They don't want to have like a full-on discussion. Growing up, I have heard of the war . . . like I keep hearing about an older brother [of my dad] who passed away, and my grandma would mention him and his name. But I only got just bits and pieces of it." Jennifer Lê's parents also deflected her questions about their past: "My dad especially never talked about his personal experiences with the war. It was always like, 'Oh yeah, I went to America,' but he never really said why. . . . I was thinking that the war had a role to play in it, but I don't really know what."

Ruth Wajnryb has written eloquently about the difficulty of transmitting knowledge about trauma across generations: "From the parents' perspective, the dilemma was how to tell what they could not bear their children to have to hear."[27] In the case of Holocaust survivors, Anna Neumann reports that "protected stories," sanitized and marked by silences, are often told to children in bits and pieces, in an effort to *protect* them from the brutal realities of the Holocaust.[28] Yet, as Eva Hoffman reminds us, within the space of the family, survivors *speak* even when they utter no words: "The past broke through in the sounds of nightmares, the idioms of signs and illness, of tears and acute aches."[29] For the young people we interviewed, the occasional and often caught-unawares moments when "the past broke through" and interrupted their parents' silence were unnerving. Nancy Thúy Trần remembered feeling panicky when her father started crying in the middle of a war movie: "I remember thinking, 'Don't panic!' The war was a hush-hush thing; I just didn't want to cause any more grief." Others recalled how war terrors haunted their parents' sleep in the form of recurring "screaming and yelling" nightmares about exploding bombs, gnawing hunger, capsized boats, and dead bodies. For the children of survivors and witnesses of the Vietnam War, these episodes confirm that the war is ever-present for their parents, whether they speak about it or not. In Dũng Vũ's words: "It's in their minds, it's in their sleep, and it's there in their memories."

The silence that pervades familial interactions emanates not only from the first generation but also from their children—the generation after. In her research on Japanese Canadian women's internment memories, Mona Oikawa learned that daughters take "great care" when they initiate conversations regarding the internment with their mothers, lest these discussions dredge up best-forgotten memories. As Oikawa writes, "Just as parents develop strategies to cope with the memories they live with, children also develop strategies for living with the memories shared and not shared in their own families."[30] Wajnryb concurs: "From the child's perspective, it was how to hear what they could not bear their parents to have to tell."[31] Over and over, the young Vietnamese Americans we interviewed indicated that not probing about the past was their way of protecting their parents from having to relive the terrors of wartime and its immediate aftermath. Vinh Dương, whose parents suffered greatly during the twelve-year period that his father was imprisoned in a reeducation camp, struggled with the weight of his family history:

> My parents don't talk about their history much mostly because it consists of suffering . . . and even when they do talk about it and stuff, sometimes I do try to block that out because it's so sad. . . . It's not that I'm trying to deny it, it's just that . . . I just lose hope sometimes when I hear about how my mom has suffered and all of the hardships that she went through. . . . With my dad, I asked him, "Why don't you ever talk about your time in war?" And he was like, "What is there to talk about?" And that would end the conversation. Umm, I didn't want to push it because there might be some unfortunate memories that he has that he doesn't want to share, like I don't want to open old wounds or anything like that but I was so curious.

Phượng Lê also hesitated to prod her father about the details of his seven years in a reeducation camp. Although her father, whom she did not formally meet until his arrival in the United States in 1991 when she was already eight years old, would provide general information about reeducation camps, he refused to divulge details about his own experiences:

> I know the general stories that many people know, which was that it was horrible. In the reeducation camp, you don't have enough food and they put you in a small room so that you don't have room to move. You eat a feast if you had a cockroach. You don't even have grass to eat. The stories are really terrible but they're generic. But I don't really know the specific stories about what *he* went through. He was some sort of officer but he just didn't give me that much detail. Maybe it was so traumatizing that he just wants to ignore it. I didn't want to ask him because I was afraid that I'd bring back memories that he's trying to hide or forget.

[handwritten margin note: My generation is so much more open to therapy]

These recollections suggest that, for many children of Vietnamese refugees, their silence is an implicit, and oftentimes complicit, attempt at family connectedness or at least family peace.[32] In this way, both the first and the second generations use silence, sometimes to control and hide but other times to love and protect—an attempt to shield family members from the painful grip of the past.[33]

HISTORY LESSONS

Many young Vietnamese Americans we interviewed expressed that they "just want[ed] to know how to feel about things," especially how to comprehend U.S. involvement in the Vietnam War: its role, motives, and tactics. Frustrated by the lack of a Vietnamese perspective on this issue, many questioned the objectivity of American sources that tout U.S. involvement in Vietnam as an effort to "save the country," "spread democracy," "stop Communism," and "help the people." As U.S.-born Vivian Thái expressed: "What I know is what I just learned or what I can remember in history class, which I think is obviously biased. It's not the opinion of the Vietnamese, but the opinion of the Americans. . . . They are always saying how America is the best and how they went over there and were generous and helped out so they were good. So then, are they saying that . . . the Vietnamese and the Viet Cong were the bad guys?" Some, like Thúy Lê, questioned Americans' ability to differentiate between Vietnamese "enemies" and "allies": "What I am confused about is how do Americans know if someone is from up North or in the South or something. . . . How can the Americans come and know the difference between people they are saving and not?"

As discussed in chapter 5, the first generation's war memory, when it is shared, takes two prominent forms: critique of U.S. conduct in South Vietnam, and denunciation of communist atrocities. Many of the interviewees reported that, even when their parents remained silent on most war matters, in the privacy of their homes they would occasionally impart "history lessons" about what they perceived to be U.S. "arrogance," "incompetence," and "self-interested" conduct in the Vietnam War. This practice suggests that there is no incongruity between the refugees' expressed gratitude for their new lives in the United States and their indictment of U.S. failed military efforts. Consider the following two examples:

> So my dad and I were discussing [the war] because I was studying for AP U.S. History. I asked him if the reason why the Americans stopped helping was because of the loss of support back at home. He said that the Americans didn't know what they were doing. The war was between the North and the South, and they fought in the form of guerilla warfare. The Americans didn't know the land and they didn't know what they were doing in general. My

dad said that the Americans didn't study the land hard enough. Both sides had different tactics. Compared to the Vietnamese, the Americans were much more advanced. He said that the way the Americans approached the war was very poor. He said that he felt they came in with a superior outlook like they knew they could defeat these Vietnamese people. He said that a lot of innocent people died. The Americans just killed people from both sides. They didn't care who was on whose side, so as long as they were killing someone, it was good enough. The Americans didn't have a system or a strategy for attacking at all. My dad would say things like how the U.S. were really the ones bringing the war to us and they weren't really interested in giving us our freedom.

twenty-one-year-old Hưng Dương

So war happened and the Americans decided that they were going to try and spread democracy, which I think is crap. Basically, from my stepfather's perspective and from the perspective of a lot of Vietnamese people who fought in the war, if the Americans had just helped us by giving us weapons and training us instead of trying to control the war itself, we would have won. I hear that from a lot of people in my family and from my stepfather's buddies. If it had just been a simple war, we would have won. So because outsiders got involved, it got more complicated than it should have been. From my family's perspective, the American role was to screw things up. My mom said that we were just a pawn in international politics.

nineteen-year-old Timmy Trần

But when Timmy vocalized these critiques of U.S. military efforts in a classroom setting, he was immediately rebuffed:

When I first learned about Vietnam in junior high, I got sent to the principal's office for talking back to the teacher. I think I told him that my mom told me something different, like the Americans weren't our savior or something like that, and he just got really mad. Looking back, he was in the American armed forces so that was the story that he heard. Here I am, coming in with a different perspective for the first time, probably shocked him. I remember him yelling at me, "I lost my thumb in the war. How can you say that? Go to the principal's office!" I think I got that anger about the American involvement in the war from my family, so I never cared to learn about it, and I still don't.

The teacher's (over)reaction to Timmy's version of the war exemplifies the American obsession with the Vietnam War as an *American* tragedy, and the corresponding U.S. failure to recognize that the war has its own

integrity that is internal to the history and politics of Vietnam—as articu-
lated by the parents' critiques quoted above. I am interested here less in
the validity or even frequency of these critiques and more in how they
enable the first generation, whose war deeds have been repeatedly dis-
missed or maligned, to explain or explain away their exiled, and oft-times
meager, existence in the United States.

In lieu of concrete answers, some young Vietnamese Americans have
latched onto the first-generation's intense emotions to anchor their own
tenuous relationship to the war and its aftermath. Consider Việt Dương's
moving response below:

> I never sympathized with the [Vietnamese] veterans before because I thought
> they were just stubborn people who couldn't let things go. But in 2005, when
> I went to April 30th [the anniversary commemoration], it was very traumatic
> for me. At that point, I realized that even after 30 years, they were still hang-
> ing on to it. People were crying over their sons, other veterans, brothers, peo-
> ple around them. I began to empathize with them. I realized that they still
> can't let something go. I started to understand them more. I used to think
> why didn't they stay there and fight then? Why did they come to America and
> parade around to fight Vietnamese communism because in America, no one
> really cares. But then I realized that they lost a lot and they were traumatized
> by the war. I didn't really sympathize with them until this year when I saw
> that man cry and people still pursuing these rights for Vietnam.

When asked if he would attend anticommunist protests in the future, he
replied:

> I would, not because I think it's going to change anything that's happening
> in Vietnam. But it's more a statement of defiance. A lot of those people are
> older and so I wonder what's going to happen once they get even older and
> they're gone. Are we going to keep the memory of Vietnam, the war, the
> people who have died, and the people who are living here, alive? My inter-
> pretation of it is that the older people want to keep all the memories alive,
> basically to let the world know that those things did happen and we can't
> forget about it. . . . That would be an important message to all different peo-
> ple—to remind them of the war and to tell them that it did happen and that
> there are still people who are affected by it.

Việt's passionate but reasoned response counters the popularized image of
the "fanatical" anticommunist protestor. It also calls attention to the range

of possible motives for participating in anticommunist protests. In Việt's case, these protests are about the making of public history—a strident reminder to all passerbys that the war "did happen and that there are still people who are affected by it."

However, many interviewees did not share the first generation's idealization of a pre–Communist Vietnam that no longer exists. At the time of the interviews, which began in 2005, Vietnam boasted a flourishing economy and deepening ties with the United States, and thus it did not resemble the rogue state demonized by the first generation. Hương Lâm's comment is typical: "Older Vietnamese Americans are so occupied with the war that they don't even realize that there are people living in Vietnam and have lives there. It's not like Vietnam ended and there isn't anything else that is going on now." Some young people felt frustrated that their parents' generation would expend so much effort on what they perceived to be the futile enterprise "of going back to Vietnam, kicking out the Communists, and taking back the country." While the virulent anticommunist protests convey the first generation's charged emotions, they leave many questions unanswered. As U.S.-born Hiền Lâm asked: "All the homeland politics makes me wonder why I would want to be so anti-Communist and what about the Communism am I against? Is it because my family came over here and we had to leave everything behind, so are we mad about that? Or are we mad about the fact that human rights are being violated? Or are we mad about how people are not getting educated properly, and how they don't have enough to eat? What and why exactly are we anti-Communist?"

The 1.5 generation who migrated to the United States in the 1990s as part of the Orderly Departure Program[34] were especially disheartened by the hostility directed against contemporary Vietnam. Hạnh Phạm, who came to the United States in 1995 at the age of fourteen, considered it a "personal attack" when Vietnamese Americans denigrate the Socialist Republic of Vietnam and its people:

> I'm thinking about the group that came here in 1975 and soon after. These are the people who have never been back to Vietnam. . . . When I hear those people talk about the people in Vietnam now, it sounds like they think that those people are not as good. Because of the Communist influence, they are no longer good Vietnamese people. They are talking about Vietnam in a way

that says whatever happened before 1975 is good and whatever happened
after 1975 is bad. I'm part of the after, so I take it as an attack on me, when
the old Vietnam is romanticized. I have seen the changes and evolution, so
I feel like being stuck in that one period is not really helping us to understand who we are.

Hùng Hồ, another 1.5 generation, whose family still lives in Vietnam, also
charged that "if you consider everything that is there now to be Communist,
then you consider my family to be Communist. If you hate Communism,
then you hate my family and if you hate my family, then you hate me. So I
can't identify with that." These narratives call attention to the increasing
intergenerational and political diversity that defines the contemporary
Vietnamese American community—a marked contrast to the one-note
anticommunist stories that often appear in national media.

"DANGEROUS STORIES": FAMILY SECRETS AND TRANSGRESSIONS

Sometimes, parents remain silent because their war years involved personal transgressions best left untold since the telling would wound loved
ones. In an achingly beautiful chapter on war-related family secrets, Thuy
Vo Dang recounts the painful moment when, on a trip back to Vietnam,
she inadvertently learned about her father's "other family." Though deeply
troubling, this startling news helped explain her father's reticence about
his war experiences: "My father could not talk to us too much about the
war, lest these dangerous stories accidentally spill from his liquored lips."
The "dangerous stories" and the father's war duties were entangled, as the
"other woman" was the one who cared for him when he was injured and
hospitalized in Saigon. This entanglement meant that to hide one, he had
to hide the other; thus he had to assiduously "avoid the topic of his service
in the army and all that he must have witnessed, endured, experienced
during the war."[35] In another example, Trí Nguyễn related that his mother
had a brief but passionate affair with a wealthy married man immediately
before and after the Fall of Saigon—an affair made possible in part due to
the chaos of wartime. Because she steadfastly refuses to discuss the affair,
she shares no details about this crucial period of her life, including her

feelings about the Fall of Saigon and leaving the country. One can imagine her conflicting emotions at the time: the sadness of losing a country mixed uncomfortably with the sweetness of an illicit relationship. As a result, there is a lot about the war that her son cannot glean from his mother: "I know that's a big piece of her life during the war, but she doesn't want to talk about it, so I still don't know much about the war. Everything is so vague, and it's hard to ask my mom questions about it. How can I bring it up without bringing up bad memories?" Family secrets such as these make visible the ways that war and migration "create ruptures in the family narrative that can never be wholly contained by an artificial peace in the refugee home."[36]

The hard-won peace in the refugee home is just that: a fragile truce that is fraught with lingering suspicion and unresolved hurts and that threatens to unravel at the slightest provocation. In Nhi Lý's family, her mother still has not forgiven her husband—Nhi's father—for his failure to escape with the family in 1983, as planned. Ethnically Chinese, Nhi's mother was part of the exodus of hundreds of thousands of Chinese Vietnamese who left Vietnam by boat in the early 1980s in response to the Vietnamese government's attempt to reduce their economic influence and to force their integration into the new nation. Amid the chaos of their escape, Nhi's father ended up staying behind, leaving his wife, who was pregnant with Nhi at the time, and two younger siblings, to fend for themselves. After drifting at sea for several days, their boat was picked up by a Hong Kong Navy ship. Nhi's mother then spent a year at a Hong Kong refugee camp, where Nhi was born, and then another six months at the Philippine Refugee Processing Center in Bataan before settling in Westminster, California. It would take another ten years before the father finally rejoined the family. In the intervening years, her mother's resentment had grown, hardened by the harshness of life as a single mother in a foreign country, and then fueled by the news that her husband's mother had asked permission for him to remarry while the couple was apart:

> My dad's mother asked my mom's mother for her permission and my mom got really pissed off cuz she was here by herself and she was supporting everybody, and she never dated. . . . When she and my dad fight, she would get snappy with my dad, she'd say something like, "I wonder why you didn't get on the boat?" Something like that, and my dad *never* answers. And like now

when my dad wants to visit his mom [in Vietnam], my mom would say stuff like, "You want to go back because you want to visit the other family you have when I wasn't there!"

These stories of "personal transgressions"—and the silence that shrouds them—are instructive in another way: they remind us that even amid the horrors of war, people continue to *live* their lives, with warts and all. In these stories, we see men and women engaging in the age-old act of initiating and dodging relationships; in some ways, war seemed to have prodded them to risk more, such as when women upended sexual mores and became involved with married men, or when married men took advantage of chaotic times to shirk family obligations. These very human (in)actions make a larger point: that war experiences are not only tragic or spectacular but also mundane and familiar. Trung Phạm underscores this point—the ordinariness of life during wartime—when he recounts his parents' day-to-day life in Saigon during the early 1970s:

> My dad would still go to cafes and get coffee even though there was a threat of getting bombed or having some sort of sniper attack and the other things that happen in war. Even though there were threats, he was able to continue on with his daily life like teaching. Both my parents got their degrees in school during the war, and began to work as teachers during the war. Then they got married after the war. So even though it was a devastating event that occurred, and there were a lot of repercussions and all the deaths and destruction all around, there were still things that went on and continued to go on. I don't think that that's told enough because it's not as interesting to people.

While it is true that "things [go] on and continue to go on" even in the midst of war, it is also important to note that Trung's parents lived in cosmopolitan Saigon, which remained mostly calm and stable during the war—a reminder of the range of war experiences sustained by Vietnamese of different regions and socioeconomic classes across the country.

These stories about "personal transgressions" and everyday-ness of wartime remind us that, even in the midst of war, people are always more than victims of their circumstances; they are also desiring subjects with both simple and complex needs and wants. Our task as scholars is to figure out how to "communicate the depth, density, and intricacies of the dialectic of subjection and subjectivity."[37] We do this not only for the sake of accuracy but also out of respect for people's multifaceted and often-contradictory humanity and subjectivity.

PRIVATE GRIEF AND PUBLIC ACHIEVEMENTS

The media often hold up Vietnamese as an example of the quintessential American immigrant success story, but the socioeconomic conditions in which most Vietnamese children found themselves were greatly insecure, "comparable only to those encountered by children of the most under-privileged native minority group."[38] In 1990, the poverty rate of Vietnamese in the United States stood at 25 percent, down from 28 per-cent in 1980 but still substantially higher than the national average of 12 percent.[39] According to the 2010 U.S. Census, Vietnamese families living below the poverty line had dipped to 12 percent but were still higher than the national average of 10 percent.[40] Reflecting this economic trend, the majority of my respondents reported that they grew up in economically struggling households: 91 percent of the respondents' parents held non-professional jobs such as gardener, custodian, construction worker, and manual laborer for men, and manicurist, seamstress, housecleaner, and child or elderly caretaker for women. A number of respondents reported that their parents did "random" or "odd" jobs or that they were "jacks of all trades." Several unemployed fathers stayed home and took care of their children while their wives worked. Nonetheless, at the time of the inter-views, 95 percent of the respondents were in college or had earned a col-lege degree. As discussed in chapter 4, the media and social scientists fuel the "good refugee" narrative by singling out the academic and professional accomplishments of (some) Vietnamese refugees' children, citing them as evidence of cultural assimilation and economic integration. Below, I show that these attempts at prosperity are often valiant (if not always success-ful) efforts to manage and compensate for the personal and material losses incurred by their families during and after the war.

For the majority of the interviewees, economic insecurities haunt their home life. In chapter 4, I showed that American newspapers tend to over-state Vietnamese economic successes in the United States, bolstered by a "before" (shot) of the refugees languishing in backward and impoverished Vietnam, and an "after" (shot) of them flourishing in cosmopolitan and affluent United States. The young Vietnamese Americans in my study also offered "before" and "after" family stories, but they often flipped the script, depicting migration to the United States, the "after," as a move toward economic instability, replete with unstable, minimum-wage employment, lack of health insurance, and welfare dependency. The downward spiral was especially bitter for formerly well-to-do refugees and their families. Liên Ngô, who came to the United States in 1982 at the age of ten, stated that her childhood ended abruptly when she witnessed her father's humiliating downward mobility:

> My dad, he was really wealthy in Vietnam, and he supported all of his thirteen brothers and sisters. Well, when he came over here and got a mechanic job, the mechanics discriminated against him. They thought that he didn't know anything so they gave him the janitor's job of cleaning the shop. My mom told me that . . . when she saw him cleaning the mechanics shop, she just started crying in the car. So that made me cry too. He was the boss and now he came over to America and he's a janitor.

Growing up, many of my respondents were hyper-aware of and anxious about their dire economic circumstances. Take Lan Hoàng's case, for example. Since coming to the United States as a boat refugee in 1983, Lan's monolingual father toiled as a janitor for a hotel, a school, and a supermarket; he also had a second job delivering pizza. Their chronic poverty crushed her father's spirit: "When my dad gets really drunk, he gets so emotional and he starts talking about his life, about what he accomplished and not accomplished, coming to America. Mostly what we hear is that he feels like he works so hard but he gets nowhere. He compares us to other people like people who have houses and everything and we don't have anything and we live paycheck by paycheck." Lan's mother contributed to the family's meager income by working as an electronic assembler, even when working with a microscope made her physically sick: "It can make you nauseous. And so she'd like throw up and she'd come home and tell my dad. And my dad just said, 'Well, you can't throw up all the time because if you keep doing that they won't let you work there.'" Because Lan's mother did not have a full-time position, she received no employer-provided health insurance. Lan described the anxiety of life without health insurance:

> I think my dad has health insurance but he doesn't buy it for my mom because it costs too much. My dad just said, "Just make sure you take care of yourself. When it's cold, make sure you're warm." My dad is like, "You just can't get sick." So one time my mom had stomach pain or something, I'm not sure what, she was crying and then she ended up crawling and stuff, and my dad didn't know what to do, so he had me call his insurance, Kaiser, and set up an appointment for him, but really it was for my mom. So then my mom went with him, and when they called my dad's name, he said, "No, it's for my wife." They were all like, "Are you okay? Is there something wrong?" My mom was like, "No, I'm not ok." After that, we got billed like a lot, like a thousand something, for running tests. . . . So I just didn't want to bring more troubles [for my parents], so I just watched TV and try to learn English from there. I didn't like to complain to them about not having things because there was no point. We were just poor.

It is true that downward mobility and economic insecurity is an immigrant story, not a refugee-specific one. However, our interviewees invariably traced their family's economic hardship back to war-related events, not to migration. For Erin Dương, learning about the war helped her to understand her parents better:

> I think early on I recognized that my stories, my family, my culture are different. How much so, how abnormal or how unnatural these things were, I didn't really fully grasp until I was much more mature. Probably not until I got to college and then I started to fully understand that this doesn't happen to everyone. I mean my family, they were refugees and they came from a country that was ravaged by war and their lives were endangered. There were broken families and my dad was born in 1950 and the country was at war in 1954 and then until 1975. So all of his life basically, there was war and that he had to grow up in. So it wasn't until I started to understand the context of what my family came from and when they were raised, that I began to understand their perspective and why they came here. And why they are so harsh on me and wanting me to excel and take advantage of the opportunities that I have. So it's a long process of understanding.

The war appeared to have affected men and women differently, saddling the latter with family responsibilities that at times required them to stay behind in Vietnam for years. Lisa Hồ's mother, as the oldest daughter, had to remain in Vietnam to take care of her ailing mother while the rest of the family left in 1975; she did not join them until 1993—eighteen years later. In another case, the oldest daughter had to manage all of the fallout from the war:

> My aunt was the oldest girl who didn't have a family yet, so she still had to take care of her brothers and sisters. Her oldest brother was in the military, and the other two sisters had families already, so they moved out. Once, their house was raided and all of their important papers were taken. Like papers for the house and the cars were taken. My aunt was the one who had to deal with it. My grandpa gave her those responsibilities. She also had to make sure that all of her younger brothers and sisters were safe. When my dad and my uncles were in the military, she had to go to this place to ask if they were still alive and if they were okay. I guess that was a lot of pressure and she felt like she was always in charge.

As a consequence, even when life was at its harshest in the United States, this aunt still refused to visit Vietnam because "she didn't want to return to a place where so much of her life and her youth was gone and taken from her."

Having witnessed their parents' economic anxiety and experienced its tolls on all of their lives, many interviewees felt deeply and personally responsible for realizing their parents' dream of "making it" in the United States. Their sense of responsibility was palpable: it had cost their parents too much to get here; it was their responsibility to fulfill their parents' dream of family success via intergenerational mobility. Below are some examples of this sentiment:

> I compare my life to what my parents had to go through. It's amazing, what they had to go through and the life that they built, from nothing to everything that they have given us. I don't think a lot of people my age have to think about that stuff. They don't think about what their parents did and how hard they worked. That's part of the reason why I try to work hard to make my parents proud. It's because I think about all they've given me. Just to make them happy everyday for them to look at their children and know that *they* made a difference.
> twenty-year-old Ngiệp Ngô

> When the Communists came, there were no opportunities. There was nothing for my dad to do. When he talks about how he grew up, there is a certain

mentality that he has which is that there is a whole generation of young men like him whose futures were just wasted. He lived almost twenty years under Communist rule, and no one could be an intellectual. There was just no room for that, and I think that he really regretted it. It was a waste. My dad came here in his late forties and he had to catch up with the rest. And he'd had a really hard time. So he kept telling me and my brother that you need to go to school, graduate, work, and have a great life. I feel that they came here for our future and so now it's up to us to make it happen.

twenty-two-year-old Thảo Hồ

I think that the only reason why I intended to be pre-med was because of my parents and what they went through. I thought that this was the only way that I would be able to repay them.

twenty-one-year-old Hiền Dương

In recent years, scholars have begun to explore how marginalized groups, and not only elites, use money and consumption to raise or secure their social standing. As Alex Kotlowitz reports, it is primarily as consumers—as "purchasers of the talisman of success"—that poor black youth claim social membership to the larger U.S. society.[41] In her insightful study of children of Asian immigrant entrepreneurs, Lisa Sun-Hee Park likewise shows that it is through conspicuous consumption that young Asian Americans attempt to claim their, and by extension their parents', social citizenship or belonging as Americans.[42] In other words, college and career choices are less, or not only, a sign of Vietnamese assimilation and social acceptance and more a sign of a complex and strategic response to their and their parents' forcible and "differential inclusion" into U.S. society. Having grown up in dire poverty, young Vietnamese Americans like Lan Hoàng knew that they needed to make money: "I was like who says money is not everything? Money is everything, you know. If you get sick and need to go to the doctor, how do you go to the doctor? Money, you know. The food you eat and the clothes you wear, you need money. And so if someone says money isn't everything, they're wrong. *Money is everything.*" For the majority of the young people whom I interviewed, their investment in success and money is meant to improve the lot and status of their families; it is not only or primarily about the pursuit of personal achievements. This investment in intergenerational economic mobility is much more than a reflection of "Vietnamese core cultural values": their alleged strong work ethic, high regard for education, and family values.[43] Rather, it exhibits the poignant and complex ways in which Vietnamese refugees and their children use public achievements to address the lingering costs of war, to manage intimacy, to negotiate family tensions, and to ensure their social position and dignity in the racially and economically stratified United States.

No matter their resolve, living for their parents—for their dreams— exacts a high personal cost. For some, such as Lan Hoàng, the cost came in the form of a stunted childhood:

> I had to translate not just for my family but for my grandma. Everything that's sent to them, and then I got so stressed and sometimes I hated it. I was like eleven years old and I had to translate things like letters and papers and fill out forms and I didn't know anything . . . [starts to cry]. But it seems that they will never be satisfied, ok? Everything I do is like their standards and expectations are set way too high I guess . . . [sniffle] . . . and I feel like . . . I'm still bitter towards my parents even now because I think when I was a kid, you know, I shouldn't be doing that stuff like I should be having fun.

Some interviewees related that their childhood years were spent working alongside their parents to help improve the family's economic situation:

> I helped out my mom with the sewing jobs. I've done that ever since we came when I was in fourth grade up until high school. So yeah, I remember a lot of things, like how we would stay up until five or six in the morning to make the deadline. Probably one of the reasons why she did that is so that she can stay home and take care of the family. With the sewing job, she can do it anytime. It's funny because whenever I go to sleep, I would hear the machine and the noise. So when we quit, which was pretty recent since it was only a few years ago, I still keep on hearing the noise. I would still hear it, until I left for college and I was away from the machine. That's when I stopped hearing it.

For many others, their financial obligation to their parents influenced their job and other economic decisions. As Vân Nguyễn recounted:

> My brother and sister worked as young as they could when they were fourteen. So did I. We did different jobs like work in the supermarkets and at flea markets. My brother is the oldest and when he came [to the United States], he was fifteen. He had a hard time adjusting. He went to a community col-

lege. He's very smart, but he somehow felt isolated. So he joined the U.S. Navy when he was nineteen. . . . My sister stayed and went to a state university and graduated with a business degree. With this business degree, she works enough to make money to support my parents. We recently bought a house which was split evenly between my brother and my sister. My brother is paying more just because he's in the military and he has more of the federal income. . . . My brother recently tried to get out of the military because your contact ends every four years and you renew it every four years. So we are all trying to get him to leave, but he feels an obligation. He said that if he comes back now, then how will he find a stable income to pay the mortgage. So he feels a deep financial obligation. We told him that we will work together as a family and figure something out. Financially, it is always a family decision. We don't really think about who that house will go to or whose name that house will go under. It's a family house and we will do whatever to support it.

The pressure to contribute to the family economic well-being has, at times, led to unwise and desperate undertakings such as gambling. As Hiếu Trường related:

My parents had random jobs. They didn't speak English. My mom sewed clothes for a couple of years. My dad helped her and then did other random jobs including being a gardener, working at McDonalds, and being a home caretaker. Then my older brother was really smart so he was taking classes, but then he realized that the family needed more money. He was in college at that time, so he just said that he would take a year off to make some money and then he would go back to school. But he didn't. He went into gambling mode, but I think it was out of good motivation. He really wanted to help out the family. My other brother went into gambling mode too, so it was really bad. The stress just affected us in all different ways. All of us have good intentions to help out the family. But we were all helpless in a way. My brothers didn't know what else to do. They know that they had to get a good education, but at the same time they wanted to help out the family. They felt trapped so they went into that gambling mode.

An irony in refugee life—indeed, in immigrant life generally—is that the steep sacrifices intended to achieve mobility for the family can end up tearing the family apart. In the following excerpt, Loan Dương recounted how her family grew apart as family members scrambled "just to survive" in the United States:

When we came here, we understood that there were lots of opportunities here, but at the same time, we were lost. You know how Vietnamese people are: We are very family oriented. Our family in Vietnam was really strong. We're huge, yet when we came here, we were the only family here. There was no one else. In a way we felt really stranded and lost. We didn't know how to drive, we didn't know a lot of the stores around us, we didn't know how to eat a hamburger, and other little things. But those little things do add up. It makes you stress when you try to adapt. I think that stress permeated into our family and in a way disrupted it. In Vietnam, we were okay. But I think the stress from such a big transition divided us for a year or two. Some of us thought that maybe this was a wrong decision and we should have stayed in Vietnam. This place is horrible since we go to work eight hours a day and then go back. We hardly see each other since we work so much just to survive. For our family, meal times are important. We eat breakfast, lunch, and dinner together. All of our meals are together. Here, we had to eat separately because we all had to work. We felt strange since we thought that mealtime was really important. That was a big transition.

In this section, I have offered an alternative explanation for the postwar generation's seeming drive to succeed: what appears to be an act of economic assimilation on the part of the "generation after"—an act of moving beyond the war—is in actuality an index of the ongoing costs of war, not only for the witnesses and survivors but also for their children. When asked what Americans should know about the Vietnam War, many respondents offered this answer: that the war did not end in 1975. As Hiếu Trường exclaimed: "For my family, [the war] never really ended. People said it ended, but it still went on even after the takeover." Many interviewees insisted that Americans should pay attention to "not only what happened during the war but also what happened after the war" and "to know about the people and what happened to them when they came here." In the end, for these young Vietnamese Americans, when they consider the Vietnam War, they think most about what happened to their families after they came to the United States. This is the part of the war that they knew most intimately and shared most freely. Their insistence that we pay heed to family life is an important reminder that wars affect not only the realms of politics and economics but also "people's intimate social ecologies."[44] As such, the domains of the intimate—in this case, Vietnamese family life—constitute a key site to register the lingering costs of war that often have been designated as over and done with in the public realm.

"THE GANGSTER WE ARE ALL LOOKING FOR": ABOUT INTERGENERATIONAL TENSIONS AND SHARED LIVES

Most popular and scholarly writings on immigrant and refugee families tend to naturalize intergenerational tension, attributing it to the "culture clash" between "traditional" immigrant parents and their more Americanized children.[45] My discussion thus far suggests that intergenerational strain, even when it is seemingly unrelated to war, is not a private matter between refugee parents and their children but a social, historical, and geopolitical affair that exposes multiple and interrelated forms of power relations. In this section, I turn to lê thi diem thúy's 2003 novel, *The Gangster We Are All Looking For,* for a critical rendering of family dynamics within refugee families. As Lisa Lowe has argued, "Culture is a ... mediation of history, the site through which the past returns and is remembered, however fragmented, imperfect, or disavowed."[46] This critical remembering is key to the formation of oppositional narratives and "to the imagination and rearticulation of new forms of political subjectivity, collectivity, and practice."[47] In recent years, Vietnamese American artists such as lê have begun to grapple with the war's disastrous consequences for Vietnam and its people, giving rise to often-haunting artistic and cultural representations that imagine, remember, and trace the complex genealogies of war and forced displacements that precede and shape Vietnamese resettlement in the United States. As such, I am interested in Vietnamese American cultural forms for what they can reveal and expand on the tensions, irresolutions, and contradictions of Vietnamese American lives.

Told through the knowing eyes of a lonely and imaginative child, *The Gangster* is a quietly powerful account of a Vietnamese refugee family who is in America but not of it.[48] Part memoir, part novel, it is among the first book-length fictional works to come from the "boat people" generation of the late 1970s and early 1980s. In 1978, six-year-old lê and her father fled their home village of Phan Thiết in southern Vietnam in a small fishing boat, leaving behind her mother and younger siblings. After a brief stay in a refugee camp in Singapore, they were resettled in Linda Vista, a racially diverse working-class community in San Diego. In 1980, lê's mother and younger sister, after a stint in a refugee camp in Malaysia, joined them in San Diego.[49] Like many of my interviewees, growing up, lê sensed an implicit silence in her family about the Vietnam War: "When my dad got together with his friends, they would sing songs and tell stories about when they were schoolboys. But there was a way they leapt over the war and the aftermath of the war. There was no one for me to turn to with my questions: how did we get here? Why are we boat people? If my mom misses her parents, and our town, then why aren't we there? And because I had no one to ask those questions, I swallowed them inside myself."[50] At the same time, she was bombarded with media images of the Vietnam War as a spectacle—and as an American tragedy: "In mainstream narrative about Vietnam, it's usually about the American GI, while the Vietnamese are part of the landscape. They rarely get particularized as characters."[51] lê wrote *The Gangster* in part to put on record what happened to the Vietnamese people, not just during the war, but also before and after the war: "In this country . . . [t]he questions about what happened to Vietnamese people don't get brought up. . . . For America to grow in its consciousness, it needs to ask what happened to the Vietnamese."[52]

In lyrical prose that reads like poetry, lê depicts the United States not as the land of opportunities but as the breaker of families—a place where family life will never be what it could or should have been. Haunting the narrator's family is the specter of her dead older brother, who drowned in Vietnam when he was just six years old—a death made more tragic by the absence of the father who was being held in a reeducation camp. The brother's death provides lê with a narrative device to move the story back and forth between Vietnam and California and to shift time, place, and viewpoint constantly throughout the novel. As lê interweaves memories of Vietnam with incidents in the United States, she melds the past and present, conveying the fluidity of time but also the unending-ness of the war's impact on Vietnamese lives. As she reminds us: "War has no beginning and no end. It crosses oceans like a splintered boat filled with people singing a sad song."[53] Unlike other immigrant accounts, lê's novel depicts the family's arrival in the United States not as the end but as the beginning of the story, poignantly detailing the main characters' struggles with living a life not of their own design. The young narrator bemoans her parents' unfulfilled dreams and unfulfilling lives in America: "[Ma] worked as a seamstress, doing piecework at our kitchen table. [Ba] worked as a welder at a factory that made space heaters. Neither of them wanted to be doing it; Ma wanted to have a restaurant, and Ba wanted to have a garden."[54] She *sees* their poverty intensely, in the rusted gates of their small red apartment building, in her father's hopeless rage, and in her parents' "big fight[s] about nothing" and in the "awful quiet" that ensues.[55]

Most poignant are the exquisite portraits of the haunted, brooding father "who cries in the garden every night"[56] and who is "sad and broken."[57] His loneliness, sadness, and brokenness—the result of years of devastating war, punishing reeducation camp, demeaning jobs, and crushing poverty—often turn into hopeless rage: "He becomes prone to rages. He smashes televisions, VCRs, chases friends and family down the street, brandishing hammers and knives in broad daylight."[58] At night, once his rage has subsided, he sits motionless in the dark for hours, "his body absolutely still, his hands folded on his lap, penitent ... straining toward things no one can see."[59] Mindful of the father's inner turmoil, the daughter's memories of him and their relationship contain a mixture of tender and terrifying moments:

> To protect myself, I tried to forget everything: that first night at the refugee camp in Singapore; those early morning walks after we arrived in America; the sound of his voice asking a question no one could answer; the shapes his fists left along a wall; the bruises that blossomed on the people around him; the smell of the fruit he brought home from the gardens he tended; the way the air seemed charged with memories of blood; the nets we fell through, faster and faster, year after year, dreaming of land.[60]

In the following scene, which takes place in a runaway shelter, lê beautifully depicts the complexity of the father-daughter relationship, one that refuses to be privatized but calls into being the larger history and context of war, refugee resettlement, and chronic poverty:

> Before I had run away for good, my father once came to pick me up at a shelter. As we sat in a conference with two counselors, he was asked if there

was anything he wanted to say. He shook his head. When pressed, he looked
down at his hands. He apologized for what his hands had done. The counselors understood this to mean he was taking responsibility for his drunken
rages. They nodded in approval. But then he drew his palms together and
apologized for all that his hands had not been able to do. He spread his
hands wide open, and said, in Vietnamese, to anyone who could understand,
there were things he had lost grasp of.

The room seemed to shrink in the face of his sorrow. Beside him the two
counselors were like tight little shrubs no one had ever watered. I thought
they had no right to frown at my father. I could not wait to get us out of
there. I told the counselors that I was ready to go home. I remember crossing the parking lot, my hand in my father's hand, the two of us running to
the car as though we were escaping together again.[61]

In this excerpt, lê denaturalizes domestic violence among poor refugee
families by showing how it is intimately linked to the violence of war, of
urban neglect, and of poverty. In so doing, she disrupts the widespread
construction of patriarchy as particular to Asian culture, which freezes
Asian immigrant men as always-already "subjects who perpetrate violence," and foregrounds the need to theorize and situate all forms of male
violence.[62] Stressing the intersection of race, gender, and class, she makes
clear how gender differentiation and oppression is not a universal experience but is structured differently, depending on how it intersects with
other inequalities such as race and class. Thus, from their race and class
vantage point, the two social service workers understand the gesture of
the father as an apology for domestic violence—"for what his hands had
done." In contrast, the marginalized father and daughter recognize that
the apology is more for what "his hands had *not* been able to do." More
than a cultural misunderstanding, the scene evinces a power struggle in
which the feminist values of the American counselors are deemed universal while those of the powerless refugees are misrecognized—though not
entirely silenced. The novel thus exhorts us to acknowledge that economic
and social discrimination have locked many working-class men of color
into an unequal relationship with not only privileged white men but also
privileged white women.[63]

Facing the overbearing and patronizing social service workers, the
daughter abruptly and protectively took her father's hand and both fled—
away from the oppressive state system that threatened to further humili-

ate a man who has just apologized for what "his hands had not been able to do." This scene encapsulates the parent-child role reversal common in immigrant families: the night they left Vietnam, it was the father who carried the daughter down to the beach and placed her on the fishing boat; but now in America, it was the English-speaking daughter who freed the father from the prying bureaucrats in the shelter. This act—"of escaping together again"—moves the story beyond the familiar trope of intergenerational conflict to one about joint lives. Although the daughter and father are divided by generation, culture, and language, they are connected by their shared histories. The crises that have shaped the father— war trauma, reeducation camps, boat escape, and chronic underemployment in the United States—while unknown to and unheard by the social service workers, are deeply felt and lived by the daughter who has witnessed and braved many of these hardships alongside her father. It is this witnessing that enables the daughter to *see* her father as one who is never utterly defeated: "His friends fell all around him ... first during the war and then after the war, but somehow he alone managed to crawl here, on his hands and knees, to this life."[64] Avery Gordon has explained that a structure of feeling articulates "the tangled exchange of noisy silences and seething absences."[65] Therein lies the contribution of lê's novel: it makes audible and visible the "noisy silences" and "seething absences" in Vietnamese life, exposing the material, cultural, and political circumstances that constrain the refugees' everyday lives, their responses to and against these constraints, and the emotional tensions that result.

.   .   .   .   .

The focus of this chapter has been on "postmemory": how young Vietnamese Americans, born and/or raised in the United States, have created their own memories of a war that took place before they were born. I have traced the repercussions of the Vietnam War, which extended far beyond the official end of the war in April 1975, into the postwar generation, not in the visible tragedies that occur in the public realm but in the hidden injuries that play out in the "domains of the intimate."[66] Focusing on family silences and secrets, I have shown that refugee families often adopt what Park calls a "don't ask, don't tell" strategy, as children implicitly know not to ask their parents about potentially painful topics about their background and migration history; instead, they string together bits and pieces of their own memories and overheard stories to create a bearable and repeatable version of their family's war and refugee experiences—one that emphasizes academic and economic gains, which invariably, though not always intentionally, validates the myth of the United States as the land of opportunity.[67] For the postwar generation, then, the war has become a shifting specter that explains or explains away past transgressions, family tensions, and/or economic instabilities, and it is a constant motivator that pushes them to assuage private grief with public achievements. The post-war generation's practice of looking to their present conditions in order to understand their parents' past corroborates one of the strongest and most enduring premises of Walter Benjamin's conception of history: the belief that it is not history that enables us to understand the present but, con-versely, the present that enables us to understand the past.[68] This concep-tion of history suggests that there is no way to close off new understandings of the Vietnam War, even for the postwar generation(s), and that it is pre-cisely through the domains of the everyday that people remember, forge, and transform a past that has been long suppressed.

7 "The Endings That Are Not Over"

Tôi nào muốn thành người tị nạn
Sống lang thang, vất vưởng xứ người
Xa bạn hữu, gia đình ly tán
Đêm âm thầm nước mắt tuôn rơi.
[I never wanted to be a refugee
Wandering aimlessly in someone else's country
Far from friends, separated from family
Silently crying in the dead of the night.]

Vĩnh Liêm, "Người Tị Nạn" ("A Refugee")[1]

For close to ten years, Vĩnh Liêm's poem "Người Tị Nạn" has sat in my office—a reminder, a prodding, an invitation. But, for a long time, I did not know how to tell the story of the refugee. What stories could be told that would highlight the costs of war yet not reduce the refugees to mere victims, even if their losses have been significant? Over the years, I have looked for ways to tell the story of the refugee—not as an object of study but as a source of knowledge. I have looked for the refugee story through the lives of the children of working-class Mexican immigrants that I grew up with in Perris, California, an economically struggling and Latino-dominated city in Riverside County. My best friend there was an immigrant from Mexico, and it was through our shared stories about "home" and "America" that I came to recognize and name anti-immigrant practices, under- and mis-education, and language and class discrimination. Later, when I began my academic career in graduate school, I looked for the Vietnamese story through the scholarship in sociology on refugees. There, I saw that Vietnamese were pitted against poor African Americans and Latino immigrants, folded into the Asian American umbrella, probed by mental health practitioners, denigrated as welfare recipients by conservatives, and pitied and/or celebrated as the model minority by liberals. In other words, the bulk of the sociological literature on refugees locates the "refugee problem" *not* in the geopolitical conditions that produced their massive displacements and movements to the United States and elsewhere but within the bodies and minds of the refugees themselves. As I began my academic career in Asian American studies, I looked for the refugee story through the lives and deeds of other Asian Americans. I was particularly compelled by Philippine and Filipino American histories, the ways that the Philippines and Filipinos have been forcibly and differentially included in the United States—through the violence, first of war, and then of colonialism and neocolonialism, and migration.[2] Knowing this history of U.S. imperialism in Asia helped me to connect other dots. As discussed in chapter 2, I came to realize that it was not coincidental that one of the most-traveled refugee routes via military aircraft was from Vietnam to the Philippines to Guam to California—all nodes of U.S. colonial and military empire in the Asia Pacific region.

However, it was the U.S. war in Iraq—*the shock of recognition*—that brought me directly back to Vietnam and back to the figure of the refugee: the spectacle of violence; the "we need to destroy it in order to save it" mandate; the ways that peace could only come in the form of a "war without end"; and the brutal displacement of thousands of Iraqi men, women, and children from their homes and neighborhoods. For Vietnam War survivor Sonny Le, who came to the United States as a "boat person" in 1982, "the image of bombs raining down on Iraq from the belly of the B-52 bombers" brought back embedded childhood memories of "nightly artillery shelling and bombing"—a "lullaby that millions of Vietnamese children . . . fell asleep to."[3] The media chattered endlessly then, as it did during the war in Vietnam, about the capabilities of U.S. military might, especially of its "shock and awe" air power and smart bombs, but said almost nothing about the Iraqis on the ground.[4] Their deeds done; never mind the after. On November 7, 2004, as U.S. Marines surrounded the proud and historic city of Fallujah, the top enlisted Marine in Iraq called on his troops to "kick some butt." In a pep talk, he rallied the troops by referring back to U.S. destruction of another proud and historic city of another time and place, the ancient citadel of Hue: "You're all in the process of making history. This is another Hue city in the making. I have no doubt, if we do get the word, that each and everyone of you is going to do what you have always done—kick some butt."[5]

All of this is to say that, in order for me to tell the story of the Vietnamese refugees, I have had to borrow and learn from a number of places and groups. But these stories are more than personal experiences; they reflect the workings of empire as the United States crisscrosses the globe in an ever-expanding quest to increase its political, military, economic, and cultural influence across the world. Though explicitly interdisciplinary, *Body Counts* engages foremost the discipline of sociology, specifically the sociology of immigration and refugee studies, which has largely treated the refugees as a problem of immigrant integration, eliding the militarized context of their flight and resettlement. Such a decoupling of Vietnamese refugees from the Vietnam War risks assimilating Vietnamese into the myth of "immigrant America," in which Vietnamese become represented as yet another poor and desperate group descending en masse on a wealthy and benevolent nation. Conceptualizing Vietnamese refugees as an analytic for critical inquiry, *Body Counts* engages the Vietnam War as an important historical and discursive site of Vietnamese subject formation and the shaping and articulation of U.S. nationhood, highlighting the role that "U.S. world power has played in the global structures of migration."[6] Even as I write about militarized lives, I also call attention to the rich and complicated lived worlds of Vietnamese refugees and their children— to the ways in which they labor to (re)create viable lifeworlds in displacement.

TOWARD A CRITICAL REFUGEE STUDY

This book arises from a set of questions: How has the United States been able to fold the Vietnam War into its list of war triumphs from the mid- to late twentieth century? How have U.S. actions in Vietnam been re-presented to be not only successful but also just and even necessary? And why have the Vietnamese dead been absent in U.S. depictions of the Vietnam War? To answer these questions, I have turned to an unlikely source in Vietnam War studies: the Vietnamese refugees. Situating Vietnamese refugees within the long durée of U.S. military colonialism in Asia, I have argued that the refugees, as the widely publicized objects of U.S. rescue fantasies, have ironically become the featured evidence of the appropriateness and even necessity of U.S. war in Vietnam. The iconic images of desperate and frantic Vietnamese, wailing with pain, grief, and terror as they scrambled to escape "communist Vietnam" at any cost, have visually and discursively transformed the Vietnamese from a people battered by decades of U.S. warfare in Vietnam to those persecuted by the Vietnamese communist government and rescued by the United States.[7] Countering this historical revisionism, I have charted an interdisciplinary field of *critical refugee study*, which reconceptualizes "the refugee" not as an object of rescue but as a site of social and political critiques, whose emergence, when traced, would make visible the processes of colonization, war, and displacement.

Dominant U.S. narratives also control dissonant memories of the Vietnam War by representing the war and its aftermath as being contained within a specific timeframe (and space)—and as being over and done with. However, as Stephen Whitfield notes, war has a geopolitical and a social temporality: even when war has ended in the geopolitical dimension, it has not necessarily done so in the social dimension.[8] Focusing on the slow and potentially critical process of the social dimension of the Vietnam War, I have emphasized the costs borne by the Vietnamese war witnesses, survivors, and their families, both in Vietnam and in the diaspora, that linger long after the supposed ending of the war. Against this dominant remembering of the "Fall of Saigon" in April 1975 as the war's unambiguous conclusion, I ask: when does war end and who gets to decide? In *Body Counts*, I have offered an alternative temporality—one that emphasizes the war's irreconcilability and ongoingness, in order to bring to the fore the living effects of what seems to be over and done with.

Militarized Refuge(es)

A crucial source of legitimacy for sovereign power is the capacity to decide on matters of inclusion and exclusion. In the case of refugees, the decision over who will, and who will not, be granted refuge is not just a humanitarian consideration but also a moment when the sovereign state reasserts its monopoly over matters of security.[9] The admission of refugees and other asylum seekers also boosts the desirability of the sovereign state because the newcomers serve as a "supplement to the nation, an agent of national reenchantment," constituting ongoing evidence that the nation remains "choiceworthy."[10] Following this logic, the arrival of Vietnamese refugees has bolstered U.S. status as a nation of *refuge*. But this is not new: citing the examples of displaced Europeans in the wake of World War II, of East European and Soviet escapees in the 1950s, and of Cubans fleeing Fidel Castro in the 1960s, scholars have shown that the precarious condition of "refugeeness" affirms statist practices—a reminder of the importance of the state and state protection.[11] What is specific about the Vietnamese refugee case is the fact of U.S. military involvement *and* defeat in Vietnam. As Vietnam's "runaways," Vietnamese refugees ideologically do more than affirm the U.S. claim of "being a safe haven for the oppressed";[12] they also provide the United States with a powerful narrative that justifies its military intervention in Vietnam. As argued in chapter 4, Vietnamese refugees—as ideological figures—buttress not only U.S. claims of humanitarianism but also its right to military interventionism, in Vietnam and elsewhere, no matter the "collateral damage."

To make a case against U.S. militarism, both then and now, we need to expose the militarized violence behind the humanitarian ideas of "refuge(es)." Toward this goal, I have coined the term "*militarized refuge(es)*," with its intended jarring juxtaposition, in order to cast America's most celebrated story of rescue—the airlifting and routing of Vietnamese refugees through various U.S.-run processing centers in the Pacific in 1975—as a troubling history of military colonialism in the Philippines, Guam, California, and Vietnam. According to anthropologist Catherine Lutz, "The US' imperial history, especially in the second half of the 20th century, has been a military colonialism around the world."[13] Indeed, Guam, the primary staging ground for refugees in 1975, has the highest ratio of U.S. military spending and hardware and land stolen from native populations of any place in the world.[14] In connecting Vietnamese dislocation to that of Filipino, Chamorro, and Native American, I literally mapped the reach of the U.S. empire, from its nineteenth-century imperial projects to its botched Cold War goals in Southeast Asia,[15] thereby revealing the "humanitarian violence"[16] that undergirds all rescue-and-liberation projects.

The term "militarized *refuge(es)*" also conjoins *refuge* and *refugees* to signal their co-constitutiveness and their tie to U.S. militarism. In chapter 2, I showed that the practice of providing refuge following on the heels of military destruction enabled the United States to re-position itself as the benevolent rescuer of Vietnam's people. Challenging the logic of this "makeover," I detailed how the very military bases credited and valorized for providing refuge for Vietnam's runaways in 1975—Clark and Andersen Air Force Bases in the Pacific, and Marine Corps Base Camp Pendleton in California—were the very ones responsible for the massive bombings and ground combat that displaced (and killed) a large number of Vietnamese in the first place. The concept *militarized refuge(es)* thus demands that we hold the United States accountable for the epistemic or symbolic violence of its wars *and* for the actual physical violence—the guns and bombs and defoliating chemicals—unleashed on allegedly "empty" lands and "expendable" populations.

Sometimes, though, the "expendable" populations, even as refugees in the United States, erupt to interrupt the U.S. claim of refuge. On April 3, 2009, Linh Phat Voong,[17] a forty-one-year-old Chinese Vietnamese immigrant, shot and killed thirteen people at the American Civic Association, a nonprofit immigrant services center in downtown Binghamton, New York. Voong then shot and killed himself. A *Los Angeles Times* article concludes its story on the killing with this summation: "Whatever drove [him] to take his pistols to the American Civic Assn. on Friday *may never be known*."[18] Indeed, we may never know what drove Voong to commit this murder-suicide, not only because he did not leave a suicide note but more so because no one thought to connect the dots of his life. However, the clues are there: Voong's father was a South Vietnamese soldier who spent years in a reeducation camp; Voong still struggled with English, after close to two decades in the United States; he was chronically unemployed and lived in subsidized housing alongside other refugees from Bosnia, Iraq, and Somalia; and he claimed to be a victim of a string of police taunting and torture that chased him from California to New York.[19] Although newspaper reporters recounted Voong's story as an isolated incident committed by a "delusional" man, his life accounts make visible the connections between U.S. wars in Southeast Asia and U.S. racism at home, which takes the forms of language and anti-immigrant discrimination, urban poverty, and police brutality. In other words, Voong's murder-suicide occurred not in a vacuum but at the intersection of local, national, and international acts of racialized violence. As a violent feat, Voong's mass killing expands the meaning of the term *"militarized* refugee,"[20] depicting the refugee not only as an object of U.S. military violence but also as a weapon-wielding ticking time bomb intent on destroying what Achille Mbembe refers to as *"death-worlds,* new and uniform forms of social existence in which vast populations are subjected to conditions of life conferring upon them the status of *living dead."*[21] In this sense, Voong's murder-suicide was not a personal act of violence but a public (re) enactment of his militarized life in all its dimensions—a resolute refusal to keep the horrors of "war," both in Southeast Asia and in the interior of the United States, private, contained, and tamed.[22]

Refuge(e) Making

This book also originates from a set of concerns that revolve around silence: the silence of history and states; the silence of witnesses and survivors; and the silence within families and between generations. As many scholars of history and memory have pointed out, "survivors of atrocity become deeply uncomfortable signifiers for the postatrocity societies within which they live," as they challenge structures of power and of normality, both of which privilege forgetting.[23] For the war casualties that the United States inflicts or facilitates, their experiences of trauma and displacement—their losses—have rarely reached the public but remained trapped within their immediate community, lest they expose the threads and threats of U.S. imperialism and militarism. As documented in this book and elsewhere, a "determined incomprehension"[24] has remained the dominant U.S. public posture on the devastating impact of warfare destruction on Vietnam and its people. Noam Chomsky rebuked the absence of any reference to American aggression against South Vietnam in U.S. mainstream media and scholarship, proclaiming curtly that "there is no such event in history."[25] More recently, in a series of essays written after September 11, 2001, Judith Butler has likewise condemned the "failure of recognition" of the thousands of Palestinian, Afghan, and other Arab peoples who have died by military means with U.S. support, exclaiming, "None of this takes place on the order of the event. None of this takes place. In the silence of the newspaper, there was no event, no loss, and this failure of recognition is mandated through an identification with those who identify with the perpetrators of the violence."[26] Woven together into a fabric of erasure, these institutionally organized blanknesses, blind spots, and gaps in meaning cover up the traumas inflicted by U.S. wars. As a consequence of this organized erasure, in the United States, Vietnamese became a people without faces and names, family and friends, personal histories and beliefs—a people whose lives do not count.

Critics of U.S. military interventions have theorized that certain lives fall outside of Western conceptions of who is normatively human, and thus violence against them "leaves a mark that is no mark."[27] In her critique of U.S. military retribution against Arab peoples, Butler provocatively asks: "If someone is lost, and that person is not someone, then what and where is the loss, and how does mourning take place?"[28] In other words, if there had been no lives, there would have been no losses and therefore no public act of grieving.[29] For Butler, this is not simply a matter of "humans not regarded as humans"; rather, she argues that, on the level of discourse, certain lives fit no Western frame for the human.[30] As Denise Ferreira da Silva explains, to be from a non-European point of origin was to have a body and consciousness that could never fit the prerequisites for modern subjectivity and political agency. In the case of military conflicts, Silva contends that the United States distinguishes between its "true friends," those of Europe and European descent, and its "new friends" of freedom, such as the South Vietnamese, who may be rhetorically included in the territory of freedom for geopolitical necessities but can only remain there with U.S. military and economic aid. She argues that this distinction is sustained by a racial lexicon that defines freedom as the sole property of the West and the "new friends" as "always-already constitut[ing] potential 'enemies of freedom.'"[31]

The theoretical discussion on "who is normatively human" suggests that, since Vietnamese are said to exist outside the limits of human intelligibility, their life does not qualify as a life and thus fails to become "a publicly grievable life."[32] Yet, as I have documented in this book, life does exist at the place of "foreclosed humanity." As Neferti Tadiar exhorts, the place of "foreclosed humanity" is also the place "of different human becoming," which always holds the potential for the radical remaking of a proper humanity, however tentative.[33] Heeding Tadiar's insight, I have paid more attention to Vietnamese American *presence*, rather than their absence, by actively looking for and writing about Vietnamese social practices that have emerged to tend to the ongoing wounds of war, flight, and resettlement. That is, I have explored the legacy of the Vietnam War not only in the words and deeds of American state officials and public media but also in the refugees' creative, improvised, and experimental refuge-making practices. Conceptualizing the remaking of social life "as the very condition and meaning of abolition,"[34] I have looked specifically for alternative forms of life that Vietnamese people have generated on the margins of sovereign space. In Tadiar's eloquent words:

> These alternative ways of becoming human consist of tangential, fugitive, and insurrectionary creative social capacities that, despite being continuously dismissed, impeded, and illegible by dominant ways of being human, are exercised and invented by those slipping beyond the bounds of valued humanity in their very effort of living, in their making of forms of viable life.[35]

In chapter 3, I detailed efforts by "protracted refugees" to create new lifeworlds within the refugee camp, not only to survive but also to forge a viable life within it. Whereas the majority of refugee camp studies scrutinize the bio- and necropolitics of camp life, I paid close attention to the "politics of living,"[36] particularly to the making of nontraditional social relationships in the camps.[37] In chapter 5, following the diasporic commemorations of my executed uncle, I showed how first-generation Vietnamese refugees have deployed Internet memorials and commemorative street names in order to literally write their histories into the American landscape. At the same time, I have been attentive to the silencing that occurs *within* the Vietnamese refugee communities. In chapters 4 and 5, I pointed to the limitations of nationalist strategies—most visibly, ardent anticommunist sentiments practices—that have led to harsh, unrelenting, and at times fatal attacks against perceived dissidents in the diasporic community.

Finally, I have written not only about public silencing but also about self-generated silence. Hannah Arendt tells us that the hidden forces of modern body politics may become most visible within the space of intimate domestic interaction—the very realm of life that the political forces strive to reduce to privacy.[38] Accordingly, in chapter 6, I traced the lingering costs of the Vietnam War in the out-of-sight injuries—and healings— that occur in the home. Focusing on family silences and secrets, I relied on interviews with the postwar generation to show that, within the space of the family, war survivors *speak* even when they utter no words—in the unnerving nightmares, recurring illnesses, acute aches, and suddenly shed tears. The occasional moments when "the past broke through," and the fractured images, stories, and affects that get transmitted therein, constitute the indirect, quiet, or even wordless ways that subjugated histories get told. This insight suggests that we need to look for "history" outside the realms of sight and sound, which tend to privilege literacy and testimonials, respectively, and to engage other senses such as feelings and emotions in order to search for the stories that are not or cannot be spoken but are nevertheless there.

Critical Juxtaposing: Connecting the Dots

Body Counts is really about connecting the dots. My methodology revolves around what I term *critical juxtaposing*: the deliberate bringing together of seemingly different historical events in an effort to reveal what would otherwise remain invisible—in this case, the contours, contents, and limits of the U.S. empire. Explicitly interdisciplinary, *Body Counts* critically juxtaposed war studies with refugee studies in order to expose the central role that U.S. wars play in structuring the displacements, dispersions, and flight of refugees and that Vietnamese and other refugees play in shoring up the U.S. right to military interventions. Although scholars in the various fields of critical war studies have launched powerful critiques of U.S. military colonialism,[39] they have largely left the study of refugees—the war's human costs—to social scientists, who have reduced the refugees to a depoliticized "object of sociological inquiry and psychiatric correction."[40] In chapter 2, I introduced the term "*militarized* refuge(es)" in order to encapsulate this connection between war studies and refuge(es) studies. I also critically juxtaposed Vietnamese displacement to that of Filipino, Chamorro, and Native American in order to make intelligible the military colonialisms that engulf and link these spaces. Grafting the colonial histories of the Philippines and Guam and the ongoing displacement of indigenous populations onto the history of the Vietnam War also debunks the misguided nostalgia for a "gentler America"—a time of national unity, purity, and innocence—that supposedly preceded the U.S. military involvement in Vietnam, a sentiment that blatantly denies the reality of a bloody, divisive, and disruptive history that included "genocide, slavery, lynchings, the atomic bomb, race riots,"[41] all in the service of empire. This methodology of grafting offers the promise that even deliberately discarded histories will continue to be told as they bump against, intersect with, and route through the lives of kin communities. Finally, I have critically juxtaposed private loss with public commemoration and have shown how this intersection has allowed me to reread Vietnamese refugee commemoration practices in the United States as critical disruptions to the hegemonic American discourse on the war and its refugees.

(A)CROSS(ING) HISTORIES: BAO PHI ON EMERGING TIES AND LIVES

I came to the United States in August 1975 at the age of twelve. At the junior high school that I was first enrolled in, there were white students to be sure, but there were many more black and Latino students whose families were poor, struggling folks. In contrast to the rich America that I had imagined, my school had no computers, no advanced placement courses, and no state-of-the-art science equipment. It was not until much later that I realized that public schools were *not* intended to be equal and that students in nearby schools had resources and opportunities that were simply unavailable and unimaginable to us. Thus it was there, in this economically depressed and Latino-majority town, that I first learned about race and racial disparities in the United States. And as the only Vietnamese in my junior high and high schools, I often had to set aside my Vietnamese background in order to become a part of this racially diverse and largely immigrant community.

As a predominantly working poor population with limited human capital and human resources, many Vietnamese refugees, like my family, have resettled in segregated low-income neighborhoods that have borne the brunt of governmental neglect, social isolation, and persistent poverty. Their location and isolation in these neighborhoods has spawned bitter conflicts but also promising affiliations with similarly marginalized peoples of color. Since the 1960s, scholars and policy makers have wielded the model minority concept as an ideological weapon to chastise and discipline poor black and brown communities for perceived persistent problems of poverty, unemployment, and crime.[42] More insidiously, some researchers suggest that the newly arrived Vietnamese refugees, especially those who live in under-resourced and underserved neighborhoods, succeed precisely because they refuse to adopt the wayward habits of their American neighbors, many of whom are people of color. As an example, Nathan Caplan and his colleagues contend that "the refugees see not only the necessity to rely on their own cultural value system for guidance but also the need to insulate themselves from the behavioral and value standards of their nonrefugee neighbors."[43] James Freeman concurs that Vietnamese refugees "try to insulate themselves from lower-class minorities, whom they associate with low education and poor paying jobs."[44] In their study of second-generation Vietnamese youth living in a poor, biracial New Orleans neighborhood, Min Zhou and Carl Bankston similarly conclude that the most successful Vietnamese youth are those who show strong adherence to traditional family *and* who are not influenced by their African American neighbors.[45] Instead of critically interrogating interminority differentials and relations, these studies collectively represent Vietnamese Americans as "exemplars for other, culturally challenged minorities," thereby encouraging a Vietnamese American subjectivity formed in part through a competitive distancing from other groups of color.[46] Moreover, the focus on interminority competition over scarce resources leaves uninterrogated the reasons for their blighted conditions in the first place.

Because Vietnamese Americans, and Asian Americans more generally, continue to be held up as the model for others to emulate, it is important that we understand how they are racialized relative to (yet different from) other groups of color. In a generative study of black-Korean conflict, Claire

Kim argues that blacks, whites, and Koreans get positioned relative to each other, with blacks portrayed as the pathological underclass, Korean merchants as the hardworking minority, and whites as neutral enforcers of colorblind justice.[47] In another example, Leland Saito shows how interethnic contacts shape the formation of individual groups; in this case, how Asian-Latino interactions help determine what it means to be "Asian American" and "Latino" in the San Gabriel Valley.[48] Writing against the expectation of interminority conflict and competition, these scholars (among others) point to emerging "lines of affiliation, channels of communication, and spaces of transmission" among communities of color that have been forged out of their shared experiences with racialization and underclass stigmatization.[49] In so doing, they explain how the conditions of Asian American lives are connected to and shaped by the condition of others' lives—and how this recognition of interconnectedness can birth new cross-racial communities. The focus on interminority connections thus challenges traditional assumptions of communities based on nationality, ethnicity, and familial ties, and it reveals that the processes of community formation are always socially situated and (re)constituted in relation to historical and material differences.

Focusing on "lines of affiliation," spoken word artist Bao Phi's poetry eloquently calls for the forging of new ties and lives out of the ruins of America's "war zones"—both here and in Southeast Asia.[50] In a "shout-out" to Phi, Ishle Park exclaims that Phi "is on a mission to keep us all knit tight, and to remind us how we are quilted together in this cold country."[51] Park's words nicely encapsulate Phi's raw and rough-edged but also tender and quiet poetry that mixes his fearless politics about race and class with resolute optimism in the power of love and community. Born in Vietnam, Phi fled Vietnam with his family in 1975 and resettled directly in Phillips, a poor Minneapolis neighborhood that was predominantly Native American and African American. As a student in an inner-city school dominated by students of color, Phi became cognizant of race and class privilege—a recurring theme in his poetry—when he met wealthier white students who were bused into his school for "integration":

[I] noticed that they sat around talking about the cars that their parents had just bought for them and all this other stuff while the rest of us were of lower

income. I think that when you're a kid and you grow up around poor people
of color, that's just kind of your life, and then when you meet other people
whose lives are different, you're just like "damn."[52]

Coming of age during the early 1990s, Phi—and subsequently his poetry—
was also deeply affected by the interconnections between race, war, and
violence as manifested in the first Persian Gulf War, the Rodney King
beating, and the Los Angeles riots: "All of these things came to a point
where I could either shut my eyes and not see what was going on or I could
really ask why this was."[53]

In "For Colored Boys in Danger of Sudden Unexplained Nocturnal
Death Syndrome and All the Rest for Whom Considering Suicide Is Not
Enuf,"[54] a poem about growing up as a young man of color in Phillips, Phi
furiously condemns the blighted conditions of his neglected neighborhood but also tenderly discloses the fierce love and loyalty that "we boys,
colored boys" have developed for and with each other in this inner-city
"war zone":

> We boys, colored boys, who ran through the streets
> with heads spinning, languages spilling into summer
> sticking into cracks on the sidewalks,
> pulling up weeds with our laughter.

Growing up in poverty, largely unwanted and forgotten, trying to survive—these multilingual "colored boys" shielded each other against the
raining batons of police brutality and the violence of meaningless and
demeaning work:

> They told us the sky above our heads is the same
> but we knew this wasn't true
> the first time it rained
> batons
> we were the only ones getting wet.
> . . .
> We colored boys, who forged our IDs
> to lie about our age and work for minimum wage
> unpacking dirt-kissed vegetables,
> rotating daily products,
> working to pay bills that misspelled our parents' names.

It is this double move—of calling attention to both the racialized urban poverty and the emerging ties and lives—that keeps Phi's poetry from being read as a depoliticized celebration of multicultural America in which people of all colors embrace each other as equals.

Urban America has also rendered young men of color "ghostly"—leaving their seething presence un-visible and their violent death un-mourned. Phi penned "For Colored Boys in Danger" in part to expose this ghostliness: "how . . . being a young man of color meant . . . not being missed when you passed on":[55]

> I had a dream that we never woke up
> and the world didn't miss us
> the sons of fathers
> who died in their sleep
> hearts trying to keep up to the beating drum
> of a land that did not want them dancing.

Living in a world that does not "want them dancing" and does not miss their passing, these young men of color, "who have all the heart to feel love and none of the words to say it," occupy the position of self-mourners, "hid[ing] each other in the maps of [their] memory." It is there in their memory that they hold fast to each other's fears and dreams, awaiting opportunities for public retellings that sometimes come in the form of suicide/murder as they insist on being "found":

> B____, the only way he could get close to the world
> was to jump down from a bridge
> to embrace it
> like a red-winged angel
> no one came looking for him
> so he went to be found.

It is important to note that, in "For Colored Boys In Danger," Phi connects the "war zone" of urban America to that of Southeast Asia, linking the death of "colored boys" in Phillips to that of Southeast Asian refugee men who succumb to Sudden Unexplained Nocturnal Death Syndrome—a medically unexplainable sudden death that has been associated with war trauma, survivor guilt, and relocation depression:

I had a dream
that we told our stories
in sleep
and the demons came
to sleep on our chests
before we could finish.

This pairing—of the war in Southeast Asia and the war in urban America—makes visible the relationship between global and domestic structures of violence and inequality. In recent years, the best works in Asian American studies have placed the social and political formation of Asians in the United States in dialectical relation to international histories and locations.[56] This innovative body of scholarship, in situating Asian American studies within an "international" frame, rejects the domestication of Asian American studies, displaces the United States as the sole nexus of historical change, and boldfaces the history of U.S. settler colonialism and imperialism in Asia and elsewhere. In connecting the colored boys' suicide to the war-induced Sudden Unexplained Nocturnal Death Syndrome, Phi is suggesting that the U.S. wars in Southeast Asia, haphazard resettlement policies and practices, and neglect of urban neighborhoods are *linked*, and that it is this cumulative violence that has profoundly affected "colored boys" in urban America (boys like Linh Phat Voong, whose stunted life ended with murder-suicide)—both the living and the dead, as well as the living dead. Against these conditions of un-visibility, Phi implores us to ask, "What happened to their dreams?" For it is in the asking that we remember to re-tell their stories so that they would not be "lost to sleep."

Finally, in evoking the Sudden Unexplained Nocturnal Death Syndrome, the chief cause of death among Hmong male refugees in the early 1980s,[57] Phi moves beyond Vietnam(ese) to recount how other Southeast Asian refugees have opened, rearticulated, and enabled new lines of questioning about empire, war, and their aftermath. In so doing, he calls attention to both the joint and the disjoint lives of Southeast Asian refugees. In the past decade, Southeast Asian American studies scholars have charted a new field of study that centers on Cambodia, Laos, and Vietnam, whose shared history of French colonization and U.S. occupation indexes the historical role of the colonizing West in Southeast Asia.[58]

Focusing on loss, displacement, and trauma, this emerging scholarship contributes to the field of critical refugee studies by untangling the rhetoric of U.S. exceptionalism, revealing the historical formations and ongoing renewal of U.S. empire and turning our attention to "issues of war, race and violence" rather than to "questions of identity, assimilation, and the recuperation of history."[59] However, as Khatharya Um reminds us, "the pan-category of 'Southeast Asian/American' has been rendered synonymous with Vietnamese/Americans."[60] The common reference to the U.S. war in Southeast Asia as the Vietnam War, and the privileging of the "Fall of Saigon" as the official war's end, semantically locates that war—and all that it connotes—geographically in Vietnam. By confining the war there, the intertwined yet *differing* political histories and historical trauma of Cambodia and Laos has often been disappeared.[61] To take seriously the range of Southeast Asian experiences and political ideologies, we need to treat Southeast Asia as a historical site, Southeast Asian people as genuine subjects with complex personhood, and the wars in Southeast Asia as having an integrity that is internal to the history and politics of each country.

In the end, *Body Counts* is really about *(a)cross(ing)* histories: across, cross, and crossing histories.[62] My main goals have been to point to lines of convergence—and divergence—of U.S. wars in Southeast Asia, the Pacific Islands, the Middle East, and the U.S. inner city and to highlight the lessons glimpsed therein for our shared future.

.   .   .   .   .

In *Body Counts*, I have examined not only the politics but also the poetics of remembering the Vietnam War by focusing on Vietnamese American memory works that call attention to the things that are seemingly not there or barely there and that imagine beyond the limits of what is already stated to be understandable. *Body Counts* thus mourns the lives that could or would have been and offers rich and varied descriptions of the lives that did emerge out of this history. To engage in war and refugee studies, then, is to listen to "fragmentary testimonies, to barely distinguishable testimonies, to testimonies that never reach us"[63]—that is, to write ghost stories. As tellers of ghost stories, it is imperative that we always look for the "something more" in order to see and bring into being what is usually neglected or made invisible or thought by most to be dead and gone— that is, to always see the living effects of what seems to be over and done with.[64] We need to see, and then to do something with, *the endings that are not over.*[65]

Notes

CHAPTER 1

1. Sturken 1997, 122.
2. Wagner-Pacifici and Schwartz 1991, 381.
3. Yoneyama 2005.
4. M. Nguyen 2012.
5. Nguyên-Vo 2005.
6. In Sept. 1975, more than 1,500 Vietnamese refugees who were waiting in Guam insisted on being repatriated to Vietnam rather than being resettled in the United States. See Lipman 2012.
7. Lipman 2012, 5.
8. General William Westmoreland, commander of the American armed forces in Vietnam, approached the Vietnam War as a "war of attrition": the plan was to kill as many Vietnamese combatants and their civilian supporters as possible, in the hope that the remaining combatants would give up the struggle (Gibson 1986, 155; Spector 1993, 154). To determine if they were winning, American military managers devised elaborate efforts to collect "body counts" of the Vietnamese dead (Lewy 1978, 78–82).
9. Kwon 2006, 4.
10. McGranahan 2006, 580.
11. Nguyen 1997, 607.
12. Sommers et al. 2006, 2–3.

13. Masquelier 2006, 737.

14. Ibid.

15. Trinh 2010, 45.

16. Ibid., 46.

17. See Eve Tuck (2009, 409) for a scathing critique of "damage-centered" research.

18. Edkins and Pin-Fat 2005, 22.

19. DuBois 1993, 4–5. Most scholars have approached the study of Vietnamese flight to and resettlement in the United States as a "crisis." Refugee-camp studies exemplify this crisis model, as researchers repeatedly portray refugees as abject figures who suffer not only the trauma of forced departure but also the boredom, uncertainty, despair, and helplessness induced by camp life. However well intentioned, this crisis model, which fixates on the refugees' purported fragile psychosocial and emotional states, discursively constructs Vietnamese as "passive, immobilized and pathetic." See, e.g., Harding and Looney 1977; Kelly 1977; Chan and Loveridge 1987; Tenhula 1991.

20. Rumbaut 2000, 180.

21. Dunning 1989, 55.

22. Haines 1989.

23. Developed during the peak years of mass immigration from Europe at the turn of the twentieth century, this narrative predicts that, with each succeeding generation, U.S. ethnic groups will improve their economic status and become progressively more similar to the "majority culture." See, e.g., Warner and Srole 1945, 294–95; Park 1950. Although no longer bound by a simplistic assimilationist paradigm, the narrative of immigration has remained "America-centric," with an overwhelming emphasis on the process of becoming American.

24. See, e.g., Caplan, Whitmore, and Bui 1989; Rumbaut and Weeks 1986; Baker and North 1984; Gardner, Robey, and Smith 1985.

25. Finnan 1981, 301.

26. Ibid., 309, 299 (emphasis added).

27. Ibid., 300.

28. Caplan, Whitmore, and Bui 1989, 56.

29. Ibid., 136.

30. Freeman 1996, 69. See also Caplan, Whitmore, and Bui 1989; Caplan, Choy, and Whitmore 1991.

31. Gold and Kibria 1993; Ong and Umemoto 1994. The *Los Angeles Times* has also published several articles on Vietnamese "welfare cheats"; see Arax 1987a and 1987b.

32. Soguk 1999.

33. Ibid., 16.

34. Carruthers 2005, 914.

35. McAlister 2005, xii.

36. Ibid., 5.

37. M. Nguyen 2012.

38. According to Laura Barnett (2002), the "refugee problem" was not recognized as an international issue until after World War I. Responding to the rise in religious and political persecutions in Europe, the first international refugee regime emerged under the League of Nations in 1921. The league, however, created no uniform definition for a refugee, relying instead on an *ad hoc* approach that identified refugees according to group affiliation and national origin. When World War II ended, leaving 30 million people uprooted, the Allies replaced the League of Nations with the United Nations Relief and Reconstruction Agency (UNRRA) in 1944, then with the International Refugee Organization in 1948; both were charged with regularizing the status of the war's refugees. As the refugee problem sparked by World War II persisted, the United Nations established the High Commissioner for Refugees (UNHCR) in January 1951, which soon became a permanent institution that played a fundamental role in the consolidation of future developments and trends in the international refugee regime. A product of the Cold War, the UNHCR was initially Eurocentric in scope, focusing exclusively on the European and World War II origins of the refugee crises.

39. Lippert 1999, 305.

40. Barnett 2002, 245.

41. Salomon 1991; Carruthers 2005, 921.

42. Gibney 2005, 25.

43. Tempo 2008.

44. Barnett 2002, 249.

45. Tempo 2008, 4.

46. The "Fall of Saigon" is a U.S.-specific term that denotes a contained singular event and refuses to acknowledge either the *before* or the *after* of that day. Vietnamese have other names for this day: "ngày giải phóng" (Liberation Day) for Vietnamese in Vietnam; "ngày quốc hận" (Day of National Resentment) and "ngày tưởng niệm" (Day of Commemoration) for Vietnamese in the diaspora.

47. Palmieri 1980, 701. In contrast, in the early 1980s, because the United States was providing massive economic and military aid to the right-wing military regimes in El Salvador and Guatemala, the Reagan administration denied asylum status to hundreds of thousands of Salvadorans and Guatemalans who were fleeing government torture and persecution. In 1984, just under 3 percent of Salvadoran and Guatemalan asylum cases were approved. See Gzesh 2006.

48. Tempo 2008.

49. Palmieri 1980, 701–2.

50. Ibid., 702.

51. Kennedy 1981, 142.

52. Palumbo-Liu 1999, 235.

53. Soguk 1999, 10.

54. Agamben 2002.

55. Ortner 1995, 187.

56. Fujitani, White, and Yoneyama 2001, 5.

57. Arendt 1978.

58. Agamben 2000, 16.

59. Owens 2009.

60. Liu 2002, 9.

61. Soguk 1999, 194.

62. V. Nguyen 2012, 930.

63. Soguk 1999, 15.

64. Malkki 1996, 444.

65. Liu 2002, 9.

66. Edkins and Pin-Fat 2005, 18.

67. Liu 2002, 9.

68. Soguk 1999, 8.

69. Owens 2009, 578–79. Owens's claim is derived from Arendt's discussion of the stateless in *The Origins of Totalitarianism* (1986), in which Arendt proposes the recognition of a supranational "right to have rights" that would guarantee each individual the right to a political community in which one has the right to opinion and action.

70. Ortner 1995, 188.

71. Ibid., 186.

72. Tuck 2009, 417.

73. Soguk 1999, 8.

74. Ortner 1995, 176–77.

75. Malkki 1995a, 3–4.

76. Gordon 1997, 4.

77. Tuck 2009, 416.

78. Ortner 1995, 187.

79. Gordon 1997, 4.

80. Trinh 2010, 47–48.

81. Trinh 1991, 100.

82. Vo 2003, ix; Pham 2003, 136.

83. Kibria 1993. Kibria's findings indicate that Vietnamese women's employment has enhanced egalitarianism within the domestic sphere but that women's earnings have continued to be too meager to sustain their economic independence from men. As a result, working-class Vietnamese women have not used their new resources to radically restructure the traditional family system, only to redefine it in a more fulfilling manner.

84. Chan and Christie 1995; Gold 1992.

85. Truong 1993; Tran 1993; Beevi 1997; Lieu 2000.

86. Valverde 2003; Thai 2003; N. Tran 2003.

87. Chan and Christie 1995, 89.

88. Kumar 2000, xi.

89. McAlister 2005, 209.

90. Viet Thanh Nguyen, personal communication, Apr. 24, 2006. This quote comes from Nguyen's draft of the mission statement for a proposed conference on Southeast Asians in the Diaspora.

91. Kaplan 1993, 11.

92. For some key examples, see Briggs 2002; Streeby 2002; Klein 2003; McAlister 2005; Isaac 2006; Imada 2012.

93. See, e.g., the essays in Appy 2000.

94. Appy 2000, 4.

95. Bradley 2000; Shigematsu and Camacho 2010.

96. Kim 2010, 8.

97. See www.cnn.com/2013/07/01/world/vietnam-war-fast-facts/.

98. Bernd 2009.

99. Kwon 2006, 67.

100. Shigematsu and Camacho 2010, xxvi. Indeed, all of the nation-states from which the largest numbers of U.S. refugees originate—El Salvador, Cuba, Guatemala, Vietnam, Laos, Cambodia, and Somalia—have been deeply disrupted by U.S. "counterinsurgency" actions, anticommunist insurgencies, terrorism counteraction, and peacekeeping operations.

101. Kim 2010, 6.

102. Rowe 1989, 197.

103. Ellison 1981, xii.

104. Gordon 1997, 195.

105. Sturken 1997, 62.

106. Nguyên-Vo 2005, 170.

107. Butler 2004, 32.

108. Ibid., 33.

109. Ibid., 36.

110. Whitlock 2007, 80, 74.

111. Ibid., 79, 78.

112. Kim 2010, 195.

113. Morrison 1989.

114. Gordon 1997, 36.

115. Kim 2010, 235

116. Um 2012.

117. McGranahan 2006.

118. Cho 2008, 17.

119. Felman and Laub 1991, xvi.

120. Chuh 2003, 151.

121. Tadiar 2009, 5–6.

122. DuBois 1993, 5.
123. Pelaud 2005.
124. Trinh 2010, 43.
125. lê 2003, 122.
126. Gordon 1997, 7–8.

CHAPTER 2

1. My mother remembers very few details of those final days and cannot recall the exact date of our departure, only that it was "a few days" before the Fall of Saigon.

2. Liu, Lamanna, and Murata 1979, 80.

3. Sahara 2012.

4. Soguk 1999, 189.

5. Jolly 2010.

6. Liu, Lamanna, and Murata 1979, 80.

7. Shigematsu and Camacho 2010, xvii.

8. Ibid., xx.

9. Harkavey 1982, 17.

10. Francisco 1973, 2.

11. Kimlick 1990.

12. Ibid. During 1978, following negotiations that had lasted on and off since the early 1970s, the two governments agreed to establish Philippine sovereignty over former American bases in the country, and thus the Clark Air Base Command of the Armed Forces of the Philippines came into being, following the signing of a revised Military Bases Agreement on Jan. 7, 1979.

13. Padlan 2005.

14. Garcia 1967, 55, 92.

15. Padlan 2005.

16. Gonzalez 2010, 67.

17. GlobalSecurity.Org 2011a.

18. Drogin 1992.

19. The information for this paragraph is derived from Rogers 1995, 206–33.

20. The information for the first two sentences of this paragraph is derived from Rogers 1995, 214–15.

21. Bevacqua 2010, 34.

22. Lutz 2010.

23. Shigematsu and Camacho 2010, xv.

24. Moos and Morrison 2005, 34.

25. Ibid., 33.

26. Vasquez 2001; Tobin, Laehr, and Hilgenberg 1978.

27. Vasquez 2001.

28. Moos and Morrison 2005, 33.

29. Tobin 1975.

30. Bevacqua 2010, 34.

31. Moos and Morrison 2005, 34.

32. Ibid., 38.

33. Ibid., 33.

34. Guttery and Guttery 2000.

35. Knickrehm 2010.

36. Mackie 1998, 57.

37. "Guam: The First Refuge" 1976.

38. Moos and Morrison 2005, 34.

39. Carruthers 2005, 929.

40. Ibid., 929–30.

41. Dunnaway 2008, 119.

42. Lipman 2012, 3–4 (emphasis added).

43. Berryman 2001, 17.

44. Denger 2013; Berryman 2001, 17.

45. Carrico 1987.

46. "Marine Corps Base Camp Pendleton" 2013.

47. Berryman 2001, 17.

48. Jolly 2010.

49. Ibid.

50. Wandering Chopsticks 2010.

51. Jolly 2010.

52. "Refugees" 1975.

53. Chapman 2010.

54. "Refugees" 1975.

55. Ibid.

56. For Graham's obituary, see www.findagrave.com/cgi-bin/fg.cgi?page=gr&GRid=42854173.

57. Cavanaugh and Finn 2010.

58. Malkki 1995b, 499.

59. Utts 2012.

60. Rogers 1995, 252.

61. U.S. Naval Hospital 2013.

62. Broyhill 2003.

63. Lutz 2009, 15.

64. Thompson 2010, 62; Rogers 1995, 242.

65. Thompson 2010, 62.

66. Rogers 1995, 243.

67. Ibid., 252.

68. Ibid.

69. Thompson 2010, 62–63.

70. Denger 2013.

71. GlobalSecurity.Org 2011b.

72. Turley 1987, 87.

73. Young 1991.

74. Chan 1991, 56.

75. Ibid., 51.

76. Sachs 2010, xi.

77. Manney 2006.

78. GlobalSecurity.Org 2011c (emphasis added).

79. KPBS 2002.

80. Ibid.

81. Sachs 2010, 190.

82. KPBS 2002.

83. Sachs 2010, 190.

84. Ibid., 207–8.

85. Ibid., 208.

86. KPBS 2002.

87. Manney 2006.

88. Doc Bernie Duff declined permission to have his painting, "Welcome Home," used in this publication because he disagrees with its critique of the Operation Babylift Project. In an email correspondence dated Apr. 23, 2013, Duff stated that he has to decline permission because "I am among those people who believe that what was done during that operation was, if fact, done so as a humanitarian effort and more good has come from it than bad. I have spoken to many of the orphans, living here in the U.S. and abroad and I agree [with] what was done."

89. All quotes are from the video advertisement of the thirty-fifth anniversary event; see www.youtube.com/watch?v=J87rgk33X84&feature=player_embedded.

90. Naval Historical Center 2009. The USS Midway was a key participant in U.S. naval actions during the Vietnam War. The first and last air-to-air kills in Vietnam were made by aircraft flying from the Midway.

91. Bharath 2010.

92. Quotes are from the video advertisement of the thirty-fifth anniversary event; see www.youtube.com/watch?v=J87rgk33X84&feature=player_embedded.

93. Bharath 2010.

94. Ibid.

95. Ibid.

96. Cavanaugh and Walsh 2010.

97. Transcript of an interview with Shragge on KPBS (San Diego), www.kpbs.org/news/2010/apr/29/uss-midway-played-significant-role-vietnam-war/.

98. M. Nguyen 2012.

99. McGranahan 2006, 580.

100. Cavanaugh and Walsh 2010.

101. Ibid.

102. Chan 1991, 113.

103. Vo 2009, 162.

104. Lipman 2012.

105. Lowe 1996, 158.

106. See Espiritu and Wolf 2013, 2.

CHAPTER 3

1. Composed in 1962 by Trịnh Công Sơn, one of Vietnam's most esteemed composers, "Biển Nhớ" is a poignant song about lost love.

2. Lin + Lam 2010.

3. Reyes 1999, 45–46.

4. United Nations High Commissioner for Refugees 2000, 81.

5. Tran 2012.

6. See, e.g., Harding and Looney 1977, 407–11; Kelly 1977; Chan and Loveridge 1987.

7. DuBois 1993, 5.

8. Kunz 1973, 133; Liu, Lamanna, and Murata 1979; Morrison and Moos 1982.

9. DuBois 1993, 4 (emphasis added).

10. Chan and Loveridge 1987, 757.

11. Feldman 2012.

12. Tadiar 2009, 6.

13. Vance 1983.

14. United Nations High Commissioner for Refugees 2000, 82.

15. See www.refugeecamps.net/Bidong.html, accessed June 2, 2013.

16. United Nations High Commissioner for Refugees 2000, 84.

17. During May–June 1979, Malaysia alone expelled about 25,000 boat people from its shores. See Stein 1979.

18. United Nations High Commissioner for Refugees 2000, 83.

19. Sahara 2012, chap. 3.

20. United Nations High Commissioner for Refugees 2000, 84–85.

21. Sahara 2012, chap. 3.

22. Thompson 2010, 163.

23. Robinson 2004, 320; Sahara 2012, chap. 3.

24. United Nations High Commissioner for Refugees 2000, 86.

25. Robinson 2004, 320.

26. Bari 1999, 489–91.

27. As Larry Thompson (2010, 218) reports, "If one refugee was approved for resettlement after telling an interviewer that the communists killed his water buffalo, one could be certain that the others would tell the same story."

28. Reyes 1999, 55; Betts 2006, 38.

29. The low resettlement rate and the threat of repatriation contributed to the drop in the number of boat people fleeing Vietnam. In 1989, when the CPA was first implemented, roughly 70,000 Vietnamese sought asylum in Southeast Asia; by 1992, only 41 did. At its final meeting in Geneva on Mar. 5 and 6, 1996, the steering committee of the International Conference on Indo-Chinese Refugees announced the CPA's formal closure as of June 30, 1996. See U.S. General Accountability Office 1996, 4–6.

30. Sautman 1985, 484–85.

31. U.S. General Accountability Office 1996, 33.

32. Betts 2006, 40.

33. Bari 1999, 503.

34. Ibid., 503–4.

35. Sindt 2004, 94–95. Other refugees were simply deemed unfit for life in the West due to their health records, criminal histories, or lack of education.

36. Smith 2004, 38.

37. Reyes 1999, 32.

38. U.S. General Accountability Office 1985, 11.

39. Hitchcox 1990, 262.

40. Doan 2004. The Palawan camp was declared closed in 1996. With the help of the Catholic Church in the Philippines and financial support from Vietnamese communities around the world, a special village, named Viet-Ville, was set up by the local government of Puerto Princesa to house the approximately 1,500 leftover Vietnamese refugees who did not want to return to Vietnam.

41. Project Ngoc 1988, 6.

42. Diller 1988, 11.

43. Malkki 1995b, 498.

44. Doan 2004.

45. Thompson 2010, 217.

46. The total share of U.S contributions to construction of the PRPC was $15 million, or about 39 percent. See U.S. General Accountability Office, 1981.

47. Thompson 2010, 166.

48. U.S. General Accountability Office 1981.

49. Barr 2011.

50. Ong 2003, 59; Fasick 1981, 9.

51. U.S. General Accountability Office 1981, 11.

52. Vo 2009.

53. Reyes 1999, 45–46.

54. U.S. General Accountability Office 1981, 12.

55. Feldman 2012.

56. Ong 2003, 52–53.

57. Ibid., 55.

58. Although the PRPC had considerably more amenities than other first-asylum camps, including a community center where movies were shown, living conditions were still barely tolerable. As a former PRPC resident recalled: "The first disheartening sight we had was the apartment itself. The building was made of light material; walls were thin concrete and the roof of corrugated steel. There was a yard without trees in front. In the back there was a shallow moat full of black foul-smelling water that probably was draining from some sewage nearby. As we entered the apartment we were overwhelmed by a strong smell of human feces. . . . The condition of the communal outhouses, about ten yards away, later gave us an explanation as to why some people had elected not to use them" (Vo 2009, 154).

59. Feldman 2012, 155.

60. Burton and Goldstein 1993, 72.

61. Diller 1988, 4.

62. Burton and Goldstein 1993, 79.

63. Law 2011, 122; Reyes 1999, 22.

64. Project Ngoc 1988, 11.

65. Agier 2010, 36.

66. Hansen 2011, 87.

67. Law 2011, 123–24.

68. Hansen 2011, 87.

69. Vo 2009, 146.

70. Law 2011, 123.

71. Sahara 2012, chap. 3.

72. Nyers 2010, 1069–71; Rajaram and Grundy-Warr 2004, 39.

73. Childs 2009, 276.

74. Cited in Ibid.

75. Childs 2009, 285–86.

76. Dayan 2011, 63.

77. Childs 2009, 289.

78. Knudsen 1985, 40.

79. Diller 1988, 50–51.

80. Ibid.; Project Ngoc 1988, 8.

81. Project Ngoc 1988, 8.

82. Thompson 2010, 217.

83. Diller 1988, 41.

84. Robinson 2004, 323.

85. Law 2011, 125.

86. Feldman 2012, 156–57; Dudley 2010, 2.

87. Malkki 1996; Dudley 2010, 8.

88. Dudley 2010.

89. The website for the Vietnamese American Oral History Project is vaohp.lib.uci.edu.

90. See, e.g., www.youtube.com/watch?v=PuWBYW2yZ6Y.

91. lê 2003.

92. See https://sites.google.com/a/bataan.gov.ph/tourism/interest/bataan-technology-park-inc.

93. See ibid.

94. Doan 2004, 56.

95. Ibid., 55.

96. Chan and Loveridge 1987, 749.

97. Project Ngoc was a U.C. Irvine student-led organization whose decade of activism (1987–97) raised awareness and support for the plight of the Vietnamese refugees detained in refugee camps throughout Asia (including Hong Kong, Thailand, Indonesia, Malaysia, and the Philippines). One of the group's many activities included sending student volunteers to refugee camps in Hong Kong, Thailand, and the Philippines to teach English classes and to work with the refugees. The organization's photographs of the camps are housed in the Project Ngoc Collection in the nationally recognized Southeast Asian Archive, which is part of the U.C. Irvine Libraries Special Collections and Archive Department.

98. Hansen 2011, 87.

99. Chan and Loveridge 1987, 749.

100. Doan 2004, 36.

101. Ibid., 8.

102. Reyes 1999, 26–27.

103. Reyes 1999, 42; www.refugeecamps.net/BAStory.html (accessed June 2, 2013).

104. See www.refugeecamps.net/GalangStory.html (accessed June 2, 2013).

105. Doan 2004, 80.

106. See www.refugeecamps.net/BAStory.html (accessed June 2, 2013).

107. "Guam: The First Refuge" 1976, 9.

108. Espiritu 2008, 50–54.

109. Beswick 2001.

110. L. Nguyen 2012.

111. Ha 2012.

112. Tran 2012, 82.

113. Ibid., 88–89.

114. Ibid., 95–96.

115. Ibid., 109.

116. Long 2012.

117. See www.refugeecamps.net/Songkhla.html (accessed June 13, 2013).

118. Vo Dang 2011.

119. Duran 2012.

120. See www.flickr.com/photos/tinyhaus/4290909309/in/pool-1310226@N25/ (accessed Dec. 20, 2012).

121. Ibid.

122. See www.flickr.com/photos/tinyhaus/4357779803/in/pool-1310226@N25/ (accessed Dec. 20, 2012).

123. *Stand By Me* is a popular 1986 American coming-of-age drama-comedy film directed by Rob Reiner. It is a story about the adventures of four boys, inseparable friends, who set out in search of a dead body.

124. See www.flickr.com/groups/1310226@N25/discuss/72157635468430757/ (accessed Decc 20, 2012).

125. See www.flickr.com/groups/1310226@N25/discuss/72157623437225314/ (accessed June 6, 2013).

126. Reyes 1999.

127. Thompson 2010, 224.

128. Vo 2009, 155–56.

129. See www.pulaubidong.org/about/pulau-bidong-island/ (accessed June 2, 2013).

130. Reyes 1999, 26–27.

131. See www.pulaubidong.org/about/pulau-bidong-island/ (accessed June 2, 2013).

132. Quoted in Hardy 1991.

133. Vo 2009, 155–56.

134. Doan 2004, 103.

135. Vo 2009, 155–56.

136. See www.flickr.com/photos/tinyhaus/4358525574/in/pool-1310226@N25 (accessed Dec. 20, 2012).

137. Long 2012.

138. Doan 2004, 32.

139. Reyes 1999, 26–27.

140. Quoted in Hardy 1991.

141. See www.pulaubidong.org/about/pulau-bidong-island/; www.terengganutourism.com/pulau_bidong.htm (accessed June 2, 2013).

142. Reyes 1999, 26–27.

143. Ibid., 30.

144. Hitchcox 1990, 231.

145. Reyes 1999, 30.

146. Ibid., 49.

147. Agamben 1998, 83.

148. Ibid.

149. Feldman 2012.

150. Agamben 1998.

151. Isin and Rygiel 2007.

152. Rajaram and Grundy-Warr 2004, 37.

153. Mortland 1987, 386.

154. Isin and Rygiel 2007, 186.

155. Ibid., 193; Pugliese 2002.

156. Nyers 2010, 1072–73, 1089.

157. Isin and Rygiel 2007, 186.

158. Ibid., 184.

159. Robinson 2004, 323.

160. Law 2011, 126–27.

161. Burton and Goldstein 1993, 75.

162. Law 2011, 126–27; Gargan 1996; Inquirer Wire Services 1996.

163. Tsang 2004, 104. I thank Pierrette Hondagneu-Sotelo for insisting that I
pay attention to the signs of life in these artworks that reveal the refugees' creative capacities to live, survive, and maybe even thrive in the camps.

164. Agier 2010, 29.

165. DuBois 1993, 4 (emphasis added).

166. Diamant 1997, 109.

CHAPTER 4

1. Chomsky 1987, 225.

2. For a brief timeline of the U.S. war in Vietnam, see www.pbs.org/
battlefieldvietnam/timeline/index.html.

3. McAlister 2005, 209.

4. Brinsfield 1998.

5. Rose 1985, 205.

6. Sturken 1997, 117.

7. Nguyen 2002, 113.

8. Sturken 1997; Rowe 1989; Nguyen 2002.

9. I thank Jody Blanco for this point.

10. In 2000, a Gallup poll found that, though 70 percent of Americans knew
the United States had lost the Vietnam War, nearly 20 percent believed incor-
rectly that U.S. troops had fought on the side of North Vietnam. Underscoring
the generational disconnect, Americans over the age of 30 were more able than
younger respondents to place the United States correctly on the side of South
Vietnam. www.sad17.k12.me.us/teachers/bburns/com/documents/ttc/gallup_
poll_on_vietnam.htm.

11. McAlister 2005, 186; Sturken 1997, 143.

12. Sturken 1997, 122–23.

13. Bacevich 2005.

14. Johnson 2004a.

15. Johnson 2004b.

16. President George H. W. Bush first enunciated his vision of the "New World Order" in a speech before a joint session of Congress in Sept. 1990 and then in a State of the Union address in Jan. 1991.

17. Johnson 2004a.

18. Ibid.; Bacevich 2005; "U.S. Military Bases and Empire" 2002.

19. See, e.g., http://articles.latimes.com/2000/apr/28/news/ss-24829.

20. Rathi 2005; "Vietnam Celebrates War's End" 2005; Lamb 2005; Cheng 2005.

21. Paddock and Tran 2005.

22. Richter 2005.

23. Ibid.

24. Johnson 2000, 19–23.

25. Sturken 1997, 1. See also Yoneyama 1999.

26. Sturken 1997, 2.

27. Yoneyama 1999, 33, 28.

28. Sturken 2001, 33; Fujitani, White, and Yoneyama 2001, 2.

29. Yoneyama 1999, 32.

30. Ibid.

31. Van Dijk 1991; Hall et al. 1978; Martindale 1986.

32. Van Dijk 1991, 10.

33. An analysis of the coverage of the thirty-fifth anniversary from the same newspapers and magazines yielded only thirty-two articles: four from the *Los Angeles Times*; seven from the *New York Times;* two from the *Washington Post;* eight from the *Orange County Register;* five from the *San Diego Union Tribune;* five from the *San Jose Mercury News;* one from *Time Magazine;* and none from *Newsweek.* Of the thirty-two articles, four focused on the American veterans; fourteen on Vietnamese refugees; eleven on U.S. rescue efforts during the Fall of Saigon; and three on Vietnam's friendship with the United States. Collectively, the articles confirm that the figure of the grateful and assimilated Vietnamese refugee has become the familiar featured evidence of the appropriateness of U.S. military actions in Vietnam and elsewhere. Some examples of the trope of the grateful Vietnamese: "To her, the journey was worth it. Even if she had died, it would still have been worth it, Lan says now. 'We didn't come here for money, food or nourishment,' she says. 'We came here for freedom. Here, we can live our lives and do what we want. And no one can put you in jail for that'" (Bharath 2010). "These people excel in school, love our country, speak English fluently, demand no special rights and privileges, pay their taxes, serve on our juries and carry their civic burdens. Last Fourth of July at Mass I was touched firsthand by

the patriotism and gratitude of these people. That day an elderly Vietnamese grandfather with his three grandsons sat next to me. Each wore a red tie, white shirt and blue pants. They were proud to be Americans" (Buckley 2010). "Pham is yet another golden product of the American immigrant dream, a member of what is among the largest diasporas in modern history—the Vietnamese 'boat people'. . . . 'The American soldiers loved kids,' she said. 'They were tall, nice-looking guys who would give us chocolate and gum'" (Newman 2010). I thank my research assistant Sally Le for her work in compiling these articles.

34. McAlister 2005, 191.

35. Wagner-Pacifici and Schwartz 1991, 392.

36. Brinsfield 1998.

37. See www.sad17.k12.me.us/teachers/bburns/com/documents/ttc/gallup_poll_on_vietnam.htm.

38. McAlister 2005, 237.

39. The quotes, in order, are from Lamb 2000; Turan 2000; Thomas 2000; and Goldstein 2000.

40. Silva 2001.

41. The quotes, in order, are from Prochnau 2000; Lamb 2000; Turan 2000; and Templer 2000.

42. Arnett 2000a.

43. McAlister 2005, 209.

44. Lessner 2000; King 2000; Sauer 2000.

45. Jensen 2000.

46. Mariscal 1999, 20–21; Appy 1993, 28–30.

47. Briggs 2003.

48. I thank Lisa Yoneyama for this point. In recent years, soldiers of color have also been held up as representatives of the nation. However, as in the case of Colin Powell, he represented the nation "not because the United States was figured as black but because it was figured as open-minded, as multicultural, as pluralist" (McAlister 2005, 255).

49. Fujitani, White, and Yoneyama 2001, 5.

50. Silva 2001, 423.

51. The quotes, in order, are from McCombs 2000; "Bittersweet Remembrance" 2000; and Goldsborough 2000.

52. Lamb 2000.

53. Vogel 2000.

54. Ibid.; Prochnau 2000; Karnow 2000.

55. Vogel 2000; Prochnau 2000.

56. Tomb 2000; Morello 2000.

57. Chandrasekaran 2000b; McCombs 2000.

58. Chandrasekaran 2000b.

59. Cohen 2000a.

60. From 1961 to 1971, U.S. forces sprayed approximately twenty million gallons of Agent Orange and other herbicides over 10 percent of the land area of what was then South Vietnam. The Vietnamese who were exposed to the herbicide suffered numerous health problems, from liver damage and severe physical deformities to heart diseases and cancer, which shortened their life spans considerably. The ecological effects were also devastating: rivers and underground water were contaminated; forests and jungles were denuded; and animals that inhabited these areas became extinct (Cohn 2009).

61. Chandrasekaran 2000c.

62. Minzesheimer 2001; Fujitani, White, and Yoneyama 2001.

63. Karnow 2000.

64. Cohen 2000b; Becker 2000.

65. Cohen 2000b.

66. Palumbo-Liu 1999, 235.

67. I thank Lisa Yoneyama for this argument (personal correspondence, Jan. 25, 2005).

68. White House 2003.

69. Ong 2003, 12.

70. In a widely publicized 1966 article published in the *New York Times Magazine,* anthropologist William Petersen coined the term *model minority* to refer to Japanese Americans who, despite being a minority group who suffered wartime incarceration, still managed to gain upward mobility, "leading generally affluent, and for the most part, highly Americanized life. . . . [T]here is no parallel to their success story" (Petersen 1966, 38). See also "Success Story" 1966.

71. Ong 2003, 77. It is important to note that, though Asian Americans are lauded for their alleged successes, they continue to face white racism in the political, economic, and social arenas as well as white resentment and violence for being "too successful." See Okihiro 1994, chap. 2; Caplan, Whitmore, and Bui 1989, 136.

72. Freeman 1996, 69; See also Caplan, Choy, and Whitmore 1991.

73. Freeman 1996, 9.

74. Caplan, Choy, and Whitmore 1991, 138.

75. Zhou and Bankston 1998.

76. The *Washington Post, New York Times,* and *San Diego Union* had no Vietnamese American writers. In contrast, 30–40 percent of the articles in the *Los Angeles Times, Orange County Register,* and *San Jose Mercury News* were authored or coauthored by Vietnamese American writers.

77. Dao 2000.

78. Since the end of the Vietnam War in 1975, the current government of Vietnam has categorically refused to incorporate South Vietnamese perspectives on the war or to provide any critical evaluation of the war, particularly regarding the violence committed by northern troops on the people of South Vietnam. See Nguyên-Vo 2005.

79. Vo Dang 2005.

80. Nguyên-Vo 2005, 172.

81. Karnow 2000.

82. Wexler 1992.

83. Ibid., 19–26.

84. Arnett 2000b.

85. Ibid. Other examples of "would have been" stories: Nguyen 2000a and 2000b; Curnutte 2000.

86. Curnutte 2000.

87. Gold and Tran 2000a.

88. Gold and Kibria 1993; Ong and Umemoto 1994. See also Arax 1987b.

89. Pan and Ly 2000 (emphasis added).

90. Alexander and Mohanty 1997, xxx.

91. Silva 2005.

92. Tran 2000.

93. Martelle and Tran 2000; "Protestors Urge Boycott" 2000; Harris 2000; Hong 2000; Truong 2000.

94. "House Passes Resolution Remembering the Fall of Saigon" (press release, www.house.gov/royce/vietnamfall.p.htm, posted June 19, 2001).

95. Ibid.; Curnutte 2000; Mangaliman 2000.

96. Alexander and Mohanty 1997, xxix, xxxiii.

97. Fiske 2000, 324.

98. Karnow 2000.

99. White House 2003.

100. Fujitani 2001; McAlister 2005.

101. Sturken 1997, 113; McAlister 2005, chap. 6.

102. Sevrens 2000.

103. Ahmad 2002.

104. Leahy 2000.

105. Bush 2001.

106. For instance, "The war took everything from the Nguyens that a war can take, and paradoxically, gave [their daughter] Janet everything—American schools, American opportunity, American affluence and indulgence" (Leahy 2000).

107. Yoneyama 2005, 886.

108. Sturken 1997, 122.

CHAPTER 5

1. Nor did one speak of men like my uncles Minh and Hùng, who spent most of their youth in "reeducation camps" and returned home broken men. Once amiable and hardworking, Uncle Minh had turned into an angry and unemploy-

able man after more than a decade in the camp. Uncle Hùng, a popular young man with natural good looks and charm, was sent to the camp at the young age of seventeen. When he was released about six years later, he was no longer the same carefree person, and he eventually died of alcoholism.

2. Tai 2001a, 191.

3. Nguyên-Vo 2005.

4. Butler 2004, 30.

5. Tai 2001b, 228.

6. Ibid.

7. Tai 2001a, 191.

8. Gordon 1997, 63.

9. Ibid., 17–23, 63.

10. Nguyên-Vo 2005, 159.

11. Atkinson 2007, 521.

12. Zizek 2006. I thank Nguyễn-võ Thu-hương for calling my attention to Zizek's work on the parallax and for suggesting that I make more explicit my argument about the public and private divide in memory.

13. Gordon 1997, 112, 124.

14. The figure of the 200,000 ARVN dead is from Beidler 2007, 306.

15. Tai 2001a, 177.

16. Nguyên-Vo 2005, 160.

17. Beidler 2007, 306.

18. Butler 2004, 34.

19. Beidler 2007, 315.

20. Ibid.

21. Brigham 2007.

22. Nguyên-Vo 2005, 161. As Nguyên-Vo Thu Huong recalls: "I remember South Vietnam as a place where political dissent was very alive against first Diem, then Thieu, and the Americans, and also many independent views against the North's war-making in the South. And Vietnamese suffered or prospered at the hands of the U.S. and the governments of the two Vietnams in myriad ways" (2005, 171).

23. Davey 2009.

24. Herman 2012.

25. Ibid.

26. See www.gopetition.com/petitions/please-return-to-the-initial-texas-capitol-vietnam-mon.html. By Mar. 14, 2013, the petition had generated 314 signatures. However, the executive committee decided to proceed with the revised version of the monument, with the South Vietnamese soldier omitted, and celebrated its groundbreaking that same month.

27. Herman 2012.

28. Nguyen 2004, 157.

29. Ibid., 159.

30. Hicks 2001; LeTran 2002.

31. Nguyen 2004, 159.

32. LeTran 2002.

33. Nguyen 2004, 157.

34. M. Tran 2003.

35. Nguyen 2004, 159.

36. Ibid., 153.

37. Quoted in Reyes 2003.

38. Socolovsky 2004.

39. See, e.g., http://legacymultimedia.com/2012/03/05/our-top-six-online-memorial-websites/, accessed Mar. 25, 2013.

40. Socolovsky 2004, 469.

41. Haskins 2007, 405.

42. Palfrey and Gasser 2008.

43. Featherstone 2006, 595.

44. Lê Espiritu 2013, chap. 2.

45. Gordon 1997, 64.

46. Ibid., 66.

47. Ibid., 110.

48. Socolovsky 2004.

49. Nguyên-Vo 2005, 170.

50. Barthes 1982, 20.

51. Ibid., 26.

52. Gordon 1997, 107.

53. Ibid., 102.

54. Email interview with Timothy Pham, Mar. 24, 2013.

55. Blight 2001.

56. Nguyên-Vo 2005, 157.

57. Enloe 1990, 454.

58. Nguyên-Vo 2005; Tai 2001a.

59. See www.themovingwall.org, accessed Feb. 13, 2013.

60. These search engines include Yahoo, Bing!, Ask, AOL, MyWebSearch, Blekko, Lycos, Dogpile, Webcrawler, Info, Infospace, Search, Excite, and Goodsearch. I thank my research assistant, Sally Le, for her help in compiling this database.

61. VNQDD has its own webpage, which is much more extensive and is exclusively in Vietnamese.

62. Tucker 2000.

63. Although my uncle did not commit suicide on Apr. 30, 1975, his widely publicized death at the hands of the Communists is repeatedly lumped in with the deaths of these high-ranking officers.

64. Email interview with Michael Do, Mar. 23, 2013. In 2009, his website (michaelpdo.com) ranked in the top 15 percent of the more than 10 million web pages based on the number of readers.

65. Email interview with Timothy Pham, Mar. 24, 2013.

66. I thank Nguyễn-võ Thu-hương for this insight.

67. Nguyen van Nga, Canada, Mar. 23, 2008, translated from Vietnamese.

68. www.vietquoc.com/INTRODUC.HTM, accessed Mar. 24, 2013.

69. See http://namrom64.blogspot.com/2012/08/nhung-vi-tuong-vnch-tu-sat-30041975.htm, accessed Mar. 23, 2013.

70. Nora 1989.

71. Beidler 2007, 317.

72. Anderson 1991.

73. Benjamin 1973.

74. Azaryahu and Foote 2008.

75. Alderman 2000, 674.

76. Lefebvre 1992; Alderman 2000 and 2003.

77. Gade 2003; Azaryahu 1996.

78. Alderman 2000, 674.

79. Nguyên-Vo 2005, 160.

80. Herman 1999, 76.

81. Yeoh 2003.

82. Wood 1997; Wood 2006, 32–33.

83. Meyers 2006, 68. Eden is now the name of the new, posh shopping/office/residence building owned by Vietnam's largest conglomerate, Vin Com, which evicted residents and demolished the old plaza in 2010.

84. See www.fairfaxtimes.com/article/20110930/ENTERTAINMENT/7093 09757&template=fairfaxTimes, accessed May 10, 2012.

85. The information for this sentence and the rest of this paragraph is from Wood 2006, 25–26.

86. Meyers 2006. Anticommunism appears to be a widely shared sentiment among diasporic Vietnamese who left Vietnam after the Fall of Saigon. For example, in France, the older wave of Vietnamese immigrants who came before 1975 did not share the same anticommunist fervor as the Vietnamese refugees who arrived after the end of the Vietnam War. See Skaife 2011.

87. Wood 2006, 37.

88. Wood 1997.

89. See www.fairfaxtimes.com/article/20110930/ENTERTAINMENT/7093 09757&template=fairfaxTimes, accessed May 10, 2012.

90. Meyers 2006.

91. Wood 2006, 23.

92. Email interview with Alan Frank, Mar. 4, 2013.

93. Nguyên-Vo 2005, 167.

94. Khalili 2005, 39.

95. Alderman 2003.

96. Alderman 2000, 675.

97. Alderman 2003.

98. Phone interview conducted by Evyn Lê Espiritu, Mar. 3, 2013.

99. Email interview conducted by Evyn Lê Espiritu, Mar. 4, 2013.

100. See www.fairfaxtimes.com/article/20110930/ENTERTAINMENT/7093 09757&template=fairfaxTimes, accessed May 10, 2012. Note the illogic of his statement: he grafted the nationalist discourse of military defense of the South to the immigrant discourse of gratitude; yet, had the generals succeeded in defending the Republic of Vietnam, Vietnamese refugees like himself would not have had to leave for America. I thank Nguyễn-võ Thu-hương for pointing this out.

101. See www.washingtonpost.com/local/trafficandcommuting/months-after-police-raid-eden-centers-vietnamese-community-worried-about-image/2012/03/30/gIQA5paTlS_story_1.html, accessed May 10, 2012.

102. See http://pigsnblanket.blogspot.com/2010/01/eden-center.html, accessed May 11, 2012.

103. See www.yvonnecaruthers.com/main/Blog/Entries/2012/10/8_withing _walking_distance_3,_Eden_Center.html, accessed May 11, 2012.

104. See http://adventurecreature.wordpress.com/category/eden-center/, accessed May 11, 2012.

105. See http://dcist.com/2007/10/out_of_eden_cen.php, accessed May 11, 2012.

106. See http://sights2cplaces2b.blogspot.com/2011/05/eden-center.html, accessed May 11, 2012.

107. See www.midweek.com/exploring-the-chesapeake-region/, accessed May 11, 2012.

108. See www.flickr.com/photos/mjlaflaca/296076637/, accessed May 11, 2012.

109. Gordon 1997, 22.

110. Nguyên-Vo 2005, 170–71.

111. The information in this paragraph is culled from Ly 2000.

112. Ly 2000.

113. Ong and Meyer 2008; Duong and Pelaud 2012.

114. Ong and Meyer 2008, 95.

115. Duong and Pelaud 2012, 251–52.

116. Khalili 2005.

117. The list includes Lieutenant Colonel Vương Văn Trổ, Nguyễn Sĩ Tấn, American Advisory Lieutenant Colonel Craig Mandeville, Major Lê Nguyễn Thiện Truyền, Trần Văn Khiết, Captain Phạm Văn Tiết, and Mr. Diệp Bửu Long (former deputy chief of Province Chương Thiện).

118. "Phu Nhân Cố Đại Tá Hồ Ngọc Cẩn" 2010. In the text below, I have translated all her statements, spoken in Vietnamese, into English.

119. According to interviews conducted by Evyn Lê Espiritu, my uncle's remains had been moved at least four times: "After Colonel Cẩn was publicly executed, his body was driven off and buried in an unmarked grave. However, a loyal friend followed the car and unobtrusively marked the grave so that Colonel Cẩn's parents could at least honor their fallen son. Later though, the government decided to raze the cemetery. Colonel Cẩn's relatives went to ask for his remains. . . . They then transferred the remains to a Church cemetery in Long Xuyên. But he remained there only a year, until that cemetery was leveled as well. The family then had to move Colonel Cẩn's body to private land: a relative's place. Finally in 1995, Colonel Cẩn's wife and son sent money home for the family to send his remains on to the United States. Thus Colonel Cẩn's remains were dug up once again, cremated, and carried to the U.S." See Lê Espiritu 2013.

120. lê 2003, 122.

121. Gordon 1997, 4–5.

CHAPTER 6

1. Cubilié 2005, xi.
2. Shigetmatsu and Camacho 2010, xxvii; Enloe 1990.
3. Williams 1977, 132.
4. Eagleton 1991, 48.
5. Williams 1977, 129.
6. Ibid., 131.
7. Burchardt 1993.
8. Hirsch 2008.
9. Hirsch 1996, 659.
10. Hirsch 2008, 107, 109.
11. Hirsch and Spitzer 2003, 257.
12. Um 2012, 842.
13. We interviewed Vietnamese Americans in these counties: San Diego, Riverside, Orange, and Los Angeles. I thank the following transcribers: Maya Espiritu, Evyn Espiritu, Niko Arranz, Mimosa Tonnu, Hao Tam, and Sally Le.
14. Seidman 2012, 9.
15. Both of the preceding quotes are from Cho 2008, 17.
16. Hirsch 2008, 112.
17. Espiritu and Wolf 2013.
18. Le 2005, 22.
19. Nguyen-Lam 2008, 2.
20. Ibid.

21. Ibid. In 2002, at the urging of educators, community leaders, and law enforcement officers, the California Legislature passed AB 78, which emphasized the need for schools to include the Southeast Asian immigration experience in their social history curriculum. However, the bill provided no funding to ensure that instruction of these subjects would actually be implemented.

22. To protect the privacy of the individuals we interviewed, I have given them fictitious names.

23. Vo Dang 2008.

24. Wajnryb 2001, 51.

25. Nagata 1993; Sturken 1997; Neumann 1997; Hirsch 2008; Oikawa 2012; Um 2012.

26. *History and Memory* 1991.

27. Wajnryb 2001, 223.

28. Neumann 1997, 93.

29. Hoffman 2004, 9, 10.

30. Oikawa 2012, 243.

31. Wajnryb 2001, 223.

32. Nguyen 2008, 73.

33. Ibid., 65.

34. Established in May 1979 under the auspices of the United Nations High Commissioner for Refugees, the Orderly Departure Program permitted Vietnamese to immigrate legally to the United States in a safe and orderly manner.

35. Vo Dang 2008, 191.

36. Ibid., 187.

37. Gordon 1997, 8.

38. Zhou 2001, 194.

39. Ibid., 193.

40. In 2011, the U.S. poverty level was defined by the federal government for a family of four as income under $22,350 a year.

41. Kotlowitz 2000, 257.

42. Park 2005.

43. Zhou and Bankston 1998.

44. Stoler 2006, xi.

45. Lowe 1996, 60–63.

46. Ibid., x.

47. Ibid., 158.

48. An earlier version of this analysis was published in Espiritu 2010.

49. lê's biography is culled from Mehegan 2003.

50. Moore 2004.

51. Mehegan 2003.

52. Moore 2004.

53. lê 2003, 87.

54. Ibid., 43.

55. Ibid., 66–67.

56. Ibid., 27.

57. Ibid., 117.

58. Ibid., 116.

59. Ibid., 116.

60. Ibid., 117–18.

61. Ibid., 118–19.

62. Mohanty 1991, 58.

63. Cheung 1990, 246; Kim 1990, 74.

64. lê 2003, 103.

65. Gordon 1997, 200.

66. Stoler 2006.

67. Park 2005.

68. Benjamin 1973.

CHAPTER 7

1. My translation.

2. Espiritu 2003.

3. Le 2003.

4. Ibid.

5. McCarthy 2004.

6. Ngai 2004, 11.

7. In a study of the representation of Southeast Asian refugees in academic and popular discourse, Thomas DuBois notes a fascination in particular with refugee escape narratives, with "the events belonging to the escape itself . . . presented in minute detail" while the events preceding or following the escape "are narratively telescoped into mere hints or allusion" (1993, 5). Popular oral history collections that detail the refugees' traumatic escape, all done in the name of "helping" the refugees to "express themselves in their own terms," further reinscribe the refugees as only victims in the U.S. imaginary. See Freeman 1989, 10.

8. Whitfield 1991.

9. Nyers 2010, 1071.

10. Honig 2001, 74.

11. Soguk 1999; Carruthers 2005, 914; Haines 2010.

12. Office of Refugee Resettlement: www.acf.hhs.gov/programs/orr/about/history, accessed Aug. 27, 2013.

13. Lutz 2010.

14. Ibid.

15. Lipman 2012, 3–4.

16. Weizman 2012; Atanasoski 2013.

17. He was also referred to as Jiverly Wong.

18. Drogin, Baum, and Tran 2009 (emphasis added).

19. Ibid.

20. My thanks to Jennifer Mogannam for calling my attention to this expanded reading of the term "militarized refugee."

21. Mbembe 2003, 40 (emphasis in original).

22. Many thanks to Lisa Park for suggesting that Voong's story be better incorporated into the book's analysis of militarized refuge(es).

23. Cubilié 2005, xii.

24. McAlister 2005, 209.

25. Chomsky 1987, 225.

26. Butler 2004, 36.

27. Ibid., 46.

28. Ibid., 32.

29. Ibid., 36.

30. Ibid., 33.

31. Silva 2005, 124.

32. Butler 2004, 34.

33. Tadiar 2009, 9.

34. Ibid., 10.

35. Ibid., 5–6.

36. Feldman 2012.

37. Tadiar 2009, 10.

38. Arendt 1998, 71.

39. Lutz 2009 and 2010; Shigetmatsu and Camacho 2010; Butler 2004.

40. Ngô, Nguyen, and Lam 2012, 677.

41. Dunnaway 2008, 128.

42. As an example, researchers repeatedly pit Vietnamese accomplishments against those of other communities of color: "[T]he Indochinese had already begun to move ahead of other minorities on a national basis" (Caplan, Whitmore, and Bui 1989, 75). By attributing Vietnamese students' achievements to their "emphasis on education and achievement through hard work and the willingness to delay immediate satisfaction for future gains," scholars imply that African Americans and Latinos fail because they do not possess these core values that are prerequisites for success (Ibid. 1989, 131).

43. Caplan, Whitmore, and Bui 1989, 132.

44. Freeman 1996, 73.

45. Zhou and Bankston 1998.

46. Kim 2000/01, 35, 44.

47. Kim 2000.

48. Saito 1998.

49. Machida 2003, xv.

50. A graduate of Macalester College, Phi has twice won the Minnesota Grand Poetry Slam and has also won two poetry slams at the Nuyorican Poets Café in New York. He remains the only Vietnamese American man to have appeared on HBO's Russell Simmons Presents Def Poetry and the National Poetry Slam Individual Finalists Stage, where he placed sixth overall out of more than 250 national slam poets.

51. His quotation can be found at http://www.baophi.com/page/5/?p=can. Park is a *Def Poetry Jam* star and Poet Laureate of Queens, New York.

52. Chen 2005.

53. Ibid.

54. Phi 2011, 82. The title for this poem was inspired by Ntozake Shange's choreopoem, "For Colored Girls Who Have Considered Suicide."

55. From Bao Phi's "notes" on the poem: www.baophi.com/liner_notes.html, Sept. 7, 2006.

56. Lowe and Kim 1997; Palumbo-Liu 1999; Nguyen 1997.

57. Centers for Disease Control and Prevention 1981.

58. See Ngô, Nguyen, and Lam 2012. See also Vang 2012; Um 2012; Schlund-Vials 2012.

59. V. T. Nguyen 2012, 930.

60. Um 2005, 134.

61. Um 2005.

62. I thank Evyn Lê Espiritu for helping me to coin "(a)cross(ing) histories."

63. Gordon 1997, 36.

64. Ibid., 4–5.

65. Ibid., 195.

References

Agamben, Giorgio. 1998. *Homo Sacer: Sovereign Power and Bare Life*. Translated by Daniel Heller-Roazen. Stanford: Stanford University Press.

———. 2000. *Means without End: Notes on Politics*. Translated by Vincenzo Binetti and Cesare Casarino. Minneapolis: University of Minnesota Press.

———. 2002. "What Is a Paradigm?" Lecture at European Graduate School, Aug. 20. www.egs.edu/faculty/agamben/agamben-what-is-a-paradigm-2002.html.

Agier, Michel. 2010. "Humanity as an Identity and Its Political Effects (A Note on Camps and Humanitarian Government)." *Humanity: An International Journal of Human Rights, Humanitarianism, and Development* 1 (1).

Ahmad, Muneer. 2002. "Homeland Insecurities: Racial Violence the Day After September 11." *Social Text* 20 (3): 101–15.

Alderman, Derek. 2000. "A Street Fit for a King: Naming Places and Commemoration in the American South. *Professional Geographer* 52 (4): 672–84.

———. 2003. "Street Names and the Scaling of Memory: The Politics of Commemorating Martin Luther King Jr. Within the African American Community." *Royal Geographical Society* 35 (2): 163–73.

Alexander, M. Jacqui, and Chandra Talpade Mohanty. 1997. "Introduction: Genealogies, Legacies, Movements." In *Feminist Genealogies, Colonial Legacies, Democratic Futures,* edited by M. Jacqui Alexander and Chandra Mohanty, xiii–xlii. New York: Routledge.

Anderson, Benedict. 1991. *Imagined Communities: Reflections on the Origin and Spread of Nationalism*. New York: Verso.

217

Appy, Christian. 1993. *Working Class War: American Combat Soldiers and Vietnam*. Durham: University of North Carolina Press.

———, ed. 2000. *Cold War Constructions: The Political Culture of United States Imperialism, 1945–1966*. Amherst: University of Massachusetts Press.

Arax, Mark. 1987a. "Many Refugees Work While Getting Welfare." *Los Angeles Times*, Feb. 9.

———. 1987b. "Refugees Called Victims and Perpetrators of Fraud." *Los Angeles Times*, Feb. 10.

Arendt, Hannah. 1978. "We Refugees." *The Menorah Journal* 31 (1943). Reprinted in *The Jew as Pariah: Jewish Identity and Politics in the Modern Age*, edited by R. H. Feldman, 55–66. New York: Grove Press.

———. 1973. *The Origins of Totalitarianism*. Orlando, Fl.: Harcourt, Brace, Jovanovich.

———. 1998 [1958]. *The Human Condition*. Chicago: Chicago University Press.

Arnett, Elsa. 2000a. "The Final U.S. Casualties." *San Jose Mercury News*, Apr. 23.

———. 2000b. "The Boat People." *San Jose Mercury News*, Apr. 23.

Atanasoski, Neda. 2013. *Humanitarian Violence: The U.S. Deployment of Diversity*. Minneapolis: University of Minnesota Press.

Atkinson, David. 2007. "Kitsch Geographies and the Everyday Space of Social Memory." *Environment and Planning* 39: 521–40.

Azaryahu, Maoz. 1996. "The Power of Commemorative Street Names." *Environmental and Planning D: Society and Space* 14 (3): 311–30.

Azaryahu, Maoz, and Ken E. Foote. 2008. "Historical Space as Narrative Medium: On the Configuration of Spatial Narratives of Time at Historical Sites." *GeoJournal* 73: 179–94.

Bacevich, Andrew. 2005. *The New American Militarism: How Americans Are Seduced by War*. Oxford: Oxford University Press.

Baker, Reginald, and David North. 1984. *The 1975 Refugees: Their First Five Years in America*. Washington, D.C.: New TransCentury Foundation.

Bari, S. 1999. "Refugee Status Determination under the Comprehensive Plan of Action (CPA): A Personal Assessment." *International Journal of Refugee Law* 4 (4): 487–511.

Barnett, Laura. 2002. "Global Governance and the Evolution of the International Refuge Regime." *International Journal of Refugee Law* 14 (2–3): 238–62.

Barr, Gaylord. 2011. "Bataan Philippines Refugee Processing Center—PRPC." http://bataan-prpc.blogspot.com/2011_08_01_archive.html (accessed May 20, 2010).

Barthes, Roland. 1982. *Camera Lucida: Reflections on Photography*. New York: Hill and Wang.

Becker, Elizabeth. 2000. "Vietnam Circles Slightly Closer to Military Ties to U.S." *New York Times*, Apr. 27: A8.

Beevi, Mariam. 1997. "The Passing of Literary Traditions: The Figure of the Woman from Vietnamese Nationalism to Vietnamese American Transnationalism." *Amerasia Journal* 23: 27–53.

Beidler, Philip. 2007. "The Invisible ARVN: The South Vietnamese Soldiers in American Representations of the Vietnam War." *War, Literature, & the Arts: An International Journal of the Humanities* 19 (1/2): 306–17.

Benjamin, Walter. 1973. "Theses on the Philosophy of History." In *Illuminations,* edited by Hannah Arendt, 245–55. London: Collins/Fontana.

Bernd, Greiner. 2009. *War Without Fronts: The USA in Vietnam.* New Haven, Conn.: Yale University Press.

Berryman, Stan. 2001. "NAGPRA Issues at Camp Pendleton." *Cultural Resources Magazine* 3: 17–18.

Beswick, Stephanie. 2001. "'If You Leave Your Country, You Have No Life!' Rape, Suicide, and Violence: The Voices of Ethiopian, Somail, and Sudanese Female Refugees in Kenyan Refugee Camps." *Northeast African Studies* 8: 69–98.

Betts, A. 2006. *Comprehensive Plans of Action: Insights from the CIREFCA and the Indochinese CPA.* Geneva: U.N. High Commissioner for Refugees.

Bevacqua, Michael L. 2010. "The Exceptional Life and Death of a Chamorro Solider." In *Militarized Currents: Toward a Decolonized Future in Asia and in the Pacific,* edited by Setsu Shigematsu and Keith L. Camacho, 33–62. Minneapolis: University of Minnesota Press.

Bharath, Deepa. 2010. "Refugees 'Come Home' to the Midway After 35 Years." *Orange County Register,* Apr. 30. www.ocregister.com/articles/midway-246797-leechambers.html (accessed May 23 2010).

"Bittersweet Remembrance: Vietnam War Leaves a Powerful but Mixed Legacy." 2000. *San Diego Union-Tribune,* Apr. 30.

Blight, David W. 2001. *Race and Reunion: The Civil War in American Memory.* Cambridge, Mass.: Harvard University Press.

Bradley, Mark Philip. 2000. *Imagining Vietnam and America: The Making of Postcolonial Vietnam, 1919–1950.* Chapel Hill: University of North Carolina Press.

Briggs, Laura. 2002. *Reproducing Empire: Race, Sex, Science, and U.S. Imperialism in Puerto Rico.* Berkeley: University of California Press.

———. 2003. "Mother, Child, Race, Nation: The Visual Iconography of Rescue and the Politics of Transnational and Transracial Adoption." *Gender and History* 15 (2): 179–200.

Brigham, Robert K. 2007. *ARVN: Life and Death in the South Vietnamese Army.* Lawrence: University of Kansas Press.

Brinsfield, John W. 1998. "Army Values and Ethics: A Search for Consistency and Relevance." *Parameters* (autumn): 69–84.

Broyhill, Marvin T. 2003. "SAC Bases: Andersen Air Force Base." www.strategic-air-command.com/bases/Andersen_AFB.htm (accessed May 10, 2010).

Buckley, Patrick. 2010. "Letters: Arizona Law in Perspective." *Orange County Register*, Apr. 28.

Burchardt, Natasha. 1993. "Transgenerational Transmission in the Families of Holocaust Survivors in England." In *Between Generations: Family Models, Myths and Memories (Memory Narrative)*, edited by Daniel Berteaux and Paul Thompson, 121–38. Oxford: Oxford University Press.

Burton, Eve B., and David B. Goldstein. 1993. "Vietnamese Women and Children Refugees in Hong Kong: An Argument Against Arbitrary Detention." *Duke Journal of Comparative and International Law* 4: 71–92.

Bush, George W. 2001. "Address to a Joint Session of Congress and the American People." Sept. 20. http://georgewbush-whitehouse.archives.gov/news/releases/2001/09/20010920-8.html.

Butler, Judith. 2004. *Precarious Life: The Power of Mourning and Violence*. London: Verso.

Caplan, Nathan, Marcella H. Choy, and John K. Whitmore. 1991. *Children of the Boat People: A Study of Educational Success*. Ann Arbor: University of Michigan Press.

Caplan, Nathan, John K. Whitmore, and Quang L. Bui. 1989. *The Boat People and Achievement in America: A Study of Family Life, Hard Work, and Cultural Values*. Ann Arbor: University of Michigan Press.

Carrico, Richard. 1987. *Strangers in a Stolen Land: Indians of San Diego County from Prehistory to the New Deal*. Newcastle, Calif.: Sierra Oaks Publishing.

Carruthers, Susan L. 2005. "Between Camps: Eastern Bloc 'Escapees' and Cold War Borderlands." *American Quarterly* 57: 911–42.

Cavanaugh, Maureen, and Pat Finn. 2010. "Camp Pendleton's Tent City Housed 50,000 Vietnamese Refugees." *KPBS*, Apr. 29. www.kpbs.org/news/2010/apr/29/camp-pendletons-tent-city-housed-50000-vietnamese-/ (accessed May 10, 2010).

Cavanaugh, Maureen, and Natalie Walsh. 2010. "Fall of Saigon Bittersweet for Vietnamese Refugee." *KPBS*, Apr. 29. www.kpbs.org/news/2010/apr/29/fall-saigon-bitter-sweet-vietnamese-refugee/ (accessed May 10, 2010).

Centers for Disease Control and Prevention. 1981. "Sudden, Unexpected, Nocturnal Deaths among Southeast Asian Refugees." *Morbidity and Mortality Weekly Report* 30: 581–84, 589.

Chan, Kwok Bun, and Kenneth Christie. 1995. "Past, Present and Future: The Indochinese Refugee Experience Twenty Years Later." *Journal of Refugee Studies* 8: 75–94.

Chan, Kwok Bun, and David Loveridge. 1987. "Refugees in 'Transit': Vietnamese in a Refugee Camp in Hong Kong." *International Migration Review* 21: 745–59.

Chan, Sucheng. 1991. *Asian Americans: An Interpretive History*. Woodbridge, Conn.: Twayne.

Chandrasekaran, Rajiv. 2000a. "Vietnam's Tours of Duty." *Washington Post,*
    Apr. 9, p. A16.
———. 2000b. "In Vietnam." *Washington Post,* Apr. 15, p. A9.
———. 2000c. "War's Toxic Legacy Lingers in Vietnam." *Washington Post,* Apr.
    18, p. A1.
Chapman, Bruce. 2010. "As Governor, Jerry Brown Was Vociferous Foe of
    Vietnamese Immigration." *Discovery News,* Oct. 2. www.discoverynews.
    org/2010/10/as_governor_jerry_brown_was_vo038821.php (accessed Dec.
    10, 2010).
Chen, Elaine. 2005. "Straight Up with Poetry Slam Champion, Bao Phi." *Nha
    Magazine,* Q&A, June 11.
Cheng, Scarlet. 2005. "Echoes of War, 30 Years Later." *Los Angeles Times,* Apr.
    8, p. E18.
Cheung, King-Kok. 1990. "The Woman Warrior Versus the Chinaman Pacific:
    Must a Chinese American Critic Choose between Feminism and Heroism?"
    In *Conflicts in Feminism,* edited by M. Hirsch and E. F. Keller, 234–51. New
    York: Routledge.
Childs, Dennis. 2009. "'You Ain't Seen Nothing Yet': Beloved, the American
    Chain Gang, and the Middle Passage Remix." *American Quarterly* 61 (2):
    271–97.
Cho, Grace M. 2008. *Haunting the Korean Diaspora: Shame, Secrecy, and the
    Forgotten War.* Minneapolis: University of Minnesota Press.
Chomsky, Noam. 1987. "Afghanistan and South Vietnam." In *The Chomsky
    Reader,* edited by James Peck, 223–26. New York: Pantheon Books.
Chuh, Kandice. 2003. *Imagine Otherwise: On Asian Americanist Critique.*
    Durham, N.C.: Duke University Press.
Cohen, Richard. 2000a. "Vietnam Revisited." *Washington Post,* Apr. 28,
    p. A31.
———. 2000b. "The Lone, Wobbly Domino." *Washington Post,* May 4, p. A25.
Cohn, Marjorie. 2009. "Agent Orange Continues to Poison Vietnam." *Global
    Research: Center for Research on Globalization.* www.globalresearch.ca/
    agent-orange-continues-to-poison-vietnam/13974 (accessed Jan. 11, 2014).
Cubilié, Anne. 2005. *Women Witnessing Terror: Testimony and the Cultural
    Politics of Human Rights.* Bronx, N.Y.: Fordham University Press.
Curnutte, Mark. 2000. "Victories Follow a Lost War: Many Vietnamese Have
    Built Successful Tristate Lives." *Cincinnati Enquirer,* Apr. 30.
Dao, Ken. 2000. "Teaching Freedom to Children Raised in a Free Country."
    Orange County Register, Apr. 28.
Davey, Monica. 2009. "In Kansas, Proposed Monument to a Wartime Friend-
    ship Tests the Bond." *New York Times,* Aug. 3, p. A12.
Dayan, Colin. 2011. *The Law Is a White Dog: How Legal Rituals Make and
    Unmake Persons.* Princeton: Princeton University Press.

Denger, Mark. 2013. "A Brief History of the U.S. Marine Corps in San Diego." The California State Military Museum. www.militarymuseum.org/SDMarines. html (accessed Mar. 15, 2011).

Diamant, Anita. 1997. *The Red Tent.* New York: Picador USA.

Diaz, Vicente M. 2001. "Deliberating Liberation Day: Identity, History, Memory, and War in Guam." In *Perilous Memories: The Asia-Pacific Wars,* edited by T. Fujitani, Geoffrey White, and Lisa Yoneyama, 155–80. Durham, N.C.: Duke University Press.

Diller, J. M. 1988. *In Search of Asylum: Vietnamese Boat People in Hong Kong.* Washington, D.C.: Indochina Resource Action Center.

Doan, Brian. 2004. *The Forgotten Ones: A Photographic Documentation of the Last Vietnamese Boat People in the Philippines.* Westminster, Calif.: Vietnamese American Arts and Letters Association.

Drogin, Bob. 1992. "Hopeful Filipinos Foresee a Boom as U.S. Exits Subic Bay." *Los Angeles Times,* Aug. 18.

Drogin, Bob, Geraldine Baum, and My-Thuan Tran. 2009. "N.Y. Gunman Wore Body Armor, Police Say." *Los Angeles Times,* Apr. 5, p. A16.

DuBois, Thomas A. 1993. "Constructions Construed: The Representation of Southeast Asian Refugees in Academic, Popular, and Adolescent Discourse." *Amerasia Journal* 19: 1–25.

Dudley, Sandra H. 2010. *Materializing Exile: Material Culture and Embodied Experiences among Karenni Refugees in Thailand.* New York: Berghahn Books.

Dunnaway, Jen. 2008. "'One More Redskin Bites the Dust': Racial Melancholy in Vietnam War Representation." *Arizona Quarterly: A Journal of American Literature, Culture, and Theory* 64: 109–29.

Dunning, Bruce. 1989. "Vietnamese in America: The Adaptation of the 1975–1979 Arrivals." In *Refugees as Immigrants: Cambodians, Laotians, and Vietnamese in America,* edited by David W. Haines, 55–85. Totowa, N.J.: Rowman and Littlefield.

Duong, Lan, and Isabelle Thuy Pelaud. 2012. "Vietnamese American Art and Community Politics: An Engaged Vietnamese Perspective." *Journal of Asian American Studies* 15 (3): 241–69.

Duran, Daisy Herrera. 2012. "Oral History of Paul Chi Hoang." Vietnamese American Experience Course Oral Histories. http://hdl.handle. net/10575/5910, Dec. 1.

Eagleton, Terry. 1991. *Ideology: An Introduction.* New York: Verso.

Edkins, Jenny, and Véronique Pin-Fat. 2005. "Through the Wire: Relations of Power and Relations of Violence." *Millennium: Journal of International Studies* 34: 1–26.

Ellison, Ralph. 1981 [1952]. *Invisible Man.* New York: Verso.

Enloe, Cynthia. 1990. *Bananas, Beaches, Bases: Making Feminist Sense of International Politics.* Berkeley: University of California Press.

Espiritu, Yen Le. 2003. *Home Bound: Filipino American Lives Across Cultures, Communities, and Countries*. Berkeley: University of California Press.

———. 2006. "The 'We-Win-Even-When-We-Lose' Syndrome: U.S. Press Coverage of the Twenty-Fifth Anniversary of the 'Fall of Saigon.'" *American Quarterly* 58 (2): 329–52.

———. 2008. *Asian American Women and Men: Labor, Laws, and Love*. 2nd ed. Lanham, Md.: Rowman and Littlefield.

———. 2010. "Negotiating Memories of War: Arts in Vietnamese American Communities." In *Art in the Lives of Immigrant Communities in the U.S.*, edited by Paul DiMaggio and Patricia Fernandez-Kelly, 197–213. New York: Rutgers University Press.

———. 2012. "Militarized Refuge: A Transpacific Perspective on Vietnamese Refuge Flight to the United States." *Pacific and American Studies* 12: 20–32.

———. 2014. "Militarized Refuge: A Critical Rereading of Vietnamese Flight to the United States." In *Transpacific Studies: Framing an Emerging Field*, edited by Janet Hoskins and Viet Thanh Nguyen. Honolulu: University of Hawaii Press.

Espiritu, Yến Lê, and Diane Wolf. 2013. "The Appropriation of American War Memories: A Critical Juxtaposition of the Holocaust and the Vietnam War." *Social Identities: Journal for the Study of Race, Nation and Culture*. doi: 10.1080/13504630.2013.789213.

Fasick, J. 1981. *Construction and Operation of the Refugee Processing Center in Bataan, the Philippines*. Washington, D.C.: U.S. General Accounting Office.

Featherstone, Mike. 2006. "Archive." *Theory Culture Society* 23 (2–3): 591–96.

Feldman, Ilana. 2012. "The Humanitarian Condition: Palestinian Refugees and the Politics of Living." *Humanity: An International Journal of Human Rights, Humanitarianism, and Development* 3 (2): 155–72.

Felman, Shoshana, and Dori Laub. 1991. *Testimony: Crises of Witnessing in Literature, Psychoanalysis, and History*. New York: Routledge.

Finnan, Christine. 1981. "Occupational Assimilation of Refugees." *International Migration Review* 15: 292–309.

Fiske, John. 2000. "Shopping for Pleasure: Malls, Power, and Resistance." In *Consumer Reader*, edited by Juliet B. Schor and Douglas B. Holt, 306–28. New York: The New Press.

Francisco, Luzviminda. 1973. "The First Vietnam: The U.S.-Philippine War of 1899." *Bulletin of Concerned Asian Scholars* 5: 2–15.

Freeman, James M. 1989. *Hearts of Sorrow: Vietnamese American Lives*. Stanford: Stanford University Press.

———. 1996. *Changing Identities: Vietnamese Americans 1975–1995*. Upper Saddle River, N.J.: Pearson.

Fujitani, T. 2001. "Go for Broke, the Movie: Japanese American Soldiers in U.S. National, Military, and Racial Discourses." In *Perilous Memories: The*

Asia-Pacific War(s), edited by T. Fujitani, Geoffrey M. White, and Lisa Yoneyama, 239–66. Durham, N.C.: Duke University Press.

Fujitani, T., Geoffrey M. White, and Lisa Yoneyama. 2001. "Introduction." In *Perilous Memories: The Asia-Pacific War(s),* edited by T. Fujitani, Geoffrey M. White, and Lisa Yoneyama, 1–29. Durham, N.C.: Duke University Press.

Gade, Daniel W. 2003. "Language, Identity and the Scriptorial Landscape in Quebec and Catalonia." *Geographical Review* 94: 429–48.

Garcia, Voltaire E., II. 1967. "U.S. Military Bases and Philippine-American Relations." *Journal of East Asiatic Studies* 11: 1–116.

Gardner, Robert, Bryant Robey, and Peter Smith. 1985. "Asian Americans: Growth, Change, and Diversity." *Population Bulletin* 40.

Gargan, Edward A. 1996. "200 Vietnamese Refugees Flee Detention Camp in Hong Kong." *New York Times,* May 11.

Gibney, Matthew J. 2005. "Asylum." In *Immigration and Asylum,* edited by Matthew J. Gibney and Randall Hansen, 23–29. Santa Barbara, Calif.: ABC-CLIO.

Gibson, James William. 1986. *The Perfect War: Technowar in Vietnam.* New York: The Atlantic Monthly Press.

GlobalSecurity.org. 2011a. "Clark Air Base." Last modified Sept. 7. www.globalsecurity.org/military/world/philippines/clark.htm (accessed May 20, 2013).

———. 2011b. "1st Marine Regiment." Last modified May 7. www.globalsecurity.org/military/agency/usmc/1mar.htm (accessed Aug. 31, 2012).

———. 2011c. "Operation New Life." Last modified May 7. www.globalsecurity.org/military/ops/new_life.htm (accessed Aug. 31, 2012).

Gold, Scott, and Mai Tran. 2000a. "The Echo of War." *Los Angeles Times Magazine,* Apr. 30, p. 10.

———. 2000b. "Vietnam Refugees Finally Find Home." *Los Angeles Times,* Apr. 24, p. A1.

Gold, Steve. 1992. *Refugee Communities: A Comparative Field Study.* Newbury Park, Calif.: Sage Publications.

Gold, Steve, and Nazli Kibria. 1993. "Vietnamese Refugees and Blocked Mobility." *Asian and Pacific Migration Review* 2: 27–56.

Goldsborough, James O. 2000. "The Saddest Chapter in America's History." *San Diego Union Tribune,* May 1, p. B9.

Goldstein, Patrick. 2000. "Vietnam: A Seismic Cultural Shift." *Los Angeles Times,* Apr. 16, p. A1.

Gonzalez, Vernadette V. 2010. "Touring Military Masculinities: U.S.-Philippines Circuits of Sacrifice and Gratitude in Corregidor and Bataan." In *Militarized Currents: Toward a Decolonized Future in Asia and in the Pacific,* edited by Setsu Shigematsu and Keith L. Camacho, 63–90. Minneapolis: University of Minnesota Press.

Gordon, Avery. 1997. *Ghostly Matters: Haunting and the Sociological Imagination*. Minneapolis University of Minnesota Press.

"Guam: The First Refuge for Vietnamese Refugees." 1976. *Nashua Telegraph*, Apr. 29, p. 9.

Guttery, Randy, and Sherry Guttery. 2000. "TenderTale: Operation New Life April 23–October 16, 1975." www.tendertale.com/ttonl/newlife.html (accessed May 27, 2011).

Gzesh, Susan. 2006. "Central Americans and Asylum Policy in the Reagan Era." *Migration Information Source*, April 1. www.migrationpolicy.org/article/central-americans-and-asylum-policy-reagan-era (accessed Mar. 16, 2014).

Ha, Ryan. 2012. "Oral History of Duc Nguyen." Vietnamese American Experience Course Oral Histories, Mar. 2. http://ucispace.lib.uci.edu/handle/10575/1636.

Haines, David W. 1989. *Refugees as Immigrants: Cambodians, Laotians, and Vietnamese in America*. Lanham, Md.: Rowman and Littlefield.

———. 2010. *Safe Haven? A History of Refugees in America*. Boulder, Colo.: Kumarian Press.

Hall, Stuart, Chas Critcher, Tony Jefferson, John N. Clarke, and Brian Roberts. 1978. *Policing the Crisis: Mugging, the State, and Law and Order*. London: Macmillan.

Hansen, Peter. 2011. "Thanh Lọc—Hong Kong's Refugee Screening System: Experiences from Working for the Refugee Communities." In *The Chinese/Vietnamese Diaspora: Revisiting the Boat People*, edited by Yuk Wah Chan, 100–114. New York: Routledge.

Harding, Richard, and John Looney. 1977. "Problems of Southeast Asian Children in a Refugee Camp." *American Journal of Psychiatry* 134: 407–11.

Hardy, Don. 1991. "Galang: Fate of the 'Boat People.'" www.twogypsies.com/html/galang.html (accessed June 3, 2013).

Harkavy, Robert E. 1982. *Great Power Competition for Overseas Bases: The Geopolitics of Access Diplomacy*. New York: Pergamon Press.

Harris, Bonnie. 2000. "Ceremony to Remember Fall of Saigon Stirs Powerful Emotions." *Los Angeles Times*, May 1, p. B5.

Haskins, Ekaterina. 2007. "Between Archive and Participation: Public Memory in a Digital Age." *Rhetoric Society Quarterly* 37: 401–22.

Herman, Ken. 2012. "Vietnamese Soldier to Be Omitted from Veterans' Memorial." *Austin American-Statesmen*, Oct. 2.

Herman, R. D. K. 1999. "The Aloha State: Place Names and the Anti-Conquest of Hawai'i." *Annals of the Association of American Geographers* 89: 76–102.

Hicks, Jerry. 2001. "War Memorial Prevails After Lengthy Battle." *Los Angeles Times*, Oct. 19.

Hirsch, Marianne. 1996. "Past Lives: Postmemories in Exile." *Poetics Today* 17 (4): 659–86.

———. 2008. "The Generation of Postmemory." *Poetics Today* 29 (1): 103–28.

Hirsch, Marianne, and Leo Spitzer. 2003. "'We Would Never Have Come Without You': Generations of Nostalgia." In *Contested Paths: The Politics of Memory*, edited by Katherine Hodgkin and Susannah Radstone, 79–95. London: Routledge.

History and Memory: For Akiko and Takashige. 1991. Film, directed by Rea Tajiri.

Hitchcox, L. 1990. *Vietnamese Refugees in Southeast Asian Camps*. Oxford: St. Antony's/Macmillan.

Hoffman, Eva. 2004. *After Such Knowledge: Memory, History, and the Legacy of the Holocaust*. New York: Public Affairs.

Hong, Binh Ha. 2000. "Scars of Vietnam Drive Hunger Strike." *Orange County Register*, May 1, p. 7.

Honig, Bonnie. 2001. *Democracy and the Foreigner*. Princeton: Princeton University Press.

Imada, Adria. 2012. *Aloha America: Hula Circuits through the U.S. Empire*. Durham, N.C.: Duke University Press.

Inquirer Wire Services. 1996. "Vietnam Rioters Burn Hong Kong Camp Forty-Nine People Were Hurt as 3,000 Protested Plans to Send Them Home. 140 Escaped." http://articles.philly.com/1996-05-11/news/25627015_1_whitehead-detention-center-new-territories-detention-camp (accessed June 9, 2013).

Isaac, Allan Punzalan. 2006. *American Tropics: Articulating Filipino America*. Minneapolis: University of Minnesota Press.

Isin, Engin F., and Kim Rygiel. 2007. "Abject Spaces: Frontiers, Zones, Camps." In *Logics of Biopower and the War on Terror*, edited by E. Dauphinee and C. Masters, 181–203. Hampshire, Engl.: Palgrave.

Jeffords, Susan. 1989. *The Remasculinization of America: Gender and the Vietnam War*. Bloomington: Indiana University Press.

Jensen, Elizabeth. 2000. "Last Man Down." *Los Angeles Times*, Apr. 29, p. A1.

Johnson, Chalmers. 2000. *Blowback: The Costs and Consequences of American Empire*. New York: Henry Holt.

———. 2004a. "Baseworld: America's Military Colonialism." *Mother Jones Magazine*, Jan. 20.

———. 2004b. *The Sorrows of Empire: Militarism, Secrecy, and the End of the Republic*. New York: Owl Books.

Jolly, Vik. 2010. "Pendleton Once Home for 50,000 War Refugees." *Orange County Register*, Apr. 8. www.ocregister.com/news/vietnamese-243238-pendleton-family.html.

Kaplan, Amy. 1993. "Left Alone with America: The Absence of Empire in the Study of American Culture." In *Cultures of United States Imperialism*, edited by Amy Kaplan and Donald Pease, 3–21. Durham, N.C.: Duke University Press.

Karnow, Stanley. 2000. "Vietnam: 25 Years After the Fall." *San Jose Mercury News* 23 April.

Kelly, Gail Paradise. 1977. *From Vietnam to America: A Chronicle of the Vietnamese Immigration to the United States*. Boulder, Colo.: Westview Press.

Kennedy, Edward M. 1981. "Refugee Act of 1980." *International Migration Review* 15: 141–56.

Khalili, Laleh. 2005. "Places of Memory and Mourning: Palestinian Commemoration in the Refugee Camps of Lebanon." *Comparative Studies of South Asia, Africa, and the Middle East* 25: 30–45.

Kibria, Nazli. 1993. *Family Tightrope: The Changing Lives of Vietnamese Americans*. Princeton: Princeton University Press.

Kim, Claire. 2000. *Bitter Fruit: The Politics of Black/Korean Conflict in New York*. New Haven, Conn.: Yale University Press.

———. 2000/01. "Playing the Racial Trump Card: Asian Americans in Contemporary U.S. Politics." *Amerasia Journal* 26: 35–65.

Kim, Elaine. 1990. "'Such Opposite Creatures': Men and Women in Asian American Literature." *Michigan Quarterly Review* 29: 68–93.

Kim, Jodi. 2010. *Ends of Empire: Asian American Critique and the Cold War*. Minneapolis: University of Minnesota Press.

Kimlick, Michael F. 1990. "U.S. Bases in the Philippines." http://www.globalsecurity.org/military/library/report/1990/KMF.htm.

King, Peter H. 2000. "Wall's U.S. Tours Bring War's Pain, Pride Home." *Los Angeles Times*, Apr. 30, p. A1.

Klein, Christina. 2003. *Cold War Orientalism: Asia in the Middlebrow Imagination, 1945–1961*. Berkeley: University of California Press.

Knickrehm, Dan. 2010. "The 43rd and Operation New Life." *The Official Website of Pope Air Force Base*. www.pope.af.mil/news/story.asp?id_123207835 (accessed May 27, 2011).

Knudsen, Christian John. 1985. *Boat People in Transit: Vietnamese in Refugee Camps in the Philippines, Hong Kong and Japan*. Washington, D.C.: Lilian Barber Press.

Kotlowitz, Alex. 2000. "False Connections." In *The Consumer Society Reader*. Center for 21st Century Studies/University of Wisconsin-Milwaukee.

KPBS. 2002. "People and Events: Operation Babylift (1975)." www.pbs.org/wgbh/amex/daughter/peopleevents/e_babylift.html (accessed May 20, 2010).

Kumar, Amitava. 2000. *Passport Photos*. Berkeley: University of California Press.

Kunz, E. F. 1973. "The Refugee in Flight: Kinetic Models and Forms of Displacement." *International Migration Review* 7 (2): 125–46.

Kwon, Heonik. 2006. *After the Massacre: Commemoration and Consolation in Ha My and My Lai*. Berkeley: University of California Press.

Lamb, David. 2000. "Reflections on Fall of Saigon." *Los Angeles Times*, Apr. 9, p. A17.

———. 2005. *"War Is History for Vibrant Vietnam." Los Angeles Times*, Apr. 30, p. A1.

Law, S.S. 2011. "Vietnamese Boat People in Hong Kong: Visual Images and Stories." In *The Chinese/Vietnamese Diaspora: Revisiting the Boat People*, edited by Yuk Wah Chan, 116–32. New York: Routledge.

———. 2005. "A Reading and Conversation." Reading sponsored by the Department of Ethnic Studies and the Department of Literature, U.C. San Diego, Apr. 11.

Le, Sonny. 2003. "Embedded in My Mind: A Vietnam War Survivor Reflects on Iraq." *Asian Week*, Mar. 21.

Le, Viet. 2005. "The Art of War: Vietnamese American Visual Artists Dinh Q. Lê, Ann Phong and Nguyen Tan Hoang." *Amerasia Journal* 31 (2): 21–35.

Leahy, Michael. 2000. "25 Years After Saigon, An American Future." *Washington Post*, Apr. 2, p. A1.

Lê Espiritu, Evyn. 2013. "'Who Was Colonel Hồ Ngọc Cẩn?' Theorizing the Relationship between History and Cultural Memory." Senior thesis, Department of History, Pomona College.

Lefebvre, Henri. 1992. *The Production of Space*. Oxford: Blackwell Publishers.

Lessner, Lori. 2000. "Memorial Draws New, Old Alike." *San Jose Mercury News*, Apr. 30.

lê thi diem thúy. 2003. *The Gangster We Are All Looking For*. New York: Knopf.

LeTran, Vivian. 2002. "Vietnam War Memorial Gives Alliance Its Due." *Los Angeles Times*, Sept. 21.

Lewy, Guenter. 1978. *America in Vietnam*. New York: Oxford University Press.

Liêm, Vĩnh. 1982. "Người Tị Nạn." *Tị Nạn Trường Ca ; Tập Hai: Thơ*. Self-published.

Lieu, Nhi. 2000. "Remembering 'The Nation' Through Pageantry: Femininity and the Politics of Vietnamese Womanhood in the Hoa Hau Ao Dai Contest." *Frontiers: A Journal of Women's Studies* 21: 126–51.

Lin + Lam. 2010. "Tomorrow I Leave." http://linpluslam.com/index/Tomorrow_I_ Leave.html (accessed May 20, 2012).

Lipman, Jana K. 2012. "'Give Us a Ship': The Vietnamese Repatriate Movement on Guam, 1975." *American Quarterly* 64: 1–31.

Lippert, Randy. 1999. "Governing Refugees: The Relevance of Governmentality to Understanding the International Refugee Regime." *Alternatives: Global, Local, Political* 24: 295–328.

Liu, Robyn. 2002. "Governing Refugees 1919–1945." *Borderlands e-journal* 1 (1). www.borderlands.net.au.

———. 2004. "The International Government of Refugees." In *Global Govern-mentality: Governing International Spaces,* edited by Wendy Larner and William Walters, 116–35. London: Routledge.

Liu, William T., Mary Ann Lamanna, and Alice K. Murata. 1979. *Transition to Nowhere: Vietnamese Refugees in America.* Nashville, Tenn.: Charter House.

Long, Nina Mai Thi. 2012. "Oral History of Mary Hoang Long." Vietnamese American Experience Course Oral Histories. http://hdl.handle.net/10575/5913.

Lowe, Lisa. 1996. *Immigrant Acts: On Asian American Cultural Politics.* Durham, N.C.: Duke University Press.

———. 1998. "The International within the National: American Studies and Asian American Critique." *Cultural Critique* 40: 29–47.

Lowe, Lisa, and Elaine Kim. 1997. "Guest Editors' Introduction." *Positions* 5 (2): v–xiv.

Lutz, Catherine. 2009. "Introduction: Bases, Empire, and Global Response." In *Bases of Empire: The Global Struggle Against U.S. Military Posts,* edited by Catherize Lutz, 1–44. New York: New York University Press.

———. 2010. "US Military Bases on Guam in Global Perspective." *The Asia-Pacific Journal* 30 (July 26).

Ly, Phuong. 2000. "Death Reopens War Wounds: Vietnamese Divided Over Man Who Died after Brawl in Va." *Washington Post,* May 27.

Machida, Margo. 2003. "Visual Art and the Imagining of Asian America: An Editorial View." In *Fresh Talk, Daring Gazes: Conversations on Asian American Art,* edited by Elaine H. Kim, Margo Machida, and Sharon Mizota, xi–xv. Berkeley: University of California Press.

Mackie, Richard. 1998. *Operation Newlife: The Untold Story.* Concord, Calif.: Solution.

Malkki, Liisa. 1995a. *Purity and Exile: Violence, Memory, and National Cosmology in Tanzania.* Chicago: University of Chicago Press.

———. 1995b. "Refugees and Exile: From 'Refugee Studies' to the National Order of Things." *Annual Review of Anthropology* 24: 495–523.

———. 1996. "National Geographic: The Rooting of Peoples and the Territoriali-zation of National Identity Among Scholars and Refugees." In *Becoming National,* edited by Geoff Eley and Ronald Grigor Suny, 434–55. Oxford: Oxford University Press.

Mangaliman, Jessie. 2000. "Vietnamese Shine in the Lone Star State." *San Jose Mercury News,* Apr. 29.

Manney, Kathy. 2006. "Operation Babylift: Evacuating Children Orphaned by the Vietnam War." HistoryNet, Sept. 13. www.historynet.com/operation-babylift-evacuating-children-orphaned-by-the-vietnam-war.htm (accessed May 20, 2010).

"Marine Corps Base Camp Pendleton." 2013. www.pendleton.marines.mil /About/HistoryandMuseums.aspx (accessed May 20, 2010).

Mariscal, George. 1999. *Aztlan and Viet Nam: Chicano and Chicana Experiences of the War*. Berkeley: University of California Press.

Martelle, Scott, and Mai Tran. 2000. "Vietnam TV Broadcasts Anger Emigres." *Los Angeles Times*, Apr. 27, p. A1.

Martindale, Carolyn. 1986. *The White Press and Black America*. New York: Greenwood.

Masquelier, Adeline. 2006. "Why Katrina's Victims Aren't *Refugees*: Musings on a 'Dirty' Word." *American Anthropologist* 108: 735–43.

Mbembe, Achille. 2003. "Necropolitics." *Public Culture* 15 (1): 11–40.

McAlister, Melani. 2005. *Epic Encounters: Culture, Media, and U.S. Interests in the Middle East since 1945*. Berkeley: University of California Press.

McCarthy, Rory. 2004. "Go Kick Some Butt and Make History, Vietnam-Style, US Troops Urged." *The Guardian*, Nov. 9.

McCombs, Phil. 2000. "The Haunting." *Washington Post*, Apr. 30, p. F1, F4.

McGranahan, Carole. 2006. "Truth, Fear, and Lies: Exile Politics and Arrested Histories of the Tibetan Resistance." *Cultural Anthropology* 20: 570–600.

Mehegan, David. 2003. "Refuge in Her Writing." *Boston Globe*, June 2, p. B7.

Meyers, Jessica. 2006. "Eden Center as a Representation of Vietnamese American Ethnic Identity in the Washington D.C. Metropolitan Area, 1975–2005." *Journal of Asian American Studies* 9: 55–85.

Minzesheimer, Bob. 2001. "Books and Movies Bulge With 'Last Good War' Stories." *USA Today*, May 15.

Mohanty, Chandra. 1991. "Under Western Eyes: Feminist Scholarship and Colonial Discourse." In *Third World Women and the Politics of Feminism*, edited by Chandra Talpade Mohanty, Ann Russo, and Lourdes Torres, 51–80. Bloomington: Indiana University Press.

Moore, Judith. 2004. "Art Is Slow." *San Diego Weekly Reader* (Feb. 5): front page, 32–46.

Moos, Feliz, and C. S. Morrison. 2005. "The Vietnamese Refugees at Our Doorstop: Political Ambiguity and Successful Improvisation." *Review of Policy Research* 1: 28–46.

Morello, Carol. 2000. "Ritual Awash in Symbolism." *Washington Post*, Apr. 30, p. C5.

Morrison, G. S., and Felix Moos. 1982. "Halfway to Nowhere: Vietnamese Refugees on Guam." In *Involuntary Migration and Resettlement: The Problems and Responses of Dislocated People*, edited by Art Hansen and Anthony Oliver-Smith, 49–68. Boulder, Colo.: Westview Press.

Morrison, Toni. 1989. "Unspeakable Things Unspoken: The Afro-American Presence in American Literature." *Michigan Quarterly Review* 28: 1–34.

Mortland, Carol A. 1987. "Transforming Refugees in Refugee Camps." *Urban Anthropology and Studies of Cultural Systems and World Economic Development* 16: 375–404.

Nagata, Donna. 1993. *Legacy of Injustice: Exploring the Cross-Generational Impact of the Japanese American Internment.* New York: Springer.

Naval Historical Center. 2009. "USS Midway (CVB 41)." *Dictionary of American Fighting Ships and United States Aviation, 1910–1995.* Last modified June 15. www.navy.mil/navydata/ships/carriers/histories/cv41-midway/cv41-midway.html (accessed June 21, 2009).

Neumann, Anna. 1997. "Ways Without Words: Learning from Silence and Story in Post-Holocaust Lives." In *Learning from Our Lives: Women, Research, and Autobiography in Education,* edited by Anna Neumann and P. L. Peterson, 91–123. New York: Columbia University, Teachers' College Press.

Newman, Bruce. 2010. "After the Fall: Vietnamese Remember 'Black April' 35 Years Later." *San Jose Mercury News,* Apr. 28.

Ngai, Mae M. 2004. *Impossible Subjects: Illegal Aliens and the Making of Modern America.* Princeton: Princeton University Press.

Ngô, Fiona I. B., Mimi Thi Nguyen, and Mariam B. Lam. 2012. "Southeast Asian American Studies Special Issue: Guest Editors' Introduction." *Positions* 20: 671–84.

Nguyen, Khuyen Vu. 2004. "Memorializing Vietnam: Transfiguring the Living Pasts." In *What's Going On? California and the Vietnam Era,* edited by Marcia A. Eymann and Charles Wollenberg, 153–63. Berkeley: Oakland Museum of California and University of California Press.

Nguyen, Lena. 2012. "Oral History of Suzy Xuyen Dong Matsuda." Vietnamese American Experience Course Oral Histories, Nov. 26. http://ucispace.lib.uci.edu/handle/10575/5885.

Nguyen, Mimi Thi. 2012. *The Gift of Freedom: War, Debt, and Other Refugee Passages.* Durham, N.C.: Duke University Press.

Nguyen, Nam Hoang. 2000a. "Former Military Surgeon Feels San Jose Is Now Home." *San Jose Mercury News,* Apr. 23.

———. 2000b. "Pilot Waited for His Moment." *San Jose Mercury News,* Apr. 23.

Nguyen, Natalie Huynh Chau. 2008. "Memory and Silence in the Vietnamese Diaspora: The Narratives of Two Sisters." *Oral History* 36: 64–74.

Nguyen, Viet Thanh. 1997. "Representing Reconciliation: Le Ly Hayslip and the Victimized Body." *Positions* 5: 605–42.

———. 2002. *Race and Resistance: Literature and Politics in Asian America.* Oxford: Oxford University Press.

———. 2012. "Refugee Memories and Asian American Critique." *Positions* 20: 911–42.

Nguyen-Lam, Kimoanh. 2008. "Foreword." In *Journey from the Fall: Curriculum 7–12.* Anaheim, Calif.: Journey from the Fall Curriculum Committee.

Nguyên-Vo, Thu Huong. 2005. "Forking Paths: How Shall We Mourn the Dead?" *Amerasia Journal* 31: 157–75.

Nora, Pierre. 1989. "Between Memory and History: Les Lieux de Mémoire." *Representations* 26: 7–24.

Nyers, Peter. 2010. "Abject Cosmopolitanism: The Politics of Protection in the Anti-Deportation Movement." *Third World Quarterly* 24: 1069–93.

Oikawa, Mona. 2012. *Cartographies of Violence: Japanese Canadian Women, Memory, and the Subjects of the Internment.* Toronto: University of Toronto Press.

Okihiro, Gary. 1994. *Margins and Mainstreams: Asians in American History and Culture.* Seattle: University of Washington Press.

Ong, Aihwa. 2003. *Buddha Is Hiding: Refugees, Citizenship, the New America.* Berkeley: University of California Press.

Ong, Nhu-Ngoc T, and David S. Meyer. 2008. "Protest and Political Incorporation: Vietnamese-American Protests in Orange County, California, 1975–2001." *Journal of Vietnamese Studies* 3 (1): 78–107.

Ong, Paul, and Karen Umemoto. 1994. "Life and Work in the Inner-City." In *The State of Asian Pacific America: Economic Diversity, Issues, and Policies,* edited by Paul Ong, 87–112. Los Angeles: LEAP Asian Pacific American Public Policy Institute and University of California at Los Angeles, Asian American Studies.

Ortner, Sherry. 1995. "Resistance and the Problem of Ethnographic Refusal." *Comparative Studies in Society and History* 37: 173–93.

Owens, Patricia. 2009. "Reclaiming 'Bare Life'?: Against Agamben on Refugees." *International Relations* 23: 567–82.

Paddock, Richard C., and Mai Tran. 2005. "Vietnamese Premier Planning a Trip to U.S." *Los Angeles Times*, May 5, p. A6.

Padlan, Mark. 2005. "US Militarism in the Philippines." *Peacemaking*, Nov. 28. http://peacemaking.kr/english/news/view.php?papercode=ENGLISH&newsno=134&pubno=142.

Palfry, John, and Urs Gasser. 2008. *Born Digital: Understanding the First Generation of Internet Natives.* New York: Basic Books.

Palmieri, Victor H. 1980. "Statement by Ambassador Victor H. Palmieri, U.S. Coordinator for Refugee Affairs, Before the House Judiciary Committee in Washington D.C., April 30, 1980." *Current Policy* 178. Washington D.C.: U.S. Department of State, Bureau of Public Affairs, Office of Public Communication.

Palumbo-Liu, David. 1999. *Asian/American: Historical Crossings of a Racial Frontier.* Stanford: Stanford University Press.

Pan, Philip P., and Phuong Ly. 2000. "3 Roads from Vietnam." *Washington Post*, Apr. 30.

Park, Lisa Sun-Hee. 2005. *Consuming Citizenship: Children of Asian Immigrant Entrepreneurs.* Stanford: Stanford University Press.

Park, Robert. 1950. *Race and Culture.* Glencoe, Ill.: Free Press.

Pelaud, Isabelle Thuy. 2005. "Entering Linh Dinh's *Fake House:* Literature of Displacement." *Amerasia Journal* 31: 37–50.

Petersen, William. 1966. "Success Story: Japanese-American Style." *New York Times Magazine,* Jan. 6.

Pham, Vu. 2003. "Antedating and Anchoring Vietnamese America: Toward a Vietnamese American Historiography." *Amerasia Journal* 29: 135–52.

Phi, Bao. 2011. "For Colored Boys in Danger of Sudden Unexplained Nocturnal Death Syndrome and All the Rest for Whom Considering Suicide Is Not Enuf." In his *Sông I Sing: Poems.* Minneapolis: Coffee House Press.

"Phu Nhân Cố Đại Tá Hồ Ngọc Cẩn." 2010. *Viễn Đông,* Aug. 10.

Prochnau, William. 2000. "Shadows and Mirrors." *Los Angeles Times,* Apr. 23, p. M3.

Project Ngoc. 1988. *The Forgotten People: Vietnamese Refugees in Hong Kong: A Critical Report.* Irvine: Project Ngoc, University of California, Irvine.

"Protestors Urge Boycott of Vietnamese Media." 2000. *Los Angeles Times,* Apr. 30, p. B3.

Pugliese, Joseph. 2002. "Penal Asylum: Refugees, Ethics, Hospitality." *Borderlands* 1 (1).

Rajaram, P. K., and C. Grundy-Warr. 2004. "The Irregular Migrant as Homo Sacer: Migration and Detention in Australia, Malaysia, and Thailand." *International Migration* 42 (1): 33–63.

Rathi, Rachana. 2005. "They Put All Hope in Tiny Boats: A Boat's U.S. Tour Rekindles Memories of Fleeing Vietnam." *Los Angeles Times,* May 1, p. B1.

"Refugees: A Cool and Wary Reception." 1975. *Time,* May 12. www.time.com /time/magazine/article/0,9171,917419-3,00.html (accessed June 12, 2009).

Reyes, Adelaida. 1999. *Music and the Vietnamese Refugee Experience: Songs of the Caged, Songs of the Free.* Philadelphia: Temple University Press.

Reyes, David. 2003. "Vietnam War Memorial Stirs Memories." *Los Angeles Times,* Apr. 28.

Richter, Paul. 2005. "Vietnam's Premier Gest VIP Treatment." *Los Angeles Times,* June 22.

Robinson, C. W. 2004. "The Comprehensive Plan of Action for Indochinese Refugees, 1989–1997: Sharing the Burden and Passing the Buck." *Journal of Refugee Studies* 17 (3): 319–33.

Rogers, Robert F. 1995. *Destiny's Landfall: A History of Guam.* Honolulu: University of Hawaii Press.

Rose, Peter. 1985. "Asian Americans: From Pariahs to Paragons." In *Clamor at the Gates: The New Immigration,* edited by Nathan Glazer, 181–212. San Francisco: Institute of Contemporary Studies.

Rowe, John Carlos. 1989. "Eyewitness: Doumentary Styles in the American Representations of Vietnam." In *The Vietnam War and American Culture,* edited by John Carlos Rowe and Rick Berg, 148–74. New York: Columbia University Press.

Rumbaut, Rubén. 2000. "Vietnamese, Laotian, and Cambodian Americans." In *Contemporary Asian America: A Multidisciplinary Reader,* edited by Min Zhou and James Gatewood, 175–206. New York: New York University Press.

Rumbaut, Rubén, and John Weeks. 1986. "Fertility and Adaptation: Indochinese Refugees in the United States." *International Migration Review* 20: 428–66.

Sachs, Dana. 2010. *The Life We Were Given: Operation Babylift, International Adoption, and the Children of War in Vietnam.* Boston: Beacon Press.

Sahara, Ayako. 2012. "Globalized Humanitarianism: US Imperial Formation in Asia and the Pacific through the Indochinese Refugee Problem." Ph.D. diss., University of California, San Diego.

Saito, Leland. 1998. *Race and Politics: Asian Americans, Latinos and Whites in a Los Angeles Suburb.* Champaign: University of Illinois Press.

Salomon, Kim. 1991. *Refugees in the Cold War: Towards a New International Refugee Regime in the Early Postwar Era.* Lund, Sweden: Lund University Press.

Sauer, Mark. 2000. "Refurbishing the Past: Vietnam Vets Turning a Swift Boat into a Memorial." *San Diego Union Tribune,* Apr. 20, p. E1.

Sautman, B. 1985. "The Meaning of 'Well-Founded Fear of Persecution' in United States Asylum Law and in International Law." *Fordham International Law Journal* 9 (3): 483–539.

Schlund-Vials, Cathy J. 2012. *War, Genocide, and Justice: Cambodian American Memory Work.* Minneapolis: University of Minnesota Press.

Seidman, Irving. 2012. *Interviewing as Qualitative Research: A Guide for Researchers in Education and the Social Sciences,* 4th ed. New York: Teachers College Press.

Sevrens, Don. 2000. "The Melting Pot Is Seasoned Anew." *San Diego Union Tribune,* Apr. 30, p. G1.

Shigematsu, Setsu, and Keith L. Camacho. 2010. "Introduction: Militarized Currents, Decolonizing Futures." In *Militarized Currents: Toward a Decolonized Future in Asia and the Pacific,* edited by Setsu Shigematsu and Keith L. Camacho, xv–xlviii. Minneapolis: University of Minnesota Press.

Silva, Denise Ferreira da. 2001. "Towards a Critique of the Socio-Logos of Justice: The Analytics of Raciality and the Production of Universality." *Social Identities* 7 (3): 421–54.

———. 2005. "A Tale of Two Cities: Saigon, Fallujah and the Ethical Boundaries of Empire." *Amerasia Journal* 31: 121–34.

Sindt, R. H. 2004. "The Vietnamese Diaspora." In *The Forgotten Ones: A Photographic Documentation of the Last Vietnamese Boat People in the Philippines,* by B. Doan. Westminster, Calif.: Vietnamese American Arts and Letters Association.

Skaife, Jane Le. 2011. "A Divided Vietnamese Community in France and Its Political Repurcussions." *New Geography*, July 15.

Skinner, Kenneth, and G. Hendricks. 1979. "The Shaping of Ethnic Self-Identity among Indochinese Refugees." *Journal of Ethnic Studies* 7: 25–41.

Smith, Merrill. 2004. "Warehousing Refugees: A Denial of Rights, a Waste of Humanity." *World Refugee Survey Warehousing Issue*: 38–56.

Socolovsky, Maya. 2004. "Cyber-Spaces of Grief: Online Memorials and the Columbine High School Shootings." *JAC* 24 (2): 467–89.

Soguk, Nevzat. 1999. *States and Strangers: Refugees and Displacements of Statecraft*. Minneapolis: University of Minnesota Press.

Sommers, Samuel R., Evan P. Apfelbaum, Kristin N. Dukes, Negin Toosi, and Elsie J. Wang. 2006. "Race and Media Coverage of Hurricane Katrina: Analysis, Implications, and Future Research Questions." *Analyses of Social Issues and Public Policy* 6: 1–17.

Spector, Ronald H. 1993. "'How Do You Know If You Are Really Winning?': Perception and Reality in America's Military Performance in Vietnam, 1965–70." In *The Vietnam War: Vietnamese and American Perspectives*, edited by Jayne S. Werner and Luu Doan Huynh, 152–64. Armonk: M. E. Sharpe.

Starr, Paul, and Alden Roberts. 1985. "Community Structure and Vietnamese Refugee Adaptation: The Significance of Context." *International Migration Review* 16: 595–613.

Stein, B. 1979. The Geneva Conferences and the Indochinese Refugee Crisis. *International Migration Review* 13 (4): 716–23.

Stoler, Ann Laura. 2006. "Preface." In *Haunted by Empire: Geographies of Intimacy in North American History*, edited by Ann Laura Stoler, xi–xiii. Durham, N.C.: Duke University Press.

Streeby, Shelley. 2002. *American Sensations: Class, Empire, and the Production of Popular Culture*. Berkeley: University of California Press.

Sturken, Marita. 1997. *Tangled Memories: The Vietnam War, the AIDS Epidemic, and the Politics of Remembering*. Berkeley: University of California Press.

———. 2001. "Absent Images of Memory: Remembering and Reenacting the Japanese Internment." In *Perilous Memories: The Asia-Pacific War(s)*, edited by T. Fujitani, Geoffrey M. White, and Lisa Yoneyama, 33–49. Durham, N.C.: Duke University Press.

"Success Story of One Minority in the U.S." 1966. *U.S. News and World Report*, Dec. 26, p. 73.

Tadiar, Neferti. 2009. "Lifetimes in Becoming Human." Keynote panel address, presented at "Angela Davis: Legacies in the Making," Nov. 1. University of California, Santa Cruz.

Tai, Hue-Tam Ho. 2001a. "Faces of Remembrance and Forgetting." In *The Country of Memory: Remaking the Past in Late Socialist Vietnam*, edited by Hue-Tam Ho Tai, 167–95. Berkeley: University of California Press.

———. 2001b. "Afterword: Commemoration and Community." In *The Country of Memory: Remaking the Past in Late Socialist Vietnam*, edited by Hue-Tam Ho Tai, 227–30. Berkeley: University of California Press.

Templer, Robert. 2000. "'Namstalgia': Baby Boomers Should Put Old War Stories to Rest." *San Jose Mercury News*, May 3.

Tempo, Carl J. Bon. 2008. *Americans at the Gate: The United States and Refugees During the Cold War*. Princeton: Princeton University Press.

Tenhula, John. 1991. *Voices from Southeast Asia: The Refugee Experience in the United States*. New York: Holmes and Meier.

Thai, Hung Cam. 2003. "The Vietnamese Double Gender Revolt: Globalizing Marriage Options in the Twenty-first Century. *Amerasia Journal* 29: 51–75.

Thomas, Evan. 2000. "The Last Days of Saigon." *Newsweek*, May 1, p. 38.

Thompson, Larry C. 2010. *Refugee Workers in the Indochina Exodus, 1975–1982*. Jefferson, N.C.: McFarland.

Tobin, Thomas G. 1975. "Indo-China: Now On to Camp Fortuitous." *Time*, May 12. www.time.com/time/magazine/article/0,9171,917414,00.html (accessed June 12, 2009).

Tobin, Thomas G., Arthur E. Laehr, and John F. Hilgenberg. 1978. "Last Flight from Saigon." In *USAF Southeast Asia Monograph Series*, edited by Lt. Col. A. J. C. Lavalle, 107–9. Vol. 4, no. 6. Washington, D.C.: U.S. Government Printing Office.

Tomb, Geoffrey. 2000. "Past Recalled; Present Honored." *San Jose Mercury News*, Apr. 30.

Tran, Mai. 2000. "Poll Finds Paradox among Vietnamese in Orange County." *Los Angeles Times*, Apr. 20, p. B5.

———. 2003. "Statue Donors Asked to Give Again: Why Is Still More Needed for the Westminster Memorial Featuring American and South Vietnamese Soldiers Together, They Wonder." *Los Angeles Times*, Mar. 8, p. B1.

Tran, Ngoc Angie. 2003. "Transnational Assembly Work: Vietnamese American Electronic and Vietnamese Garment Workers." *Amerasia Journal* 29: 4–28.

Tran, Quan Tue. 2012. "Remembering the Boat People Exodus: A Tale of Two Memorials." *Journal of Vietnamese Studies* 7: 80–121.

Tran, Qui-Phiet. 1993. "Exile and Home in Contemporary Vietnamese American Feminine Writing." *Amerasia Journal* 19: 71–84.

Trinh, T. Minh-ha. 1991. *When the Moon Waxes Red*. New York: Routledge.

———. 2010. *Elsewhere, Within Here: Immigration, Refugeeism and the Boundary Event*. New York: Routledge.

Truong, Monique Thuy-Dung. 1993. "The Emergence of Voices: Vietnamese American Literature 1975–1990." *Amerasia Journal* 19: 27–50.

Truong, Noelle. 2000. "The Time's Not Right for Reconciliation." *Orange County Register*, May 14, p. 4.

Tsang, Daniel. 2004. "Visions of Resistance and Survival from Hong Kong Detention Camps." In *The Chinese/Vietnamese Diaspora: Revisiting the Boat People*, edited by Yuk Wah, 99–115. New York: Routledge.

Tuck, Eve. 2009. "Suspending Damage: A Letter to Communities." *Harvard Educational Review* 79: 409–27.

Tucker, Spencer. 2000. *Encyclopedia of the Vietnam War: A Political, Social and Military History*. Santa Barbara, Calif.: ABC-CLIO.

Turan, Kenneth. 2000. "The Horror, the Madness, the Movies." *Los Angeles Times Calendar*, Apr. 16, p. 91.

Turley, William S. 1987. *The Second Indochina War: A Short Political and Military History, 1954–1975*. New York: Signet.

Um, Khatharya. 2005. "The 'Vietnam War': What's in a Name?" *Amerasia Journal* 31 (2): 134–39.

———. 2012. "Exiled Memory: History, Identity, and Remembering in Southeast Asia and Southeast Asian Diaspora." *Positions: Asia Critique* 20 (3): 831–50.

United Nations High Commissioner for Refugees (UNHCR). 2000. *The State of the World's Refugees: Fifty Years of Humanitarian Action*. New York: Oxford University Press.

U.S. General Accountability Office. 1981. *Construction and Operation of the Refugee Processing Center in Bataan, the Philippines*. Washington, D.C.: Office of Public Affairs.

———. 1985. *Problems in Processing Vietnamese Refugees from the Dong Rek Camp in Cambodia*. Washington, D.C.: Office of Public Affairs.

———. 1996. *Vietnamese Asylum Seekers: Refugee Screening Procedures under the Comprehensive Plan of Action*. Washington, D.C.: Office of Public Affairs.

"U.S. Military Bases and Empire." 2002. *Monthly Review*, March 20.

U.S. Naval Hospital. 2013. "Command History." www.med.navy.mil/sites /usnhguam/information/Pages/CommandHistory.aspx (accessed Mar. 27, 2010).

Utts, Thomas C. 2012. "Gateway." *Clark Air Base Scrapbook*. http://zcap. freeyellow.com/pix3.htm (accessed Sept. 9, 2013).

Valverde, Kieu Linh Caroline. 2003. "Making Vietnamese Music Transnational: Sounds of Home, Resistance and Change." *Amerasia Journal* 29: 29–50.

Vance, Cyrus. 1983. "Statement by Secretary of State Cyrus Vance before the Sub-Committee on Immigration, Refugees, and International Law of the House Judiciary Committee, July 31, 1979." In *American Foreign Policy: Basic Documents, 1977–1980*, 989–41. Washington, D.C.: Bureau of Public Affairs.

Van Dijk, Teun. 1991. *Racism and the Press*. London: Routledge.

Vang, Ma. 2012. "Displaced Histories: Refugee Critique and the Politics of Hmong Remembering." Ph.D. diss., Department of Ethnic Studies, University of California, San Diego.

Vasquez, Tim. 2001. "Clark Air Base: History and Significant Events." www. clarkab.org/history/ (accessed Aug. 31, 2010).

"Vietnam Celebrates War's End 30 Years Ago." 2005. *Los Angeles Times,* May 1, p. A14.

Vo, Linda. 2003. "Vietnamese American Trajectories." *Amerasia Journal* 29 (1): ix–xviii.

Vo, Nghia M. 2009. "Guam, the Transit Island." In *The Viet Kieu in America: Personal Accounts of Postwar Immigrants from Vietnam,* edited by Nghia M. Vo, 157–64. Jefferson, N.C.: McFarland.

Vo Dang, Thuy. 2005. "The Cultural Work of Anticommunism in the San Diego Vietnamese American Community." *Amerasia Journal* 31 (2): 65–86.

———. 2008. "Anticommunism as Cultural Praxis: South Vietnam, War, and Refugee Memories in the Vietnamese American Community." Ph.D. diss., Department of Ethnic Studies, University of California, San Diego.

———. 2011. "Oral History of Dan Nguyen." Thuy Vo Dang Oral Histories, Dec. 5. University of California, Irvine, Libraries. http://ucispace.lib.uci.edu/handle /10575/5228.

Vogel, Steve. 2000. "Out of the Jaws of the Dragon." *Washington Post,* Apr. 29, p. B1.

Wagner-Pacifici, Robin, and Barry Schwartz. 1991. "The Vietnam Veterans Memorial: Commemorating a Difficult Past." *American Journal of Sociology* 97: 376–420.

Wajnryb, Ruth. 2001. *The Silence: How Tragedy Shapes Talk.* Crows Nest, Australia: Allen and Unwin.

Wandering Chopsticks. 2010. "Images at War's End: Refugee & Marine Images from Col Waterhouse Collection & Marine Staff Photographs from Camp Pendleton - Camp Pendleton." http://wanderingchopsticks.blogspot. com/2010/09/images-at-wars-end-camp-pendleton.html (accessed Mar. 17, 2011).

Warner, W. Lloyd, and Leo Srole. 1945. *The Social System of American Ethnic Groups.* New Haven, Conn.: Yale University Press.

Weizman, Eyal. 2012. *The Least of All Possible Evils: Humanitarian Violence from Arendt to Gaza.* London: Verso.

Wexler, Laura. 1992. "Tender Violence: Literary Eavesdropping, Domestic Fiction, and Educational Reform." In *The Culture of Sentiment: Race, Gender, and Sentimentality in Nineteenth-Century America,* edited by Shirley Samuels, 9–38. New York: Oxford University Press.

White House, Office of the Press Secretary. 2003. "President Bush Discusses Freedom in Iraq and Middle East." Remarks by the President at the 20th Anniversary of the National Endowment for Democracy United States Chamber of Commerce, Nov. 6. Washington, D.C.

Whitfield, Stephen J. 1991. *The Culture of the Cold War*. Baltimore, Md.: Johns Hopkins University Press.

Whitlock, Gillian. 2007. *Soft Weapons: Autobiography in Transit*. Chicago: University of Chicago Press.

Williams, Raymond. 1977. *Marxism and Literature*. Oxford: Oxford University Press.

Wood, Joseph. 1997. "Vietnamese America Place Making in Northern Virginia." *Geographical Review* 87: 58–72.

———. 2006. "Making America at Eden Center." In *From Urban Enclave to Ethnic Suburb: New Asian Communities in Pacific Rim Countries*. Honolulu: University of Hawaii Press.

Yeoh, Brenda S. A. 2003. *Contesting Space in Colonial Singapore: Power Relations and the Built Environment*. Singapore: Singapore University Press.

Yoneyama, Lisa. 1999. *Hiroshima Traces: Time, Space, and the Dialectics of Memory*. Berkeley: University of California Press.

———. 2005. "Liberation under Siege: U.S. Military Occupation and Japanese Women's Enfranchisement." *American Quarterly* 57: 885–910.

Young, Marilyn Blatt. 1991. *The Vietnam Wars, 1945–1990*. New York: HarperCollins.

Zhou, Min. 2001. "Straddling Different Worlds: The Acculturation of Vietnamese Refugee Children." In *Ethnicities: Children of Immigrants in America*, edited by Rubén Rumbaut and Alejandro Portes, 187–227. New York: Russell Sage Foundation.

Zhou, Min, and Carl L. Bankston III. 1998. *Growing Up American: How Vietnamese Children Adapt to Life in the United States*. New York: Russell Sage.

Zizek, Slavoj. 2006. *The Parallax View*. Cambridge, Mass.: MIT Press.

Index

absent presence, 116

African American(s), 3–4, 62–63, 131, 161, 181, 182, 183

Agamben, Giorgio: and "bare life," 76; and *homo sacer*, 76; and refugees, 11

Agency for International Development, U.S. (Saigon), 42

Agent Orange, 92, 139, 205n60

Agier, Michel, 78–79

alliances, cross racial, 181–87

Amerasians, 55–56

"American Dream," 6, 94, 101, 130

Americans, as liberators, 82, 93

American studies, 3, 16, 26, 83

Andersen Air Force Base (on Guam), 25, 28, 31; involvement in the Vietnam War, 36–38, 40; and Vietnamese refugees, 176

Anderson, Benedict, 125

Angel Island, 57

anticommunism, European, 8; association of refugees with, 8–9; and Vietnamese, 22, 55, 85, 94, 96, 101, 117–118, 120, 122, 129, 134–136, 137, 145, 150, 152–153, 179, 209n86

Archive of Vietnamese People, 69

"arc of instability," 84–85

Arendt, Hannah, 11, 180, 192n69

Argentina, 108, 114

Arlington, Virginia, 129, 135

Armed Forces of the Republic of Vietnam (ARVN), 105, 106, 113, 116, 123; American vilification of, 108–09; fallen war heroes, 116–118, 122, 124, 125, 130, 131–132; Junior Military Academy, 126; soldiers, forced disappearance of, 108–111; veterans, 123, 129, 137, 152

Asian American studies, 3, 172, 172, 186

Asians and Asian Americans, 6, 109, 171, 172; and alleged economic success, 6, 95, 172, 182, 183, 205n71; and social citizenship, 161

assimilation, 5–6, 34, 95, 96, 130, 137, 190n23

Association of Southeast Asian Nations (ASEAN), 52–53

asylum seekers. *See* refugees

Australia, 47, 54, 69, 123

Barthes, Roland, 114–116

Bataan Peninsula, Philippines, 58, 66, 67, 71, 72, 75, 155

Benjamin, Walter, 170

"Biên Nhớ," 49, 65

biopolitics, 57, 59–60

black(s). *See* African American(s)

screening of, 54–56, 198n35; and in-
betweenness, 23, 80; as solution for the
United States, 2, 18, 83, 104, 175; warehousing of, 56, 58, 61–62
refugee studies, 83, 171; critical, 10–14, 19,
173–81, 187; critique of, 3–7, 10, 17;
damage-centered approach, 3; focus on
resettlement, 11; in international relations, 7–8; in social science research, 3–7,
171–72, 173, 180; and war studies, 17–18,
173, 18
repatriation, 11, 12, 47, 54, 68, 77–78, 189n6,
198n29
representation, crisis of, 13
Republic of Vietnam Army Rangers, 105
"rescue and liberation" narrative, 1, 23, 25,
94, 96, 97, 103, 104, 174; critique of,
46–47, 48, 120–21, 150; and "humanitarian violence," 176
resettlement policies, 49, 51–53, 54–57, 62,
198n29
Reyes, Adelaida, 72
Rohrabacher, Dana, 101

Sahara, Ayako, 25, 62
Said, Edward, 13
Saigon, 24, 25, 30, 41, 42, 89, 92, 105, 115,
121, 128, 129, 145, 154, 156
Saito, Leland, 183
Samoa, Eastern, 26
San Gabriel Valley, California, 183
San Yick Closed Centre, Hong Kong, 63–64
scriptorial landscape, 125–128, 137
second-generation Vietnamese, 3, 6; and
achievements, 95, 96, 142, 157, 160–65,
170, 214n42; and anticommunism, 152–
54; daughters, 165–69; and discrimination, 171, 184–85; economic instabilities,
141, 157–59, 162–63, 170, 184; and gang
activities, 142, 143; intergenerational tensions, 141, 142, 162, 165–69, 170; in multiracial neighborhoods, 181–87; postwar
generation, 22, 124, 141, 169, 170, 180;
and suicides, 142, 185; and Vietnam War,
123, 133, 139–140, 141, 143–145, 148–149,
150–154, 164–65, 170
Seidman, Irving, 141
Sek Kong, Hong Kong, 77
settler colonialism, 47, 186
Sharpton, Al, 3
silence, 20, 142; of history, 177; self-generated,
180; silencing within Vietnamese communities, 179; within refugee families,

140, 147–149, 150, 154–57, 166, 169–70,
177, 180
Silva, Denise Ferreira da, 178
Sino-Soviet Bloc, 29
Socialist Republic of Vietnam, 70, 92, 106,
108, 119, 120, 153
socially stigmatized, 96–97
Soguk, Nevzat, 7, 12
Songkhla, Thailand, 70
South America, 84
Southeast Asia, 89, 93, 187; Cold War objectives in, 32, 175; first asylum countries in,
62; refugee camps in, 21, 49, 50, 52, 53,
54, 57, 62, 65, 70, 73; refugees from, 9–10,
25, 35, 51, 58, 60, 82, 186; U.S. military
involvement in, 36, 37, 84, 85, 91, 177;
youth, 142
South Vietnam (Republic of Vietnam), 17, 37,
39, 42, 44, 111, 124, 210n100; erasure of,
114, 118, 119–120, 125, 137; flag of, 75, 117,
118, 122, 129, 134; U.S. invasion of, 81;
military, 47, 55, 75, 105; nostalgia for, 121;
soldiers, 110–111; sovereignty, 11, 26; war
dead of, 106–07, 108, 113, 114, 116, 119,
121–122
Spanish American War, 24, 26, 27
Spivak, Gayatri, 13
State Department, 35, 59
stateless, 10, 60, 67, 74, 192n69
Statue of Liberty, 45
Strategic Air Command, 29, 37
street names, commemorative, 22, 126–128,
130–134, 135, 137, 179
"structure of feeling," 140, 169
Sturken, Marita, 82
Subic Naval Base, 27
Sudden Unexplained Nocturnal Death Syndrome, 185–86

Tadiar, Neferti, 21, 49, 51, 179
Tai A Chau, Hong Kong, 61–62.
Tajiri, Rea, 139, 147
Talcott, Burt, 34
Tân Sơn Nhất International Airport, 24
Tempo, Carl J. Bon, 9
Texas Capitol Vietnam Veterans Monument.
See memorials.
Thailand, 25, 52, 56, 57, 69, 70, 72, 200n97,
Third World, 4, 79, 97
Thuong Tin I, 68
Tran, Quan Tue, 70
transnationalism, 3, 15
Tran Tuong Nhu, 42